whom say ye that I am?

whom say ye that I am?

Lessons from the Jesus of Nazareth

James W. McConkie and Judith E. McConkie

with an essay by Dean Collinwood

GREG KOFFORD BOOKS
SALT LAKE CITY, 2018

Paperback ISBN: 978-1-58958-707-6
Also available in ebook.

Greg Kofford Books
P.O. Box 1362
Draper, UT 84020
www.gregkofford.com
facebook.com/gkbooks

Library of Congress Cataloging-in-Publication Data
available upon request.

To our children and our children's children

"We do well to remember that our duty is not only to ourselves but also to our children and our children's children. If in our time the Church were to become weak; if the Christian ethic were to be more and more submerged in the world; if the Christian faith were to be twisted and distorted, we would not be the only losers. Those of generations still to come would be robbed of something infinitely precious. We are not the possessors but also the trustees of the faith. That which we have received, we must also hand on."

William Barclay (1907–1978)

contents

acknowledgements

We would be remiss if we did not thank our family and friends who share with us a deep commitment to Jesus and the four Gospels. We have literally spent hundreds of hours conversing on this subject over the years and have been blessed by their insights and comments, especially comments from our children and their spouses. All six have been full-time Latter-day Saints missionaries. Our oldest son James, his wife Laurel, and their four children relinquished all professional ties and family associations for three years to serve their church in the Czech and Slovak Republics. Their unqualified commitment of Christ-like consecration remains a powerful example. Our son Bryant and his wife Aimee have literally devoted thousands of hours in service to their church and community. They are a constant source of sensitive, intelligent spiritual guidance. We have written about Kelly elsewhere in this book. After her mission she married Brian Stewart. They have remarkable devotion to each other, their four children, and their families, and they are filled with wit, self-discipline, and insights about Jesus and how one goes about applying his teachings.

We have enjoyed some of the finest conversations with James's siblings and their husbands. On one of our trips to Israel, Dean and Kathleen Collinwood, James's sister and brother-in-law, went along. Kathleen is an attorney who has studied in Israel at the Hebrew University of Jerusalem. Among more than a few other topics, her knowledge of modern as well as ancient Hebrew law and biblical text was such an important part of many discussions. Dean is a PhD anthropologist (a witty one at that!) and an inquisitive and careful thinker about Jesus in the context of his own times—so much so that we asked him for permission to include his essay on the personality of Jesus at the end of this volume. James is also indebted to four lunch mates who have read extensively on the life of Jesus and were always willing to engage in insightful discussion: Brad Parker, Richard Lambert, Robert Stephenson, and Brent Ward. We must also thank our skilled and patient editors.

Working together as husband and wife on this project has made all the difference. We could not have finished this book without many deeply satisfying moments of mutual encouragement. Over more than a half-century of marriage, we have had the privilege of thinking about so many far-ranging topics. We have taught the New Testament and other classes together over the years, and we have never lacked interesting ideas and thoughts to consider. That is not to say we always see eye to eye. Indeed, we might compare our collaboration more to the on-screen relationship of Spencer Tracy and Katherine Hepburn than that of scholars Will and Ariel Durant. We do always try to elevate the conversation and the work product. We count this opportunity to work as a team as one of life's choicest blessings.

A couple of introductory considerations: First, we have chosen to use several alternative translations of the Bible. For Christians who are accustomed to reading from the King James translation, these newer translations are rather like hearing familiar music in a different key. And while we love the poetic language of the King James Bible, it is not easily understood in our day when the Elizabethan language of its pages sounds strange to our ears, since the construction and meaning of words and whole sentences have changed over time. Sometimes readers may gather incomplete ideas or miss nuance or meaning of ancient or Elizabethan iconography. In addition, the King James scholars of the seventeenth century had only a handful of Greek manuscripts to work from. Since then, well over 4,000 other complete and fragmentary manuscripts have come to light, each helping the newer translators sort out what the original text actually had to say. Therefore, for purposes of clarity, accuracy, and pedagogy, we have decided to primarily use the New Living Translation in this effort.

Finally, our aim and purpose has always been to focus on what the newer scholarship calls the historical Jesus—that is, the Jesus from Nazareth in the context of first-century Palestine. Therefore, we have primarily cited, as often as possible, the most scholarly books we could find that describe his historical setting. In this way we have tried, as best we can, to strip away centuries of layers, lore, and legend that have been superimposed on the Jesus story. We hope that this approach has helped us to more clearly understand Jesus on his own terms.

J. Reuben Clark, Jr., the Undersecretary of State for US President Calvin Coolidge and prominent Mormon Church leader, described the approach we have undertaken. "You know" he said, "I am quite a believer in studying the life of the Savior as an actual personality. That is not often done. Our students of the Bible and of the New Testament seem to refrain from trying to build a biography of the Master out of those four great Gospels."[1] With this in mind, he went on to suggest that the serious student might get "some good . . . Bible that contains . . . an outline of his life, a so called harmony. It does not make much difference what Bible you take. . . . Then try to go along with the Savior, live with him, let him be an actual man, half divine, of course, but nevertheless moving as a man moved in those days."[2]

---

1. See, J. Reuben Clark, *Behold the Lamb of God*, 8. Clark was a member of the First Presidency of the Church (1933–1961).
2. Ibid.

foreword

The moment we decided to collaborate on a book of essays about Jesus of Nazareth, several challenges—as well as opportunities—presented themselves. First, the act of collaboration itself could create the opposite of joint joyful creativity: We are both strong personalities; disputes over content or style could derail a happy relationship of more than half a century. We thankfully write that we managed to come through the experience, as J. D. Salinger wrote in a wonderful short story about relationships, with "all [our] faculties in tact."[1] In fact, our mutual and individual warrants to be the disciples of the Jesus whom we know as the Savior of mankind have been immeasurably strengthened.

The second challenge we faced was choosing what and how often we would reference the sources we found to be important. We are both active members of The Church of Jesus Christ of Latter-day Saints, sometimes known as the Mormon Church. As would be expected, men and women in the leadership of our faith have written and spoken often about Jesus. Their wisdom and insights are invariably esteemed. However, we decided early on that the sources we would examine and share most often would be, as frequently as possible and appropriate, primary ones—that is, the four Gospels of the New Testament themselves, as well as those who wrote and spoke as close to the first century of the Common Era as possible. In addition, we would study the most respected scholars we could find on the subjects of the customs, beliefs, and especially contexts of the four Gospels. We admit that it was often tempting to especially lean on men and women of our faith who have made the personal commitment to read and then think critically about the Gospels and the scholars for themselves and then share their conclusions, especially by way of testimony, in written or oral form.

---

1. "For Esmé - with Love and Squalor," a touching short story by J. D. Salinger about a young girl and a traumatized soldier, was originally published in 1950 in *The New Yorker*. It has since been re-published often in American literature texts. Ours comes from an anthology of his work published in 2001 by Back Bay Books (New York City).

But we have agreed that quoting them too often would in a way have short-circuited the purpose of our efforts for both of us. Therefore, the secondary sources we have tried to employ are works written by particular experts in various fields of research about the New Testament or the contexts of those scriptures. Without question, the authors we have chosen have added to whatever insights about Jesus we may have brought to these essays. We hope that the research those scholars have added to the authoritative testimonies from our pastoral leaders will serve to be as important to those who read this work as they have been to us.

Finally, we had to decide how we would blend our two voices in a series of essays. As you read the following chapters, you may discern the personality of one writer or the other. Our personal areas of expertise may come through. Our interests may come through as well. Judith brings to the volume references to works of art about the subjects at hand. She tends to produce complex sentences populated by any number of dependent clauses, which honestly made our editor crazy. James, on the other hand, employs direct and disciplined constructions. He tends to be more interested in the scholars whose expertise is the newest historical Jesus research, and his devotion to the study of their work is obvious. With the help of an able editor, we hope that we have been able to achieve a respectable fusion. In this foreword to the essays, however, we have chosen for the moment to write separately about what brought each of us to the work at hand.

From James:

In 1997, our daughter Kelly was accepted into the Brigham Young University Study Abroad program. She packed her bags and went off to be taught at BYU's Jerusalem Center for Near Eastern Studies. The Center, a BYU satellite campus, offers coursework that focuses on the Hebrew Bible and the New Testament, Near Eastern studies, and ancient languages—particularly Hebrew and Arabic. The classroom experience is built around field trips to various parts of the Holy Land.

The BYU campus itself is located on Mount Scopus, directly across the Kidron Valley from the famous Golden Gate of the Temple Mount. The BYU complex's enormous west windows look over what is left of the more ancient City of David, as well as the level ground on Mount Zion where Jesus, at least once and perhaps twice, drove out the moneychangers and merchants and where he went to teach the crowds and heal the sick. Today, the holy shrine of the Dome of the Rock dominates the famous skyline.

Mount Scopus is not merely a spot from which to look out and admire Old Jerusalem. Over the years, it has been strategically important as well. For centuries it was used as a base from which to attack the ancient city. A Roman legion camped there in AD 66 and again four years later. And from that place the legion launched military strikes on the city. Centuries later, the Crusaders would use it for the same purpose. Today the area remains a hotly disputed part of the West Bank.

Three of the world's most influential religions converge on the Temple Mount across from the BYU Center: Judaism, Christianity, and Islam. Some believe that this was the very spot where, at the last moment, an angel stopped Abraham from sacrificing his son Isaac (or Ishmael, according to the Islamic account). It was here that Herod began his massive reconstruction and expansion of the Temple in 19 BC, and where the priests ritualistically slaughtered thousands upon thousands of animals for sacred offerings. For Christians, the Temple Mount was the spot where Jesus debated the Pharisees, inspired his followers, and proclaimed himself the "light of the world." For Muslims, this is one of the holiest places in all Islam. It is the place where the Prophet Muhammad, accompanied by the angel Jibril (Gabriel), rode to heaven on the back of a supernatural beast called a *buraq* in what is known as the Night Journey. He saw Abraham and the other patriarchs. He saw Jesus, whom he witnessed to be among the other prophets. And it was in this context of some of the world's great historical sites that my daughter Kelly would have the privilege of studying the life of Jesus, and where she would become better acquainted with two other religious traditions.

After Kelly returned from the Holy Land, our family was eager to know about her experiences. She was filled to the brim with profound insights and information. Generally, when someone comes home from a trip, things return to normal after a few days and past adventures are only occasionally referenced. This was not the case with Kelly. Our discussions continued over the next year as she shared her thoughts and impressions with all of us. We realized that our membership in The Church of Jesus Christ of Latter-day Saints gave us a deep appreciation for Jesus as our Redeemer. But this experience of speaking with Kelly caused me to want to know far more—more about the social, cultural, and political context of Jesus's life. I wanted to enrich my understanding of his ministry and mission and come to know him more deeply and more completely. I wanted to get to know the details about who he really was, how he behaved, and what distinctive attitudes and traits set him apart from others.

It was with these thoughts in mind that I decided to begin a journey to discover as much about Jesus as I could—to get a feeling for who he was. To the extent possible, I wanted to get to know him as I might know our closest friends. What gratified him? What made him angry? Where were his sympathies? For whom did he express antipathy? What issues, beliefs, and ideas were most important to him? What kind of a "kingdom" was he trying to build? I even wanted to get a better sense of his personality. Was he easy to get along with? Did he have a sense of humor? Was he always patient and kind? What would it have been like to be one of his disciples and accompany him each day as he went about conversing, teaching, and healing?

Answering these questions more fully about Jesus was important to both of us as Kelly's parents because we had always been taught that adherence to the principles he espoused was essential. After all, for Christians, "there is none other name under heaven given among men, whereby we must be saved" (Acts 4:12 KJV). Like most followers of Jesus, we believed our very happiness and fulfillment in this life and ultimate happiness and fulfillment in the life to come depended upon becoming like him. We accepted Mormon Apostle Jeffrey R. Holland's observation: "In every choice we make, [Jesus] ought to be our point of reckoning, our charted course, our only harbor ahead. He should be for us individually what he is for all men collectively—the very brackets of existence, the compass of our privilege. We should not stray outside him."[2]

I realized that as we tried to pattern our lives after him, I personally needed to learn more about what he did and said. I needed to develop a clearer view of Jesus as a person. That meant coming to understand him as thoroughly as was humanly possible so that I could more closely emulate him and come to value the things he valued and behave as he behaved.

The starting point for me, then, was to consider where I could find the most reliable information about the actual historical Jesus. Certainly, the Bible and the LDS canon of scriptures speak about him. However, it is only in the four Gospels that Jesus was presented in real-life situations—loving, teaching, forgiving, rebuking, healing, and encouraging. It is in the Gospels that Jesus exemplified the principles he taught. We see him interacting with women in ways that were uncommon to the culture of his day—such as his encounters with the woman caught in adultery and the sinful Samaritan woman at a well. We hear his sharp rebuke of

---

2. Jeffrey R. Holland, "Whom Say Ye That I Am?"

hypocrites who used their form of religion to promote themselves while condemning others. We listen to his prayers and what he prayed for—his enemies, forgiveness, the kingdom of God. We watch his inclusion of the poor, his restoration of the mental faculties of the deranged, and his renewal of the sick to good health. It is in this way, by paying particular attention to his behavior, that I wanted to come to understand what kind of a person he actually was, to come to discover what kind of a person he expects all of us to be.

Because the Gospels describe real-life situations, their pages give context and substance to Jesus's teachings—teachings that might otherwise end up becoming merely lovely-sounding phrases and moral platitudes that could be applied in so many different ways as to make them almost meaningless; or worse still, they could become insipid clichés that could seemingly support so many causes, religious predispositions, or political ideologies. Consequently, I felt it was only when I came to even minimal but deeper comprehension of *how* Jesus loved and what he considered morally reprehensible that I more fully comprehended who the Son of God is.

Whatever might be argued about the rest of the scriptural canon, it is impossible for us to ever do without the four Gospels as a guide to the real Jesus. This is why these Gospels are such a gift. As John P. Meier, a preeminent biblical scholar, says, "There are very few [reliable] sources for knowledge of the historical Jesus beyond the four canonical Gospels. Paul and Josephus offer little more than tidbits."[3] William Barclay, a well-known religious scholar of the mid-twentieth century, rightly pointed out, "It is perfectly true—as we have so often said—that Christianity is founded not on a printed book but on a living person. The fact remains that the only place in all the world where we get a first-hand account of that person and of his teachings is in the New Testament. That is why the church which has no Bible class is a church in whose work an essential element is missing."[4]

Accordingly, I began to earnestly study the life of Jesus in the Gospels. I paid attention to his daily walk. I thought about the people he befriended. I noticed who his closest friends were. I took particular note of what made him angry and what pleased him. I simply spent time observing how he lived and acted in the context of his times. After study and the long conversations with Judith and our children that followed, I realized

3. John P. Meier, *A Marginal Jew: Rethinking the Historical Jesus*, loc. 379, Kindle.
4. William Barclay, *The New Daily Study Bible Series: The Letters to Timothy, Titus, and Philemon*, 225.

that it is one thing to say, "Jesus is loving." But it was another thing to observe how and whom he loved. It is one thing to say that he condemned sin. It is another to see how he treated sinners.

I read about Jacob DeShazer, who was particularly impressive to me. He was a man who was deeply influenced by his reading of the four Gospels. DeShazer enlisted in the U.S. Army Air Corps in 1940. Following the Japanese attack on Pearl Harbor, he became a member of one of the units trained to fly modified B-25 bombers off the deck of the USS *Hornet* in the Pacific Theater as part of the famous Doolittle Raiders. After bombing Nagoya, Japan, he attempted to reach safety in China but was forced to parachute into enemy territory and he was captured by the Japanese along with the rest of the crew.

He spent forty months as a prisoner of war, thirty-four of which were in solitary confinement. He was malnourished and beaten. During his incarceration, he convinced one of the guards to give him a copy of the Bible. Over and over he read and studied the four Gospels and was converted to Christianity. At the close of the war, he studied to become a Methodist missionary, and in 1948, he returned to Japan to preach the gospel and establish a church in the city he had bombed. He spent the next thirty years of his life there. Reading about the details of Jesus's life in a concentration camp had transformed him into a disciple.

Like Jacob DeShazer, except under far less-stressful circumstances, Judith and I have become more fully acquainted with Jesus—something the two of us have vowed to do every day of the rest of our lives.

This journey we have taken over the past few years has more fully convinced us that Jesus is the Son of God. What we learned about him became our own answer to the question Jesus asked Peter and his disciples at Caesarea Philippi: "Whom say ye that I am?" (Matt. 16:15 KJV). At the time of Jesus, unlike the dry planes of Judea, the ancient city of Caesarea Philippi was a verdant, lush spot with running water. It was also a wicked cosmopolitan city full of pagans and dotted with the temples of ancient Assyrian Baal worship. There were no fewer than fourteen such temples at this spot. As Barclay poetically described it, "Here was an area where the breath of ancient religions was in the very atmosphere. Here was a place beneath the shadow of the ancient gods."[5] In Caesarea Philippi, Herod built a great temple of white marble and dedicated it to Augustus Caesar, who had declared himself a living god.

---

5. William Barclay, *The Daily Study Bible Series: The Gospel of Matthew*, 2:135.

It was at Caesarea Philippi that this "homeless, penniless Galilean carpenter, with twelve very ordinary men around him,"[6] and with the gods of this world arrayed behind him, asked his most devout followers, "Whom say ye that I am?" And it was here that they said, "Some say that thou art John the Baptist: some, Elias; and others, Jeremias, or one of the prophets." Jesus was not satisfied and said, "But whom say ye that I am?" Simon Peter stepped forward and declared, "Thou art the Christ, the Son of the living God" (Matt. 16:14–16 KJV).

Peter answered this question based upon his personal knowledge of the details of Jesus's life and upon his day-to-day observations of what Jesus did and said, which inevitably helped him conclude that Jesus was "the Son of the living God." Like Peter, we have become more fully acquainted with many of these same details, and we are more able than before to say that he is the Promised Messiah. It is with these thoughts in mind that we decided to write this book together—to express our profound appreciation for his divinity, grandeur, and beauty. We will always be grateful to our daughter Kelly, who awakened in both of us the desire to answer Jesus's question to Peter more fully for ourselves.

From Judith:

My generation of LDS women came of age shortly after the Kennedy assassination, and during the Vietnam War, protest riots at U. C. Berkeley, fallout from monumental civil rights legislation, Elvis Presley and the dance called The Twist, Andy Warhol's shakeup of the art world with a Campbell's soup can, and "women's libbers" who had a habit of burning their bras in front of the black-and-white television cameras.

I remember taking a road trip with James in our first car. We had been married just four months; we had been invited to spend Thanksgiving with the parents of James's former missionary companion who lived in tony Palo Alto, California. The companion rode with us in the impossibly small back seat of our car. I was the more naïve sophomore undergraduate from Provo, Utah, where my father was a professor of physics at BYU, and my mother a first grade public school teacher. Dad came to the university from Southern Alberta, Canada after the war. Mom was the daughter of a small college president who later became a chemistry professor. Both were

---

6. Ibid.

part of that "greatest generation" who went to war from small towns and came home to the same small towns, changed and grateful.

On that trip to San Francisco, I saw my first hippies and flower children who were of the same baby boomer generation as I was but eons apart from my experience growing up in a conservative Mormon university community. I went to my first professional symphony concert and to dinner at the top of the Mark Hopkins hotel. (I wore a beaver fur loaned to me for the occasion by our hostess. Elegant hardly describes how I felt on that night!) James had come to Provo to attend BYU after growing up in New York and London, a world of culture and "sophistication" away from mine. More importantly, however, he was a returned missionary from a family of genuinely accomplished scriptorians. I, on the other hand, had spent my last two high school years in Provo mostly skipping my early morning religion classes. I remember that my teacher, Brother King, was inordinately patient with me, even though I did other homework in the class on days when I did attend. I owned only one rarely read copy of the New Testament; I owned no Book of Mormon that I recall. My parents were active and dedicated, my father having been a lay ministry bishop as well as having served in other higher church leadership positions. Their lives were spent in devotion to their church and their family in the same way my grandparents and their parents had lived their days on earth—but not quite in the way as James's family had. I quickly realized I had considerable catching up to do where gospel scholarship was concerned, not to mention an awareness of the amenities and supposed refinement of big-city living. I wanted to know both.

I remember being awed by James's knowledge of the scriptures. I was, however, content to let him be our newly minted family leader in spiritual matters. That was the way our generation assumed the order of the universe was and ought to be.

James thought differently about my responsibility for knowing the scriptures and for continuing in my father's academic footsteps. Despite the fact that he was our children's primary tutor in gospel study, I came to know that in our marriage, my own progression depended on my initiative and dedication in that area, not his.

The five decades that have followed that first road trip have brought us three children and twelve grandchildren, civic and religious opportunities to serve others, law school for James, graduate school for me—first an MFA then a PhD. He has just described the year that our daughter Kelly returned from studying in Israel and our epiphany about knowing the historical Jesus. We cannot express the importance of this on-going journey to understand him, to become his more committed disciples, to spend the remainder of our sojourn in mortality qualifying for glory in immortality because we somehow have managed to begin to be like him. In addition to an identity as an adoring parent and grandparent, an educator and artist, I have come to be a middling scriptorian, a dedicated student, and a grateful, somewhat more sophisticated partner in the quest.

Abbreviations

Several different Bible translations are quoted in this volume, indicated by the abbreviation following the parenthetical scriptural reference.

AMP = Amplified
AMPC = Amplified Classic
Barclay = William Barclay Translation
KJV = King James Version
MSG = The Message: The Bible in Contemporary Language
NEB = New English Bible
NIV = New International Version
NLT = New Living Translation
NTWT = N. T. Wright Translation
Phi = Phillips New Testament in Modern English

chapter 1

Jesus in Historical Context

Based on our approach of looking at the details of Jesus in real-life situations to better understand who he is and what he is like, historical context is an essential ingredient. Without it, we will not be able to understand the meaning of the written text or appreciate the significance of what Jesus did and said. As Marcus J. Borg expresses it, "Setting biblical passages in their ancient context makes them come alive. It enables us to see meanings in these ancient texts that would otherwise be hidden from our sight. It unearths meanings that otherwise would remain buried in the past."[1]

Think for a moment about how difficult it would be for someone two thousand years from now to explain the World Series to a group of people unfamiliar with baseball. "Stealing third base" or "hitting the winning run at the bottom of the ninth inning" would be meaningless gibberish. Likewise, think about how difficult it would be to understand the phrase "That is a good course" if we did not know more about the setting. The phrase denotes one thing coming off of a golf course and another thing coming out of a schoolroom. The phrase takes on yet another meaning coming out of a restaurant. Or think of the word *left*. It could mean you exited a place (I *left* the room) or that an object remained behind (I *left* my credit card at home). It could be used as an adjective to identify which of your two hands you prefer to use (I am *left*-handed) or as a directional indicator (turn *left*) or even as a political preference (Joe leans *left* politically).

Not only does context help us know what is going on, but it also "helps us to avoid reading the Bible simply with our current agendas in mind and frees the Bible [Jesus] to speak with [his] own voice."[2] It should be obvious that out of historical context, Jesus could plausibly be expropriated to support almost any "good" cause, whether he would have actually endorsed it or not. For example, during the Civil War, the Confederate States often justified slavery by quoting the New Testament

---

1. Marcus J. Borg, *Reading the Bible Again for the First Time*, 39.
2. Ibid.

and the Apostle Paul. Mormons used the same sources to justify priesthood restrictions. If Jesus and his disciples could be commandeered to support such practices, there is no limit to what his name might be used to justify. N. T. Wright explains, "Plenty of people in the church and outside it have made up a Jesus for themselves, and have found that this invented character makes few real demands on them."[3]

Think about that idea. Consider the many different ways the name of Jesus is employed and for what purposes. In the words of Wright, Jesus is "almost universally approved of" but for "very different and indeed often incompatible reasons."[4] He is "wheeled in" to give support to capitalism on the one hand and socialism on the other. Some groups use him to "undergird strict morality" while others use him to offer freedom from more "constrictive moral constraints."[5] Yet still others tout him as a pacifist while others make him out to justify violence in some circumstances.

If this is the case, then what Jesus are we worshiping, and is the Jesus we are worshiping of our own making? This is why "the question as to *which* Jesus we are talking about will not go away. Nor will the impression that this question contains the deeper question as to which *god* we are talking about."[6] Wright concludes, "The point of having Jesus at the center of a religion or a faith is that one has *Jesus*: not a cipher, a strange silhouetted Christ figure, nor yet an icon, but the one Jesus the New Testament writers know, the one born in Palestine in the reign of Augustus Caesar, and crucified outside Jerusalem,"—the Jesus that died and three days later came back to life.[7] How easy it is for us to distort the picture, to "see the world through the colored spectacles of our own personal histories, backgrounds, assumptions and so on."[8]

We did not want to devise a self-validating Jesus who just happened to agree with our view of things—a Jesus that could make us feel good about whatever we happened to be thinking or doing at the time. Making Jesus in our own image makes him no god at all and certainly not one that could save us.

During the past half century, historians have made significant strides examining the most recently discovered source materials to reconstruct

3. N. T. Wright, *Following Jesus: Biblical Reflections on Discipleship*, ix.
4. N. T. Wright, *Jesus and the Victory of God*, 10.
5. Ibid.
6. Ibid.
7. Ibid., 10–11.
8. Marcus J. Borg and N. T. Wright, *The Meaning of Jesus: Two Visions*, 17.

the first-century Jesus—the Jesus that first-generation Christians would recognize. The aim is to put Jesus within the context of his own times using historical methods that place emphasis on primary sources—source material that is closest to the person being studied. This approach also involves an analysis of contemporary histories and gospels not in the biblical canon, used for historical and cultural information about the times in which he lived. The end result is, as N. T. Wright insists, a "historical jigsaw [that] must portray Jesus as a credible and recognizable first-century Jew, relating comprehensively in speech and action to other first-century Jews. No solution which claims to be talking about history can ever undo this basic move."[9]

As we mentioned in our Foreword, our interest in placing Jesus in his own historical perspective was awakened when our daughter Kelly came home from her study abroad program in Jerusalem, where she studied the New Testament. Our conversations with her put us on the lookout for good historical information about the life and times of Jesus. It was not long afterward that we were in San Francisco, where we visited a bookstore in the basement of Grace Cathedral. It was there that we became acquainted with a vein of historical scholarship on Jesus that opened up a whole new world to us and explained better than anything we had read before what Jesus was all about in the context of his times. We picked up a book by Marcus J. Borg, *Meeting Jesus Again for the First Time: The Historical Jesus and the Heart of Contemporary Faith* (1995). Once we started reading it, we could not put it down. We disagreed with his pantheistic view of God and his metaphorical approach to miracles and the resurrection narrative, but he brought to life the character, demeanor, and temperament of Jesus as a person, teacher, and social prophet. Borg convincingly portrayed Jesus as a compassionate person who was unflinching in his just criticism of the religious and socioeconomic conditions of his day. We were captivated by Borg's portrayal.

Our interest in what Borg had to say led us to read other scholars of the historical Jesus. One in particular was John Dominic Crossan, an Irish-American religious intellect and former Catholic priest. He presented Jesus as a revolutionary with an emphasis on personal action and social transformation. He believes that Jesus came from a landless peasant background and was initially a follower of John the Baptist. He was a healer and a man of wisdom who taught a message of tolerance and inclusiveness

---

9. Wright, *Jesus and the Victory of God,* 6.

and challenged the practices of the ruling classes. Crossan's book *Jesus: A Revolutionary Biography* (1994) portrays Jesus as an activist who believed in social and economic equality. This was a Jesus who was loving but also full of indignation.

We are indebted to these authors and to many others who have contributed to a historical understanding of Jesus's life and times. Included in that list are Oscar Cullmann, E. P. Sanders, J. B. Phillips, Robert E. Funk, L. Michael White, James A. Charlesworth, Raymond E. Brown, Bart D. Ehrman, Lisa Sergio, Elaine Pagels, Karen Jo Torjesen, Ian Wilson, Henry Chadwick, Rodney Stark, Garry Wills, Margaret Barker, Bruce Chilton, and many others.

favorite author N. T. Wright

Our favorite, however, is N. T. Wright, an Anglican. Now retired, he was the bishop of Durham in the Province of York. He is more literalistic in his interpretation than many other historical Jesus scholars and does not shy away from concluding that Jesus is the actual Son of God—a God of miracles who was literally resurrected from the dead. His trilogy on Christian origins—*The New Testament and the People of God* (1992), *Jesus and the Victory of God* (1996), and *The Resurrection of the Son of God* (2003)—is a must-read for any serious student of the Gospels. We started with his book on the resurrection, which was a resounding defense of the literal resurrection. Wright skillfully places Jesus within the dimensions of Jewish culture and shows a mastery of the primary and secondary materials that he uses in a search for the historical Jesus. He gives a comprehensive interpretation of the life of Jesus "that inspires a kind of awe."[10]

We are reminded of a professor of English literature Judith enjoyed during her undergraduate days at Brigham Young University. His name was Professor Thomas Cheney, and he taught a course on the short story. He made the point, which is applicable here, that a compelling short story does not rely on a few adjectives to develop its characters. Rather, he said, if you want to tell a story about a cantankerous old man, don't say he is "cantankerous." Put him in the story and let him "cantank." Chenny's point was undoubtedly based on a similar comment made by the master story-teller Mark Twain, who said, "Don't say the old lady screamed. Bring her on and let her scream."

10. Robert H. Stein, "N. T. Wright's *Jesus and the Victory of God*: A Review Article," 2017–18. Stein is a senior professor of New Testament interpretation at the Southern Baptist Theological Seminary, Louisville, Kentucky. He is the author of, among other works, *The Method and Message of Jesus' Teaching* (1977) and *Difficult Passages in the New Testament* (1990).

His point was that we learn more about the personality, character, and temperament of a person by observing what that person actually does in any given context than by generalizing—using a few adjectives to describe him. This is also true when it comes to learning about Jesus. As Borg is fond of saying, context is meaning. Therefore, it is within the pages of the four Gospels that we permit Jesus to "cantank" for himself, as it were.

One person who was unintentionally placed in a position to watch Jesus "cantank" up close was Dr. E. V. Rieu, a distinguished classical scholar who translated Homer into modern English for Penguin Classics. In his book *Ring of Truth*, J. B. Phillips reports a radio interview he had with Dr. Rieu. He said Rieu was sixty and a lifelong agnostic when Penguin asked him to do a translation of the Gospels. When his son learned about this he said, "It will be interesting to see what father makes of the four Gospels. It will be even more interesting to see what the Four Gospels make of father."[11]

The translation process demanded Rieu's careful attention to every detail of Jesus's life as he considered every word in the Greek texts along with the indispensable context to render an accurate translation. A year later, Dr. Rieu was "convinced and converted."[12] Phillips asked Dr. Rieu, "Did you not get the feeling that the whole material was extraordinarily alive?" Rieu replied, "I got the deepest feeling. . . . My work changed me. I came to the conclusion that these words bear the seal of the Son of Man and God. And they're the Magna Carta of the human spirit."[13] Phillips summed up: "I found it particularly thrilling to hear a man who is a scholar of the first rank as well as a man of wisdom and experience openly admitting that these words written long ago were alive with power. They bore to him, as to me, the ring of truth."[14]

It is with the Cheney method in mind that we will examine how Jesus conducted himself in various life situations. Part I of this book will focus on Jesus's interactions with classes or groups of people: women, members of his family, the hungry, the poverty stricken, the wealthy, the sick, the afflicted, the sinner, the lost souls, and the outcasts, along with his enemies and any others who were fearful and faced adversity and suffering. In these instances we often see a compassionate, sympathetic, and kindhearted Jesus. Part II will focus on how Jesus interacted with the powerful institutions of his day: the Pharisees, the Sadducees, and the Romans. In these

11. J. B. Phillips, *Ring of Truth*, 76–77.
12. Ibid.
13. Ibid.
14. Ibid.

instances we become acquainted with an angry, impatient, and incensed Jesus. Why did Jesus respond so differently to these two groups—the people (individuals) and the institutions (the establishment)? Why was Jesus at once compassionate or angry depending upon whom he was addressing? The answers to these two questions reveal the genuine personality and character of Jesus of Nazareth.

section one
jesus and individuals

chapter 2

Jesus and women

Arguably, some of the most striking images of medieval European Christianity are the sixteen high relief bronze panels on the Bernward Doors (circa 1015) of the cathedral in Hilldesheim, Germany. The image sides of the enormous single-cast doors face the pilgrim who approaches the cathedral. Scenes from the Book of Genesis on the left door tell the Adam and Eve story from top to bottom; the last panel shows the murder of Abel by his older brother Cain. The right door's eight-panel cycle, reading from bottom to top, connects the birth and resurrection of Jesus to the fallen state of man and mankind's need for the Savior's redemption.

The fourth panel on the left door is an appropriate metaphor to begin a chapter on Jesus and women. In it, God stands on one side of the fallen couple, a serpent-like creature below Eve on the other. God reproaches Adam, pointing an accusing finger at the first man. But Adam in turn points to Eve, who seems to still hold the fruit offered by the serpent. She cowers in absolute, abject shame behind the tree of life, trying to cover her nakedness.

There they are, caught between ultimate goodness and evil. And the weight of the sin rests with Eve, who, for us in this chapter, aptly represents the theological second-class status of women, who are to be blamed for the concupiscence—meaning the lustful and carnal appetites (as opposed to those of the spirit)—of the human family throughout Judeo-Christian history, including the culture of Jesus's day.[1] Using the same canon text, the Jewish authorities justified their pervasive attitudes and treatment of women. It was common for devout Jewish men each morning to begin their day by thanking God that they were not women. "Blessed are you, Lord, our God, ruler of the universe," they prayed, "who has not created me a woman."[2] The prayer and Bernward's panel epitomize the misogyny

---

1. *Catholic Encyclopedia*, s.v. "concupiscence."

2. The Jewish prayer book called the *siddur* contains blessings, thanksgivings, petitions, and instructions. Some traditional translations contain one prayer that devalues women in comparison to men. "Blessed are you O God, King of the Universe, Who has not made me . . . a goy [Gentile] . . . a slave . . . [or a] woman."

that existed in Jesus's day and that remains at the core of so many contemporary patriarchal religions and societies.

Women in First-Century Palestine

At the time of Jesus, women had virtually no rights. Women were considered objects, like an animal or a piece of property owned by their husbands. Some rabbis even wondered if females had souls.[3] A comment about Adam and Eve from the late Second Temple period (530 BC and AD 70) reflects the prevailing attitudes: "The Lord said: '. . . thy wife shall tremble when she looketh upon thee.' And an angel instructed Adam, 'Thus saith the Lord; I did not create thy wife to command thee, but to obey.'"[4]

A woman's world in first-century Palestine was bounded by the walls of her home—so much so that men and especially rabbis were forbidden from addressing and speaking with them in public places. The woman's job description was overtly specified. She was to nurse and raise children, grind flour, bake bread, wash clothes, cook food, and make her husband's bed.[5] In cases of abject poverty, women were allowed to work outside the home in limited settings but only as cooks, bakers, laundresses, hairdressers, or innkeepers.[6] In extreme cases, a man's wife and child could be sold as slaves. In the countryside, "economic necessity allowed some women to work outside of their homes to help with the harvest or other farm needs."[7] Because their role was limited to duties of the hearth and home, they were rarely if ever tutored or taught the Torah. Rather, their education was limited to culinary and household chores.

Dress standards were used to control women and protect men from sexual temptation. Absolute modesty was equated with sexual purity. A married woman was to be completely covered outside her home, and "if a Jewess uncovered her head in public, it was interpreted as a sign of rejecting God."[8] Veiling of the face was so prevalent that on one occasion a chief

---

3. Lisa Sergio, *Jesus and Women*, 3.

4. Lynne Hilton Wilson, *Christ's Emancipation of Women in the New Testament*, 4, citing Robert H. Charles, ed., *The Apocrypha and Pseudepigrapha of the Old Testament*, 2.134. The Jewish pseudepigrapha is a collection of religious works attributed to scribes sometime between 200 BC and AD 100.

5. Wilson, *Christ's Emancipation of Women*, 42.

6. Ibid., 45.

7. Ibid.

8. Ibid., 37.

priest in Jerusalem did not realize that the person brought before him for judgment was his mother.[9] In agricultural areas, the dress code was slightly more relaxed to take into account the practicality of helping with chores.

In or out of the home, women were expected to take counsel from their husbands. The most reliable Jewish historian, Josephus, explained that (as the Bernward doors illustrate) Adam was cursed in the Garden of Eden "because he *weakly* submitted to the counsel of his wife."[10] Therefore, "a woman is inferior to her husband in all things."[11] After a man and woman married, the husband in devout first-century Jewish households claimed the new title of *rab* or *rabbi,* which meant "Master," "my great one," or "honorable sir."[12]

Divorce was the ultimate weapon of control that husbands held over the heads of their recalcitrant wives. It was easy for a man to divorce his wife but difficult for a woman to divorce her husband. A woman could leave her husband only for rare afflictions or grievances that would make him forever "unclean," such as if he were afflicted with boils or if he collected dog excrement. On the other hand, a man could divorce a woman for a long laundry list of items, including big or small affronts: her inability to bear children, her "bold speech," or even her burning her husband's bread for dinner.[13] For the husband to undertake a divorce, all he had to do was write on a piece of paper called a *get* (a Hebrew word for a divorce document) the words, "You are hereby permitted to all men."

The implication of the statement seems clear. The divorced woman could thereafter be used or abused by any male. The divorce became final when he simply handed the *get* to her. Threats of divorce controlled every aspect of the husband-wife relationship. It was the ultimate tool of intimidation because once divorced, a woman became a pariah in the society at large. Divorce put her in the same financial category as widows and orphans, who were most often economically destitute and left to live hidden from view in the shadows of society. Because of fear and ostracism, then, marriages were full of insecurity and distrust. A woman tried to

9. Ibid., 38.
10. Ibid., 44; emphasis added.
11. Ibid.
12. Ibid., 156.
13. Ibid., 197–200.

"comply with every demand her husband made."[14] She was subservient to her spouse, and her relationship with him was unequal.[15]

The wider first-century Greco-Roman world was generally contemptuous of women as well. Just as in Jewish society, most pagan women were nonentities. A woman's duty was "to remain indoors and to be obedient to her husband."[16] A Roman husband could divorce his wife at will provided he returned her dowry.[17] Under Roman law, a woman had more status but few (if any) rights, mainly because from a Roman perspective, a wife remained on the same legal level as a child—forever. And as a child, she was under the supervision of her father—a privilege referred to as *patria potestas* (power of a father)—meaning that he had the right of life and death over her until she married, at which time the father's supervisory responsibilities vested in her husband. Cato the Censor wrote, "If you were to catch your wife in an act of infidelity, you [could] kill her with impunity without a trial."[18] Another Roman, Publius Sempronius Sophus, divorced his wife because she had been seen at the public games.[19]

Clearly, in civilizations surrounding the Mediterranean at the time of Jesus, restrictions and expectations surrounding women reflected a decidedly patriarchal view of the world as a whole. Male dominance was at the heart of patriarchy and meant that males heavily controlled all public aspects of society. As K. C. Hanson and Douglas E. Oakman point out in their book, *Palestine in the Time of Jesus,* the idea that males were privileged stemmed from the concept that a man's "seed" was what created a child,[20] A woman simply provided the womb as a place for the gestation of her husband's children. Whether justified or not, this view was legitimized throughout the Israelite story of the Creation. After all, males were created first, as we saw on Bernward's doors at Hilldesheim, and it was Eve who broke the commandment first and ate the forbidden fruit. Adam got to blame it all on her.

Historians and sociologists often argue that gender divisions were also based on male fear. A woman was potentially dangerous because the fe-

---

14. Ibid., 200.

15. Ibid., 198–200.

16. William Barclay, *The New Daily Study Bible: The Letters of James and Peter,* 252.

17. Ibid.

18. Ibid.

19. Ibid.

20. K. C. Hanson and Douglas E. Oakman, *Palestine in the Time of Jesus: Social Structures and Social Conflicts,* 50–51.

male could sexually overpower a man. Women, therefore, were seen as fundamentally sinful. On the other hand, women were praised as wives and mothers. A good wife meant her "husband was respected at the city gate, where he takes his seat among the elders" (Prov. 31:23 NIV), and mothers were deserving of their sons' respect (Ex. 20:12; Prov. 1:8; 6:20). Associating women with the home meant that "males must guard the females within the family and continually be on guard against females from the outside."[21]

The effects of these general attitudes and beliefs about males and females, husbands and wives, at the time of Jesus justified the behaviors and customs related to women's roles in the home, in the marketplace, and in worship settings.[22] The obvious result was that women functioned differently from their male counterparts. Public behaviors such as negotiating contracts, testifying in court, or even attending public events were the prerogatives of males only. Similarly, religious roles were limited. Woman could not make sacrifices or otherwise officiate at the Temple. These privileges required intermediaries in the form of male priests.

Fundamentally, the roles assigned to men and women were made clear in the ancient Mediterranean values of honor and shame. "Males [were] expected to embody the family's honor in their virility, boldness, sexual aggression, and protection of the family. . . . Females [were] expected to keep the family from shame by their modesty, restraint, sexual exclusivity, and submission to male authority."[23]

Against this backdrop, how did Jesus view and treat women?

Jesus and the Samaritan Woman

The story of Jesus and the Samaritan woman he encountered at Jacob's Well personifies Jesus's countercultural attitudes about women. Jesus was in Judea, where his disciples had been successfully baptizing converts. The account indicates that Jesus left Judea and set off to return home to Galilee through the customary route through Samaria, the province separating Judea and Galilee. On his northward journey, he stopped to rest at Jacob's Well, just outside the Samaritan town of Sychar. His disciples went into town and left him alone at the well. A Samaritan woman came to the well, and Jesus asked her for a drink. The woman was surprised because Jews

---

21. Ibid., 50.
22. William Whiston, trans., *The Genuine Works of Flavius Josephus, the Jewish Historian*, "Antiquities," 15.419.
23. Hanson and Oakman, *Palestine in the Time of Jesus*, 51.

did not associate with Samaritans or women. Jesus responded by telling her that if she knew who he was, she would have asked him to give her "living water," which would be "a well . . . springing up into everlasting life." When the woman asked for this "water," Jesus told her to find and bring her husband. The woman answered that she did not have a husband, whereupon Jesus told her that she previously had five husbands and was currently living out of wedlock with a sixth man. She perceived that he was a prophet. He then engaged her in a weighty religious discussion. He taught her about the proper worship of God and then declared himself to be the promised Messiah. She believed him. With Jesus's approbation, she returned to her village to tell her friends and relatives that the Messiah had come. The story concludes with the men and women of the town coming to hear Jesus preach the gospel (John 4:5–42).

This story, which does not seem so out of place to us in our gender-mixing society, was revolutionary in its time. It not only portrays how Jesus related to women in general, but it also illustrates how his view of women was different from his own society and culture. First, as we have established, in Jesus's day, it was inappropriate for males, let alone a rabbi like Jesus, to speak to a woman. Second, it was inappropriate for Jesus to be alone with a woman to whom he was not related or married, let alone an unclean Samaritan. And third, it was inappropriate for Jesus to approve of a woman functioning in a religious role (inviting her friends and relatives to believe that Jesus was the messiah). In this account, Jesus was seemingly indifferent to many social norms of his day. All of the boundary lines, those presumed sets of beliefs about the way men and women or Jews and Samaritans should relate, are turned upside down.

Speaking with a Woman

When Jesus spoke to the woman at the well and asked for a drink of water, she was genuinely surprised by his flouting of social protocols. She knew that customs were so deeply rooted that the most religious Pharisees would literally shut their eyes upon catching sight of a woman and stumble into walls and houses, thus deserving their popular nickname, "bruised-and-bleeding Pharisees." In public, women were to be invisible.

This interaction between Jesus and the woman at Jacob's Well was even more egregious because Jesus was a Jew and the woman a Samaritan. The antipathy between these two groups was legendary and based on centuries of Samaritans intermarrying with non-Jews. The antipathy was so great that Jews traveling in Samaria would literally shake the dust off of their feet as they exited the territory. As well, Jesus knew that he was speaking to an unsavory Samaritan woman who was living in adultery and had been divorced five times. Her reaction to Jesus when he asked for a drink of water was not surprising: "You are a Jew, and I am a Samaritan woman. Why are you asking me for a drink?" (John 4:9 NLT). She could have added, "I am also an immoral woman." Jesus had every reason to ignore her.

This story is even more remarkable and culturally atypical when we consider the fact that Jesus did far more than simply utter a few words to quench his thirst. He engaged the woman in a lengthy and serious religious conversation. After all, a woman's religious education was limited. Women were not expected to study the Torah but rather to devote their attention to household responsibilities. Yet Jesus and the woman talked extensively about the meaning of worship and what a person must do to be saved (John 4:21–24). "So tell me, why is it that you Jews insist that Jerusalem is the only place of worship, while we Samaritans claim it is here at Mount Gerizim, where our ancestors worshipped?" she asked (John 4:20 NLT). Jesus responded that the Samaritans knew little about God and that "salvation is of the Jews" (John 4:22 NLT).

During the course of their conversation, he compared his words to "living water" that leads to eternal life (John 4:11 NLT). "Anyone who drinks this water [in the well] will soon become thirsty again. But those who drink the water I give will never be thirsty again. It becomes a fresh, bubbling spring within them, giving them eternal life" (John 4:13–14 NLT). Jesus then revealed his true identity and said he was the messiah (John 4:26). The woman was so overtaken at the news that she "left her water jar beside the well and ran back to the village telling everyone" (John 4:28 NLT).

Alone with a Woman

Being alone with a woman in *public* was even more suspect than speaking with one. Being alone with a woman at a *well* reached the height of impropriety. It was scandalous and indecent. In addition to being a public place where women should not speak to men, wells had a reputation of being places for amorous encounters. Just being there with a woman was something Rabbi Jesus ought to avoid. Genesis 24 recounts the story of Abraham's servant's encounter with Rebekah at the well. He had been sent by Abraham to find a wife for Isaac (Gen. 24:15–28). Isaac's son Jacob courted Rachel at that very well, where he kissed her and fell in love so deeply that he was willing to work seven years for the privilege of marrying her (Gen. 29:1–18).

It is no wonder that when Jesus's disciples returned from the village, they were astonished to find Jesus speaking with a woman (John 4:27). Yet, none of them had the temerity to ask him, "What do you want with her?" Or "Why are you talking to her?" (John 4:27 NLT). It appears as though the woman immediately left when the disciples arrived, perhaps in haste because it was an utterly inappropriate situation.

A Woman Preaches the Gospel

There was a wall of separation between priestly duties and women. Priests were by definition men. Sacrificing animals, administering the affairs of the Temple, and expounding the Torah and Oral Law were for males only. Women were not even admitted into the most sacred precincts of the Temple, but were limited to the Women's Court. Therefore, it is of particular interest and import that Jesus approved of this woman going back to her village to tell all her friends and neighbors about her heartfelt belief that Jesus was the messiah, and by implication that the Kingdom of God was on the earth. Her efforts prompted people to come "streaming from the village to see [Jesus]" (John 4:30 NLT). Many believed that Jesus was "indeed the Savior of the world" (John 4:42 NLT), and they "begged him to stay" (John 4:40 NLT).

In this one account we see a Jesus who related to women in an entirely different way than other men in his culture. He was inclusive—he spoke to women about religion and envisioned them as emissaries who could and should carry the message about the messiah and the emerging Kingdom of God to others.

Other Encounters Jesus Had with Women

Jesus's partnership with women would continue to be a hallmark of his ministry. In the twenty-nine different passages in the four Gospels where Jesus encountered women, he continued to defy the traditional roles assigned to men and women. [24] Invariably, Jesus did not hesitate to

---

24. See Jesus and his mother at the Cana wedding (John 2:1–12); Jesus talks with Samaritan woman (John 4:1–42); Jesus on adultery and divorce (Matt. 5:28–32; 19:1–12; Mark 10:1–12; Luke 16:18); Jesus heals Peter's mother-in-law

recognize, speak with, bless, and include women in public encounters and in his closest and most intimate circles. When a woman who had suffered from constant bleeding for twelve years unobtrusively touched him in a crowd, he healed her and reassured her. "Daughter, be encouraged!" he said, "Your faith has made you well" (Matt. 9:22 NLT). On yet another occasion, contrary to tradition, Jesus involved Mary in a religious discussion instead of having her respond to Martha's plea that she perform her more traditional role to help prepare food. "My dear Martha," Jesus said, "you are so upset over all these details! There is really only one thing worth being concerned about. Mary has discovered it—and I won't take it away from her" (Luke 10:40–42 NLT).

It is not surprising that women followed Jesus and even contributed money to his ministry (Luke 8:2–3). Many were committed disciples, faithful through adversity to the end of Jesus's life (Mark 15:40–41; 16:1). In the end, there came a point in the story where his male disciples abandoned him and ran away. As far as they were concerned, Jesus's death marked the end of their hope that he was the messiah. But not the women!

(Matt. 8:14–15; Mark 1:30–31; Luke 4:38–39); Jesus raises widow's son at Nain (Luke 7:11–15); Mary and family come to take Jesus home (Matt. 12:46–50; Mark 3:20–21, 31–35; Luke 7:11–15); Jesus raises Jairus's daughter, heals woman with issue of blood (Matt. 8:18–26; Mark 5:22–43; Luke 8:40–56); daughter set against mother (Matt. 10:35; Luke 12:53); Jesus anointed by sinful woman (Luke 7:36–50); group of women supports Jesus and the Twelve (Luke 8:2–3); Jesus exorcises demon from girl (Matt. 15:21–28; Mark 7:24–30); Jesus teaches Martha an object lesson (Luke 10:38–42); woman calls Jesus's mother blessed (Luke 11:27–28); Jesus commends queen of the south (Matt. 12:42; Luke 11:31); Jesus heals crippled woman on Sabbath (Luke 13:10–17); woman hides leaven in meal (Matt. 13:33; Luke 13:20–21); woman loses piece of silver (Luke 15:8–10); widow troubles judge (Luke 18:1–8); mother of sons of Zebedee makes request (Matt. 20:20–28; Mark 10:35–45); Jesus teaches on marriage in the resurrection (Matt. 22:23–33; Mark 12:18–27; Luke 20:27–40); Jesus teaches on widow's mite (Mark 12:40–44; Luke 20:47–21:4); Jesus predicts calamities facing nursing mothers, women at mill (Matt. 24:19–21; Mark 13:17–19; Matt. 24:41; Luke 17:35); Jesus teaches parable of ten virgins (Matt. 25:1–13); Mary and Martha grieve for Lazarus (John 11:1–44); Mary anoints Jesus (Matt. 26:6–13; Mark 14:3–9; John 12:1–8); women bewail and lament Jesus (Luke 23:27–31); women behold Crucifixion (Matt. 27:55–56; Mark 15:40–41; Luke 23:49; John 19:25–27); Mary Magdalene and others attend Jesus's burial, set out to anoint his body on third day (Matt. 27:61, 28:1–11; Mark 15:47–16:8; Luke 23:55–24:12; John 20:1–18). See Margaret E. Köstenberger, *Jesus and the Feminists: Who Do They Say That He Is?*, 187.

Women were the first to come to the empty tomb, the first to see the risen Lord, and the first to run to tell the apostles that Jesus had risen from the dead (Mark 16:2–8; Luke 24:1–11; Matt. 28:1–10; John 20:11–18). As N. T. Wright emphasizes, "This is of incalculable significance. Mary Magdalene and the others are the apostles to the apostles."[25] They are the unshakable disciples and followers of Jesus.

The Role of Women in the Earliest Christian Communities

It is no wonder, after even a cursory examination of how Jesus and women related to each other, that the first Christians allowed women expanded roles in the early Church as compared to their own restrictive society. They were deacons and missionaries who worked hard in the cause of Christ (Rom. 16:1–2, 6, 12; Philip. 4:2–3). They participated in Christian meetings (1 Cor. 11:5), founded churches (Acts 18:2, 18–19; 1 Cor. 16:3–5), and acted as prophets (1 Cor. 11:5; Acts 21:9).

Given the history of the early Christian Church, feminist New Testament scholars have given considerable attention to females who were included in the inner circle of the apostles. Paul referred to a female *apostolos* when he wrote, "Greet Andronikos [husband] and Junia [wife], my fellow Jews who were in prison with me. They are highly respected *among the apostles* and became followers of Christ before I did" (Rom. 16:7 NLT; emphasis added). In this context, Junia may actually have been one of the apostles herself. Paul in his letter uses the preposition *en* that in this locution means she was a member of the group. "Had he meant to exclude her he probably would have used the dative *apostolois* without the preposition." Therefore, "what we have is a reference to a woman Paul considered not only an apostle, but an outstanding one."[26] Joel's prophecy anticipated that when the messiah came, God would "pour out [his] Spirit upon all flesh: and your sons and your *daughters* shall prophesy" (Acts 2:17 KJV; emphasis added).

One of the books that has received a great deal of attention on the subject of women and early Christianity is the Gospel of Mary, an apocryphal book discovered in 1896 in a fifth-century papyrus codex. Most believe that the Mary referred to in this non-canonical gospel is Mary Magdalene, based on her status as a known disciple of Jesus. The narrative begins in the middle of the story, so it is difficult to know the setting.

---

25. N. T. Wright, *Surprised by Scripture: Engaging in Contemporary Issues*, 69.

26. Anthony A. Hutchinson, "Women and Ordination: Introduction to the Biblical Context," 66.

But because this gospel begins with Jesus speaking with his disciples, it seems to be one of the post-resurrection accounts. Jesus departed, and his disciples became apprehensive and distraught. Mary recounted a vision she had in which Jesus communicated with her. Some of the apostles were skeptical because she was "just a woman." Yet they knew that Jesus loved Mary more than all the other disciples.

As Mary spoke to the Twelve about her vision, it was evident that her leadership was based on her superior spiritual understanding. After she finished speaking, "Andrew said, Brothers, what is your opinion of what was just said? I for one don't believe that the Savior said these things. . . . Has the Savior spoken secretly to a woman? . . . Surely he did not wish to indicate that she is more worthy than we are?" At this, "Mary wept." Levi then spoke up in defense of Mary and said to Peter, "If the Savior considered her to be worthy, who are you to discard her? For he knew her completely and loved her devotedly."[27]

Karen Jo Torjesen has written extensively about the role of women in the early Christian Church in her thought-provoking book, *When Women Were Priests*. In it she tracks the scholarship of Giorgio Otranto, an Italian professor of church history, who has shown through papal letters and various inscriptions that women participated in the Catholic priest-hood for the first millennia of that church's history as deacons, priests, and even bishops from the first to the thirteenth century.[28] For example, in a Roman basilica, the fresco of the female face of Theodora Espicopoa looks down. *Espicopoa* is the female designation for the word "bishop." Over time someone crossed out the "a" at the end of the word and replaced it with "us," an ending that changes the word from female bishop to male bishop.[29] The practice of having female bishops was prevalent enough that at the end of the fourth century, Epiphanius, the bishop of Salamis, in Cyprus, referred to women bishops and argued for their subjection.[30] Evidence of women acting in priestly roles is also found on a third-century fresco in a Greek chapel (Catacombs of Priscilla in Rome), where a woman is depicted breaking bread at an early Christian Eucharist.[31] Torjesen also documents that widow evangelists probably baptized their own converts,

---

27. Robert J. Miller, *The Complete Gospels*, 357–65.

28. Karen Jo Torjesen, *When Women Were Priests: Women's Leadership in the Early Church and the Scandal of their Subordination in the Rise of Christianity*, 2.

29. Ibid., 9–10.

30. Ibid., 44.

31. Ibid., 52.

especially if they were female, because early converts to Christianity took off all their clothing to be baptized.[32]

In the beginning, when the church was small, Christians met in homes where women had more influence and naturally assumed positions of leadership. By the third century, the process of institutionalization gradually transformed the house churches, where woman originally played prominent roles, into a body presided over by a monarchical male bishop. Over the next two centuries, the leadership of women was contested.[33] After the fourth century, the role of women changed. During the rule of Constantine, Christianity became more institutionalized, and leadership roles for women decreased. The trend continued, and in the Western Roman Empire, the Councils of Oragne in AD 441 and of Orleans in AD 533 directly targeted the role of deaconesses and forbade their ordination. In the Byzantine Church, the demise of female deaconesses happened over a longer period, with the vanishing of ordained orders for women in the twelfth century.

In the twenty-first century, when these issues are alive and controversial, Jesus's treatment of women is prescient. His example and the privileges afforded the first Christians provide important perspectives. We certainly should not rush to any conclusions or use historical material as a shortcut to a feminist agenda by turning "women into men."[34] But we must also "think carefully about where our own cultures, prejudices, and angers are taking us, and make sure we conform not to the stereotypes the world offers but to the healing, liberating, humanizing message of the gospel."[35] We live in a time when "we need to radically change our traditional pictures of what men and women are and of how they relate to one another within the church, and indeed of what the Bible says on this subject."[36]

Commenting on feminist biblical scholarship, Marcus J. Borg said, "The emergence of feminist theology seems to me to be the single most important development in theology in my lifetime."[37] Although feminist theology is important, a general consensus has not been reached on its

---

32. Ibid., 148.
33. Ibid., 6.
34. Wright, *Surprised by Scripture*, 68.
35. Ibid., 82
36. Ibid.
37. Marcus J. Borg, *The God We Never Knew: Beyond Dogmatic Religion to a More Authentic Contemporary Faith*, 70.

implications, and there is disagreement among feminist scholars on the meaning of the evidence for the acceptance of leadership roles for women in the early Christian church. Consequently, there is a considerable spectrum within feminist interpretation.[38] Regardless of where one comes down on this issue, however, there is enough evidence inside and outside the New Testament to cause a reevaluation of the role women played during Jesus's ministry and shortly thereafter.[39] The subject becomes even more intriguing as we appreciate more and more the significance of the priestly roles that women in the Mormon faith play in temples. At the founding meeting of the Relief Society, Joseph Smith said to the women there that "he was going to make of this Society a kingdom of priests as in Enoch's day—as in Pauls day."[40]

---

38. Margaret Elizabeth Köstenberger, *Jesus and the Feminists*, 216–18.

39. Letha Scanzoni and Nancy Hardesty, *All We're Meant to Be: A Biblical Approach to Women's Liberation,* 205. "Today we stand at the crossroads. As Christians we can no longer dodge the 'woman problem.' To argue that women are equal in creation but subordinate in function is no more defensible than 'separate but equal' schools for the races."

40. "Nauvoo Relief Society Minute Book," March 31, 1842.

chapter 3

JESUS, MARRIAGE, AND THE FAMILY

During World War II, the Reverend James Welch served as the BBC director of religious broadcasting. Welch had read a book by Oxford-based lay theologian C. S. Lewis called *The Problem of Pain*. It is a small meditation on one of the more abiding paradoxes in Christian theology—why an all-powerful God who loves his children allows suffering and pain. Later, Rev. Welch asked Lewis to deliver a series of radio broadcasts between 1940 and 1942 during the height of England's existential conflict with Nazi Germany.

The series, which was published later under the title *Mere Christianity,* became an instant classic for C. S. Lewis. Lewis died in 1963, yet according to his publisher, this work continues to sell more than 150,000 copies a year.[1] Toward the end of the book, Lewis mused on yet another juxtaposition of seemingly contradictory behavior for Christians. He wrote, "The only things we can keep are the things we freely give to God. What we try to keep for ourselves is just what we are sure to lose." It is, he said, "the paradox of [an authentic] Christian faith."[2]

The word paradox comes from a combination of the Greek prefix *para,* meaning "beyond" or "side by side," and the noun *dox* or *doxy,* meaning "belief" or "opinion." A shorter paradox is called an oxymoron, as in "icy hot" or "absolutely unsure." Stop to think for a moment about the use of paradox in the Old and New Testaments, and especially in the four Gospels. Clearly, a statement that seems to contradict itself is one of the more often-employed literary devices in the scriptures. Consider a few:

> Unless a kernel of wheat falls to the ground and dies, it remains only a single seed. But if it dies, it produces many seeds. (John 12:24 NIV)

> Whoever tries to keep their life will lose it, and whoever loses their life will preserve it. (Luke 17:33 NIV)

---

1. Mark Oppenheimer, "C. S. Lewis's Legacy Lives On, and Not Just through the Wardrobe."
2. Lewis, C. S., *Mere Christianity*, 180.

For those who exalt themselves will be humbled, and those who humble themselves will be exalted. (Matt. 23:12 NIV)

Is your eye envious because I am generous? So the last shall be first, and the first last. (Matt. 20:16 NIV)

But of all the paradoxes in the Gospels, it may be those times when Jesus spoke both directly and indirectly on marriage and family life that present the most difficulty. Those passages record occasions when he appears to support and yet simultaneously be at odds with what we understand to be eternal principles of binding family relationships. They are passages with seemingly contradictory views that feel at least perplexing to those of us who live in the twenty-first century. In part we perceive those scriptures as irreconcilable paradoxes because Jesus's explicit views on the topics of marital covenants and family allegiances only sparsely populate his overt teachings. And they leave many other references to parents, children, husbands, and wives in oblique contextual forms that color the narrative of a social and political world that the four Evangelists assumed would be understood. So when we read the text, we are supposed to know—like the authors and their audience—about Jewish marriage and family customs. For example, perhaps the most important parable in the Gospels—The Prodigal Son— assumes that the reader knows the constitution of a first-century Jewish household. The text in Luke 15 mentions father, inheritances, sons (older and younger), signet rings, robes, sandals, slaves, and day laborers, presupposing that the reader is aware of the complex social bonds, rituals, and obligations that provide nuance and meaning to the story.

But however much we may come to understand the various contexts of most of the four Gospels, when the authors recorded what Jesus taught about matrimony and familial relationships, the texts remain difficult because they contain at least three paradoxes—those pesky, contradictory statements or attitudes that do not seem to square with what we *think* Jesus *should* have said.

The first paradox is that he seems to value his ministry and his disciples over his own family. The Kingdom of God supplants and becomes the *new* family. The second paradox is that this new family of followers is set up as a kingdom, but it looks as if it upends how we think of a kingdom, run by a monarch, should look in the Ancient Near East. And finally, for Mormons, the third outwardly irreconcilable contradiction or paradox is that in the face of the doctrine of eternal lives, Jesus seemed to declare that there are no marriages in the eternities beyond mortality. No one, he said, "will . . . marry nor be given in marriage" after death (Matt. 22:29–30 NIV).

The first section of this chapter will approach a brief summary of the political and social context of ancient Palestine. Unless we take a moment to fill out the contours of family life during the time of Jesus, any discussion of the pairs of seemingly incongruous ideas that follow cannot be interpreted with any degree of accuracy. The notions of families and households in the larger Greco-Roman world and in the more-narrow Jewish world of first-century Palestine are followed by a section on the sayings of Jesus in those contexts. That way, we hope to lastly frame three of the many paradoxes of the New Testament that relate to marriage and family, and offer several insights about them.

Family Life in the Ancient World

In New Testament times, family life centered on households rather than on what we would call the nuclear family. Households were the domiciles or the fixed legal residences of the wealthy or nearly wealthy and their genetic descendants. But those households also included supporting servants, professional retainers, laborers, and slaves. So there could be several, if not many, non-consanguineous members of a household. And everyone in the household was under the protection of or belonged to a single living patriarch (from Greek words *pater*, "father," and *arkhein*, "to rule"). Under him were always the two broad divisions of members of a household—those who owned the goods, land, servants, and so forth, and those who in one way or another were owned.

Those who owned the household's property and wealth were affiliated in strictly hierarchical relationships as a result of kinship or descent. Gender was also an important determinant of rank for purposes of inheritance. That is, every decision moved down from the patriarch at the top to youngest child at the bottom of his family. This arrangement meant that the patriarch's wife or wives; his unmarried sons; his married sons and their wives, and their younger, unmarried children; his sons' widows or the widow of his own father; his unmarried daughters, aunts, or sisters; his married grandsons and their wives and children; and other assorted non-kinspersons might all live together. Everyone knew who was in charge. What we may well describe today as a clan was united around its one leader, whose successor was strictly determined by what was known as the right of primogeniture (unless subterfuge was involved). That right required that the firstborn son assume the role of the next generation's patriarch.

Marriages in what we refer to as the kinship family were usually *ex-ogamous,* meaning that they were generally arranged outside the kinship relationships of the household in order to benefit the patriarch and the family's well-being. Marriages were of two kinds: one was called a *cum manu.* In that marriage, the bride lost her birth-family rights of inheritance but gained other inheritance privileges in her new family. The other kind of marriage arrangement was called a *sine manu.* The young woman remained the property of her father, so until her father died, her husband's family received only the benefit of her presence in their family as a provider of the offspring of their union.

Depending on the wealth of the kinship family, when it came to the lower echelons of an Ancient Near Eastern household, people were hired, bought, and sold. These people might include tailors, barbers, cooks, bakers, and teachers. The most wealthy households might also have musicians, artists, craftsmen, farmhands, and, always, guards. The family's doctors, surgeons, and secretaries might also be attached to the patriarch by allegiance or ownership. Everyone looked to the head of the house for help and protection. Slaves might have been acquired as trophies of war and conquest. They might have been purchased or even given as gifts. The children of slave parents were given the name *vernae,* which would distinguish them from freeborn servants. But all persons belonging to one owner were called members of the family. Those who lived at a complex of attached or detached residences were *urban* families; the ones who lived in the country on a villa estate were called *rustic* families. It was common, however, for slaves to follow the kinship family's movements and to serve in both the city and the country.[3]

From the existing archaeological evidence, we know that most households with enough wealth built homes called atrium houses. They were constructed around courtyards open to the sky. Often what we would call apartment buildings, which Romans called *insulae,* housed multiple slave and servant families waiting on a household. As the number of dependents and blood-related members of the family grew, more rooms were added, but generally with a courtyard between them.[4]

The Roman name for the household was the *gens.* Even in the farthest outposts of the empire, like Judea on the most eastern shores of

---

3. David Noel Freedman, ed., *The Anchor Bible Dictionary,* s.v. "slavery."
4. A. C. Bouquet, *Everyday Life in New Testament Times,* 27–29.

the Mediterranean, the *gens* looked the same.[5] Consider, for example, the Roman army officer called Cornelius, who we are told presided over a household in Caesarea Maritima. That city should not be confused with the city called Caesarea Philippi in the north, above the Sea of Galilee. Caesarea Maritima was the luxurious Roman enclave built by Herod the Great on the shores of the Mediterranean Sea.

Cornelius and his household are an example of both spoken and unspoken Roman family practices. We are told that Cornelius was not only a Roman soldier and a captain of a regiment stationed in Caesarea, but also that he and everyone in his family, as Luke tells us, "feared God" (Acts 10:2 KJV). God-fearers were non-Jews who were sympathetic to Judaism and, although they were Gentiles and decidedly uncircumcised, shared Jewish beliefs. As a God-fearer, Cornelius had heard of Jesus as the messiah. Cornelius gave to the poor and regularly offered his devotions to Israel's God alone. One day as he was praying, he had a vision. He summoned "two of his *household servants,* and a devout soldier" (Acts 10:7 KJV; emphasis added). He asked the servants to find Peter at the town of Joppa as directed by the angel in the vision. When Peter arrived at Cornelius's home, it is evident from the account that his family consisted, as we should expect by now, of more than just Cornelius as the father, his unidentified wife, and their minor children. We read that he "called together his *relatives* [extended family] and close friends" to hear Peter (Acts 10:24 NIV; emphasis added).

After reading this story, which assumes that we would take the constitution of the household of Cornelius as unremarkable, we must keep in mind that we hear little or nothing about the lower strata of his household or any other in the society of Palestine. We almost never hear about a slave's families (the Epistle of Philemon is a great exception!), the very poor and homeless, or the diseased *except* when they had interactions with the upper-class families who either owned, punished, or shunned them.

Let us now turn to devout Jewish families in tiny Palestine or in the Diaspora—the area outside Palestine settled by the Jews. They were in many ways identical to others in the empire. All members of the Jewish household looked to the father-patriarch for leadership and authority. Just as in a Roman family, lines of inheritance were strictly hierarchical. The right to govern the family's affairs as well as a double portion of the patriarch's wealth and property were inherited by the firstborn living son upon the death of his father. Other sons received a single portion of the estate.

---

5. Lynn H. Cohick, "Women, Children, and Families in the Greco Roman World," 179.

Widows belonged to their deceased husband's households. They did not go back to their birth families. And just as in any other prosperous Near Eastern or Roman household, slaves, servants, and laborers were ubiquitous and generally invisible.

In many ways, family life in Jewish households was much like the living arrangements in other civilizations. A well-to-do *domus* (house) included adult siblings and grandparents, as well as slaves and freedmen and freedwomen who served the needs of the household. Less well-off families lived in crowded apartments, often in just one room. They were still governed by a patriarch, however. No matter the financial situation, members of a household performed a variety of culturally and ritually designated tasks. Women in a Jewish household, the *materfamilias,* would oversee household functions. Women prepared the food. They ground grain, baked bread, milked animals, and made cheese. Some women worked for menial wages in the marketplace, but most who did were poor, akin to slaves.

Children began working alongside the adults in the family before they were teenagers. Oftentimes parents were not the primary caregivers of their own children; rather, various members of the household tended their offspring. In wealthy families, slaves were hired as wet nurses who also oversaw the basic education of the children. No matter what the economic status, extended family members worked and contributed what they could to the group. Each person in a traditional, observant Jewish family had a "specific [hieratic] status within the home, and each good Jewish family member deemed the social status of the family, including its wealth and social prestige, as of equal or greater value to their personal happiness."[6]

By far and away, however, the differences between Roman or other pagan families and Orthodox Jewish families centered on religious practices that were woven into every inch of the fabric of the Jewish family's day-to-day lives. To remain unspotted from the Gentile world around them, Jewish households, including their slaves and servants, were voluntarily separated from pagan society. Virtual and literal walls were built to exclude that which was unclean. Jewish households refused participation in non-Jewish customs; in fragmented Roman polytheistic religious rituals, prayers, and sacrifices; and especially in the rituals of the state cult that required impure sacrifices and interaction with male and female temple prostitutes.

Members of Jewish households looked to Jewish customs. Their rituals were Jewish ones. Jewish theology guided their lives. Torah Law—613

---

6. Ibid.

commandments called the *mitzvot* extracted from the Hebrew Bible—
and the Oral Law governed everyone's conduct and position in the family structure. Rome and its local procurators and legions typically stood
back and accommodated Jewish religious customs, provided they did not
threaten the state, because they were aware that to oppose the centuries-
old, deeply engrained customs and practices meant bloodshed.

The First Paradox: Leaving a Family Meant Finding Another

For Jesus, the family relationships just described were not necessarily
abandoned, but rather reconfigured by means of expansion. Old segregated families were merged into the new one called God's family, or his
Kingdom. The ideal family, then, was not a nuclear one. Nor was it even
a traditional household. It was instead the entire Christian community
gathered together. Membership in the family and Kingdom came by way
of the ritual of baptism, symbolizing a new birth not always dependent
on mortal kinships. Therefore, members referred to each other as brothers and sisters, who on bended knees acknowledged "the Father . . . from
whom every family in heaven and on earth takes its name" (Eph. 3:14–15
NRSV). Therein lies the first paradox of Christianity. To leave the traditional family or household meant joining a new and liberating one.

Jesus explained the new definition of family to his own mother, brothers, and sisters. The accounts, without the context of the concept of a new
family organization, is a paradox without resolution. For example, when
Jesus was teaching a group of his followers, members of his own family
tried to summon him. "As Jesus was speaking to the crowd, his mother
and brothers stood outside, asking to speak with him." Jesus responded,
"Who is my mother? Who are my brothers?" Answering this question, he
gestured to his disciples and said, "Look, *[you] are my mother and brothers.
Anyone who does the will of my Father in heaven is my brother and sister
and mother!*" (Matt. 12:46–50 NLT; emphasis added).

Jesus undoubtedly recognized here that the idea of a kingdom led by
God rather than by the established hierarchy of the ancient household was
the true or ideal family. He also undoubtedly realized that his doctrine
would be seen as a paradox of genuine concern for his own family as well
as other families in traditional Judaism because it was a seeming renuncia-
tion of the family as it was known. It was a provocative idea in the context
of a culture where a person's identity, worth, status, and personal happiness were subordinated to an assigned place within the household. Jesus

said the new family was actually a kingdom where, amazingly, the king allowed even the very least members of a household—slaves and bondsmen and women alongside captains and patriarchs—to be his children and literal heirs. This new family in which all were considered equals was far too horizontal and inclusive for those who benefitted from an oppressive culture. It struck at the heart of a hierarchical home everyone knew by displacing patriarchy and the other vertical social arrangements in a household. Parenthetically, this may be one of the reasons that Jesus's own family members rejected his teachings. We cannot blame them for feeling that he "had taken leave of his senses and that it was time he was taken home"[7] (Mark 3:21; John 7:5). Mark comments that others even went so far as to say he was possessed by Satan (Mark 3:22).

Jesus acknowledged that this radical rearrangement of family relationships would create serious conflict. He explained: "For I am come to set a man at variance against his father, and the daughter against her mother, and the daughter-in-law against her mother-in-law. And a man's foes shall be they of his own household" (Matt. 10:35–36 KJV). The birth of the Kingdom of God—God's new family—would not come without labor pains.

As Christianity welcomed more and more diverse converts into the new family of God, conflicts inevitably arose. Consider, for example, Paul's rebuke of Peter for his refusal to sit with Gentile converts in Antioch (Gal. 2:11–16). Old habits and beliefs often die hard deaths. As time went on, and especially after the fall of Jerusalem in AD 70 (a date that marked the beginning of Gentile dominance in the Christian community) all converts seem to have been welcomed. Paul wrote that from "one man [God] created all the nations throughout the whole earth" (Acts 17:26 NLT). Even the despised Gentiles were no longer "strangers and foreigners," but "God's holy people . . . [and] members of God's family" (Eph. 2:19 NLT).

This vastly expanded idea of family may seem counterintuitive to Mormons living in the twenty-first century, who hold up the nuclear family (father, mother, and their children) as the ideal arrangement. But when we examine ideas on marriage and family in Joseph Smith's day, we see that his personal family experience was more along the lines of a multi-family household. The use of the term *nuclear family* begins to appear only in the early twentieth century, and historically speaking, it is not comprehensive enough to describe the complexity of actual family relationships. And what Joseph ultimately taught about how the family should be organized

---

7. William Barclay, *The New Daily Study Bible: Gospel of Mark,* 86.

is remarkably similar to what Jesus had in mind. Temple rituals, which were instituted in Nauvoo, Illinois, in the 1840s before Joseph's death, enlarged family relationships and, as ultimately understood, involved sealing the family together into one unbroken genealogical chain. Or, expressed differently, modern temple ceremonies brought all of God's children into the Kingdom of God as God's heirs. After all, Mormon theology teaches that almost as soon as we had been given mortal bodies, those who had once been brothers and sisters in premortality began to contend with each other and even spill each other's blood. "Sealing" his children to each other was the way to put God's heavenly family back together again.

The Second Paradox: Submission to a King Meant Liberation

As we pointed out at the beginning of this chapter, a kingdom of brothers and sisters utterly upended the existing family structure and social hierarchy of the Near East. With Jesus, under the authority of his father at its head, the vertically organized family was supplanted. And so, in the early Christian community, Onesimus, a runaway slave, was "no longer" an inferior to his master or anyone else in the Kingdom. Rather, he was to be valued as "a beloved brother" (Phil. 1:16 NLT). In God's eyes, there were no favorites. There were "no more strangers and foreigners." All were "fellow citizens with the saints, and of the household of God" (Eph. 2:19 KJV).

Social equality was reinforced by economic living arrangements. Members of the household of God held "all things common" (Acts 2:44 KJV). It was, therefore, a safe haven for the widow, the orphan, the halt and the lame, and the other most vulnerable members of society. It was the promise of this household that Jesus offered to the rich man who lived all of the commandments but was incapable of selling all that he had to "give the money to the poor" (Matt. 19:21 NLT).

Contrary to the traditions of his day, in Jesus's household, women taught, prophesied, prayed, and held office. All were invited to dine together around the same table in equal fellowship. Old food restrictions were abandoned (Mark 7:17–19). The high ideals expressed in the Sermon on the Mount governed and defined the community. Emphasis was placed on love and forgiveness, even of one's enemy. Jesus's community would never perpetrate violence. God's household was the ultimate expression of the two greatest commandments—love of God and love of neighbor. As N.T. Wright expressed it, "Through his actions and words Jesus was calling into being a people with a new identity, a new family."[8] Paul described it, and first-generation Christians lived it. "All the believers were united in heart and mind. And they felt that what they owned was not their own, so they shared everything they had" (Acts 4:32 NLT).

Divorce

At this point, it seems appropriate in a chapter on marriage and family to add a comment on Jesus's teachings on divorce. The new family—defined as the Kingdom of God—was not intended to abolish or even diminish the bonds among fathers, mothers, and children. Jesus taught that those personal relationships were fundamentally important and worth preserving for all of God's children, be they wealthy or poor or enslaved. He spoke approvingly about marriage, children, and parents, and he taught specific principles intended to fortify family relationships. So when we read that Jesus forbade divorce or exemplified love for children or taught sons and daughters to honor and care for their parents, we understand that Jesus's fundamental commitment to marriage and family relationships was ordained from the beginning. Accordingly, he said that what "God hath joined together, [man must not] put asunder" (Matt. 19:6 KJV). When challenged on his no-divorce position, he said that divorce was justified only in situations where the woman (presumably the man as well) had been unfaithful: "whosoever divorces his wife and marries someone else commits adultery—unless his wife has been unfaithful" (Matt. 19:9 NLT).

Jesus's views on divorce were far stricter than the standard Jewish practice of his day. First-century BC Rabbi Hillel expressed the norm. Rabbi Hillel relied on the Pentateuch (Deut. 24:1) and taught that a man could divorce his wife for any displeasure.[9] Women, however, could not divorce husbands so easily. They could initiate a divorce, but doing so was considered shameful.[10]

As discussed in the previous chapter, divorce in Jesus's day did not require government approval. The husband could secure a divorce simply

---

8. N. T. Wright, *The Challenge of Jesus, Who Jesus Was and Is,* loc. 1017–18, Kindle.

9. Although his was the minority view, Rabbi Shammai, a contemporary of Rabbi Hillel, disagreed. Like Jesus, he believed that divorce was justified only in the case of adultery.

10. A woman could divorce a husband if he persistently refused to fulfill his conjugal duties or was impotent.

by handing his wife a letter of divorce. Once it was delivered, the marriage was over. Some feminist scholars have pointed out that Jesus's no-divorce commandment, rather than confining women to terrible marriages, actually empowered them to be more assertive once the fear and intimidation of being cast out of the family at her husband's displeasure was eliminated.

Jesus's views on divorce were similar to those of the last-recorded Old Testament prophet, Malachi. The scriptures record that in a situation where God was not answering the prayers of his people, Malachi explained that it was because "the Lord witnessed the vows you and your wife made when you were young. But you have been unfaithful to her, though she remained your faithful partner, the wife of your marriage vows" (Mal. 2:13–14 NLT). The Lord, Malachi said, wanted "Godly children from your union. So guard your heart; remain loyal to the wife of your youth." Then by way of rebuke, he said that God "hates" divorce (Mal. 2:15–16 NLT).

For Jesus, one simple antidote to divorce was fidelity in marriage. He placed emphasis on the Ten Commandments that taught, "Thou shalt not commit adultery . . . [nor] covet thy neighbour's wife, . . . nor his maidservant" (Ex. 20:14, 17 KJV). Jesus went straightaway to one of the root causes of adultery, saying, "Ye have heard that it was said by them of old time, Thou shalt not commit adultery: But I say unto you, That whosoever looketh on a woman *to lust after her* hath committed adultery with her already in his heart" (Matt. 5:27–28 KJV; emphasis added). It was with regret that Jesus recognized that Moses permitted divorce "only as a concession to your hard hearts," but it was not what "God originally intended" (Matt. 19:8 NLT).

Children

In addition to the necessary context for Jesus's comments on divorce, we should also describe his and general attitudes about children in first-century Palestine. Small children were sometimes considered more of a nuisance than an asset until they were mature enough to work and contribute to the household. Paul reflected this attitude when, in the context of a family whose father had died, he referred to the children as "not much better off than slaves until they grow up" (Gal. 4:1 NLT). Jesus, on the other hand, did not condone treating children as if they were the household's slaves; rather, he welcomed and acknowledged them. Children epitomized attributes that members of the Christian community were to cultivate. Recall that he invited children forward so that he could bless them and wrap his arms around them. When his disciples tried to shoo the children away—something entirely consistent with their culture—Jesus was displeased. He said, "Let the children come to me. Don't stop them! For the Kingdom of God belongs to those who are like these children. I tell you the truth, anyone who doesn't receive the Kingdom of God like a child will never enter it" (Mark 10:14–15 NLT).

When the resurrected Jesus visited the Book of Mormon descendants of the Israelites, as recorded in 3 Nephi, we continue to observe a Jesus who was affectionate with the children. Just as he had done in the Old World, he invited them to come forward. In an extraordinarily moving passage, we read that he "took their little children, one by one, and blessed them, and prayed unto the Father for them." He then turned to the multitude and said, "Behold your little ones. . . . And as they looked to behold they cast their eyes towards heaven, and they saw the heavens open, and they saw angels descending out of heaven as it were in the midst of fire; and they came down and encircled those little ones about, and they were encircled about with fire; and the angels did minister unto them" (3 Ne. 17:23–24).[11]

Honoring Our Parents and the Elderly

Jesus's thoughts on fortifying families in the Kingdom of God not only required parents and others to love and value their children, but also obligated adult children to honor and care for their parents as they aged and became infirm. For example, when Jesus was in Gennesaret, a fertile plain on the western shore of the Sea of Galilee toward the northern end, some Pharisees and teachers of the religious law came from Jerusalem to confront him. As Jesus debated with the Pharisees, he pointed out that they used their own rules and regulations of the Oral Law to break one of the commandments brought by Moses from the Mount. "Honor thy father and thy mother" was an affirmative obligation (Ex. 20:12 KJV). He accused them of breaking this commandment by taking advantage of a rule that involved the giving of a gift called *Corban.* The precise meaning of the word is difficult to ascertain, but we know that it was a way of pledging money and property for the Temple and the exclusive use of God. So if an adult wanted to dedicate something of value to God in order to protect his wealth, he declared it Corban, and "thereafter it might never

---

11. Under the influence of God, the children spoke "marvelous things, even greater than he had revealed unto the people; and he loosed their tongues that they could utter" (3 Ne. 26:14).

again be used for any ordinary or secular purpose."[12] In the case of an
adult's parents, when a father or mother was in dire need, the son would
simply say, "I am sorry that I cannot give you any help because nothing
that I have is available for you; it is all dedicated to God."[13] In this way
children avoided obligations to their parents. The perverted twist to the
practice was that once the parent or parents died, it was possible to have
money or property returned to the adult child.

Jesus condemned Corban in no uncertain terms for its obvious hypocrisy. It exalted rules and regulations above one of the most fundamental
commandments. His point was that rules or the Oral Law must never
eclipse the love and assistance children should provide parents. Jesus said
of them: "These people honor me with their lips, but their hearts are far
from me. Their worship is a farce, for they teach man-made ideas as commands from God" (Mark 7:7 NLT).

Jesus honored and obeyed his parents throughout his life. As a child,
during the pilgrimage to celebrate the Passover festival in Jerusalem, he
became separated from his parents while he discussed the Torah with the
religious teachers on the Temple Mount. His parents were frantic to find
him (Luke 2:48) because they knew that during Passover the city was
crowded with people—some good, others not. When they found Jesus,
they confronted him, demanding, "Why have you done this to us?" (Luke
2:48 NLT). The young Jesus then respectfully submitted to his parents'
authority. Luke recounts that "he returned to Nazareth with them and was
obedient to them" (Luke 2:51 NLT).

Later, as an adult, he honored his mother's request at a wedding feast
in the village of Cana. She asked him to provide wine for the guests. It
might appear from the text that Jesus's response to his mother's request
was ill mannered and even curt. He said to her, "Woman, what have I to
do with thee? Mine hour is not yet come" (John 2:4 KJV). However, this
expression—"What have I to do with thee?"—was a common conver-
sational phrase in the milieu of first-century Palestine. When spoken in
anger, it indicated complete disagreement and reproach. But when spoken gently, it had a completely different connotation and meant, "Don't
worry; you don't quite understand what is going on; leave things to me,
and I will settle them in my own way."[14] And, as William Barclay has
pointed out, the word "woman" as used in in this context was a tender

---

12. Barclay, *The Gospel of Mark*, 196.
13. Ibid., 197.
14. Ibid., 114.

and respectful term of endearment. It had a softer tone than it appears to have in English. It was a title of respect and meant "my lady."[15] It is worth noting that the Joseph Smith Translation also renders this passage in more respectful tones. It says, "Woman, what wilt thou have me *to do for* thee?" (John 2:4 JST; emphasis added).

Ultimately, Jesus's concern for parents was manifest when, with great compassion, he reached out to his mother as she viewed him dying on the cross. In his agony, Jesus asked his disciple John to care for his mother. From that time forward, John took Mary "unto his own home" (John 19:26–27 KJV).

The Third Paradox: The Eternal Nature of Marriage without Marriages in Heaven

For Mormons, the greatest paradox found in Jesus's teachings on family life is the contradictory idea that marriage in mortality is the ultimate sacrament, but that in the heavenly realm, as the text seems to say, there will be no such sacrament and therefore no salvific familial binding available there. If this nearly insurmountable contradiction exists in the scriptures, as Jesus clearly taught, it would be entirely incompatible with the teachings of Joseph Smith on marriage and the family in the next life.

We can refer to the Gospel of Matthew for help in this matter. There the question of marriage in the next life came up in a discussion with the Sadducees. They confronted Jesus with a question structured to entrap him. What happens, they asked, if a woman marries, her husband dies, and then she marries another man? Whose wife will she be in and after the resurrection? Jesus's answer seemed unequivocal. "For when the dead rise, they will neither marry nor be given in marriage. In this respect they will be like the angels" (Matt. 22:30 NLT). Here is the great difficulty. The idea that in the next life all mankind will be like unmarried angels contradicts Joseph Smith's teachings that marriage and family relationships continue in and are indispensable to the next part of our eternal lives.

For Mormons, one way to solve this paradox is to look beyond the four Gospels to other Christian writings that as a matter of historical accident were never canonized or widely recognized.[16] With this in mind,

---

15. Ibid., 115.

16. In Bart D. Ehrman's *Lost Christianities: The Battles for Scripture and the Faiths We Never Knew*, his primary thesis is that what is contained in the four Gospels may not be the full story. The first Christian community, he writes, was

Everett Ferguson, a distinguished scholar in residence at Abilene Christian University and author of numerous books on early Christianity, points to some early Christians who believed that once a person was baptized, that person could receive higher ordinances (*mysteries*) that were carefully guarded from the knowledge of the profane world. In the ancient world, *mysteries* were "ceremonies of secret initiation by which persons were brought into a special relationship with deity and assured of certain benefits."[17]

Ferguson observes that the early Christian Church participated in various hidden sacraments and teachings that influenced their practices.[18] He cites Origen, one of the early Church fathers, who said that converts were initiated into the deeper mysteries of Jesus.[19] In the opening statement in the *Pistis Sophia,* an early third-century Christian work from Egypt, Origin quotes Jesus as saying that he taught his disciples certain important sacraments "after he had risen from the dead."[20] Jesus "brought the key of the mysteries of the heavens, without which no flesh on earth could be saved, since without an ordinance *(mysterion)* no one, whether righteous or unrighteous, shall enter into the kingdom of Light."[21] Similar information about Christian *mysteries* comes to us in *Cyril of Jerusalem's Lectures on the Ordinance.* Cyril, who was a venerated Saint in the Roman Catholic tradition, the Eastern Orthodox Church, and the Anglican Communion, reveals the instructions given to initiates into the secret rituals of the Church that were limited to an inner circle. These rites involved purification rituals, prayer circles, and other sacred ordinances.

We cite these early Christian sources because it appears to be their belief that marriage may have been one of these key mysteries. The Gospel of Philip, first published in an English translation in 1959, explains how marriage brought Christians into a special relationship with God. It dates

---

a cauldron of contending beliefs. Some Christian groups claimed that there was not one God but many. Others believed that the earth was not created by Jesus but by a lesser, ignorant deity. Certain sects claimed that Jesus was merely human and not divine, while others took the opposite extreme that Jesus was divine but not human. Therefore, it is not surprising, says Ehrman, that some early forms and beliefs of Christianity were suppressed, reformed, or entirely forgotten. Eternal marriage may very well be one of these forgotten beliefs.

17. Everett Ferguson, ed., *Encyclopedia of Early Christianity*, s. v. "mysteries."

18. Ibid., 791.

19. Ibid.

20. Hugh Nibley, *The Message of the Joseph Smith Papyri: An Egyptian Endowment,* 273.

21. Ibid., 274.

back to at least AD 400, though probably back further to the second century. The Gospel of Philip speaks of five rites in ascending order: baptism, chrism (the Spirit), Eucharist (sacrament), redemption, and *bridal chamber* (marriage). Against this backdrop, the Gospel of Philip explicitly tells us that Jesus was married to Mary Magdalene. "[The Lord loved Mary] more than [all] the disciples, and kissed her on her [mouth] often."[22] Furthermore, the Gospel of Philip describes marriage relationships in heaven, the purpose of which is to "beget" new life, a teaching reminiscent of Joseph Smith.[23]

The idea that the Kingdom of God is in fact an ideal universal family is an equivalence that speaks to the kind of association God's children should experience. The Kingdom, or God's family, is designed to strengthen the human bonds among fathers, mothers, and children based on compassionate, moral, and upright living. Because the Kingdom of God is ultimately open to all of humankind, it destroys discrimination of any sort based on gender, race, or social class. In the context of family, insider and outsider lines of distinction are not meaningful. All are welcome and all are loved. It is the community described by Paul: "So you are all children of God through faith in Christ Jesus. And all who have been united with Christ in baptism have been made like him. There is no longer Jew nor Gentile, slave or free, male or female. For you are all Christians—you are one in Christ Jesus" (Gal. 3:26–29 NLT).

A wise rabbi told a story about when day begins and night ends. It summarizes Jesus's teachings about how the familial relationships of the eternities will be determined.

The determination as to the moment night fell or the morning came is seemingly unimportant today. It remains of tremendous importance however to Judaism because of the holiness of the Sabbath day. Does morning dawn, asked one student, "'when you can see an animal in the distance and tell whether it's a sheep or a dog?' 'No,' answered the rabbi. Another asked, 'Is it when you can look at a tree in the distance and tell whether it's a fig

---

22. R. McL. Wilson, *Gospel of Philip*, 39.

23. The Gospel of Philip teaches that "Christ came" so that men and women would not be separated at death—this is why "the woman is united to her husband in the bridal chamber" (ibid., p. 46); in the next life gods beget children (pp. 51, 57); that marriages are a "mystery for those who have taken a wife" (p. 58); and that "the Father anointed the Son, and the Son anointed the apostles, and the apostles anointed us," and that those who are anointed "posses the All," which are the blessings given in the "bridal chamber" (p. 50).

tree or a peach tree?' 'No,' answered the rabbi. 'Then when is it?' the pupils demanded. 'It is when you can look on the face of a person and see that it is your sister or brother. Because if you cannot see this, it is still night.'"[24]

And so we have come full circle in this chapter, back to the wise insight of C. S. Lewis. He said, "The only things we keep are the things we give to God." Most assuredly then, the lives and families we give to God in order to be in his Kingdom are the relationships we keep forever. That is one of the four Gospels' great paradoxes and simultaneously one of the greatest truths Jesus revealed in them.

---

24. Deirdre Good, *Jesus' Family Values*, 149.

chapter 4

jesus and the poor, Hungry, and Destitute

Of all the writings of the Old Testament prophets, those by Isaiah are the ones Jesus quoted most often. As a book widely recognized for its profound religious importance not only for ancient Israel but also for the Palestine of Jesus's milieu, Isaiah is sometimes referred to as the fifth Gospel. Moreover, as much as any other book in the Hebrew canon, Christians believe it spoke with revelatory prescience about Jesus as the promised Messiah—the Anointed One—and about his mission to establish the Kingdom of God on earth after the pattern of his Father's Kingdom in Heaven. First-century Christians interpreted one-fourth of Isaiah's hymns, referred to as the Songs of the Suffering Servant, as prophecies about Jesus's mission, atonement, and exaltation (Isa. 52:13–53:12).

Many of us read the four New Testament Gospels without realizing how often Jesus adopted the language of Isaiah in any number of contexts. He used it to excoriate the corrupt scribes and Pharisees for their hypocrisy (Mark 7:7; Isa. 29:13). At other times he cited Isaiah to prefigure the end of times and final judgment (Mark 13:24; Isa. 13:10). It is significant that Jesus read from a passage in Isaiah as the salutatory at the commencement of his ministry. Through the words of Isaiah, he defined the purpose of his mission as one of complete philanthropy and compassion. We must stop here briefly to provide context for that singular moment.

After Jesus was baptized by John at Bethabara, or Bethany Beyond the Jordan, and after his forty-day immersion in the wilderness, it was time to formally commence his ministry. We can surmise that with this in mind, he went to the Galilee, to the meeting place for the tiny village of Nazareth where he had grown up.[1] Members of the congregation there recognized him immediately as simply Joseph's son. They must have had personal

---

1. A number of archaeologists believe Nazareth at the time of Jesus was too small for a synagogue with hand-copied scrolls. In this context, however, we will continue to refer to it as a synagogue.

memories of Jesus as a child. So, he was evidently welcomed and then invited to come forward to the raised platform, or *bimah,* at the center of the synagogue to read from the scroll prescribed for that Sabbath. Texts for every Sabbath of the calendar year were designated portions from the five books of the Torah, the Prophets, and the Writings so that in the annual cycle all the sacred texts would be read. We are told that on that day, it was the Isaiah scroll that was the set reading. We can imagine that it had been prepared and unrolled at the *bimah.* Jesus read out loud from the sixty-first chapter: "The Spirit of the Lord is upon me, for he has appointed me to preach good news to the poor. He has sent me to proclaim that captives will be released, that the blind will see, that the downtrodden will be freed from their oppressors, and that the time of the Lord's favor has come" (Luke 4:18; Isa. 61:1–2 NLT).[2]

At the conclusion of the reading, the scroll was handed back to the attendant. Jesus stepped from the *bimah* and sat down, a signal that he was about to teach. And while all eyes looked at him intently, he applied the scripture to himself. "The scripture you've just heard," he declared, "has been fulfilled this very day!" (Luke 4:21 NLT). With this sentence, and to everyone's utter amazement, he had avowed himself to be the promised messiah. More importantly, he had adopted as his mission statement Isaiah's words about bringing relief to the poor, healing the broken hearts, releasing the imprisoned, and restoring sight to the blind (Luke 4:14–30). Then he explained that in addition to God's favor already extended to the covenant children of Abraham through Isaac and Jacob, God's grace was also upon the Gentiles.

Several things stand out in this story. First, Jesus demonstrated that he was a literate individual. Next, he must have known that the reading for the day was from Isaiah, and that as a favorite son, he would be called to the *bimah* to read, an honorific responsibility. Then we must picture the small congregation's astonishment that he would proclaim himself as the long-awaited one who would save Israel. Finally, we see his audience become incensed to hear him say that God would look approvingly on the impure Gentiles, a group that most Jews would not want even to be seen with, let alone have a covenant association with. (Witness Peter's remark after Jesus's death and resurrection: "You know it is against our laws for a

---

2. When Mary visited her cousin Elizabeth, Mary sang praises to God and rejoiced in "God my Savior" (Luke 1:47 KJV). She described his mission and understood that during his life he would show "mercy" and would fill "the hungry with good things" (Luke 1:50, 53 KJV).

Jewish man to enter a Gentile home . . . or associate with [them]" (Acts 10:28).) What happened next in Nazareth on that Sabbath may surprise a modern reader today but not Jews of Jesus's day, because it was at this point that the men in the synagogue had had enough of his blasphemy. They jumped up and seized him. They took him to the top of a large hill to push him over the precipice to his death on the rocks below and then to hurl heavier stones on him, as the punishment for such talk demanded. But he slipped from their grasp (Luke 4:28–30).

Considering all that Jesus would go on to teach and accomplish in the three years of his ministry, it is remarkable that he chose as his mission statement a passage that Jews read as Isaiah speaking prophetically about a future messiah's accomplishments. Jesus could have introduced his ministry's purpose by speaking about faith, repentance, and baptism. But he did not. He could have chosen to announce the commencement of his ministry on the occasion of his sermon recorded in three chapters of Matthew delivered on the mount overlooking the Sea of Galilee. It certainly encapsulated his superlative moral teachings. Or in the synagogue in Nazareth, he might have prefigured his redemptive acts that would save all mortality from damnation and death. But he did not. Rather, he began his ministry by speaking about his concern for the poor and destitute.

The fact is that Jesus chose the day in the yearly cycle of readings when the Isaiah passages framed his mission and informed the world concerning how deeply he felt about the needs of the least economically and socially advantaged in his midst. It was a theme he would return to over and over. It was, for example, his focus in the first few paragraphs of the Sermon on the Mount: "Blessed are the poor. . . . Blessed are those that mourn. . . . Blessed are those who hunger . . . for theirs is the kingdom of heaven" (Matt. 5:3–12 NIV). And this: "Give to the one who asks you, and do not turn away from the one who wants to borrow from you" (Matt. 5:42 NIV). We should note here that some newer translations of those verses offer profound insights into exactly how the poor and the hungry would be blessed. Several suggest that Jesus did not promise a quid pro quo arrangement for those individuals, meaning that simply the condition of poverty in mortality meant the reverse—extraordinary wealth—would be the reality of heaven. Rather, the paraphrase of the original Greek by Eugene Peterson, for example, known simply as The Message (MSG), offers the idea that God exalts the poor and the destitute who can find the real meanings of justice and compassion for others in the grips of, or because of, the tragedies that beset them in this life (Matt. 5:3–12 MSG).[3]

We do not mean to suggest that blessedness of the sort he promised in the Sermon on the Mount was accomplished only by dogged acceptance and subsequent endurance of terrible conditions in this life. Elsewhere in the Gospel of Luke his message of blessedness is not metaphorical. Luke says that he preached a literal social reorganization called the Kingdom of God on earth. Whereas the celestial characters of the poor and the destitute were forged in and through earthly vicissitudes, he also taught that the solution to those same deprivations that produced hunger and poverty was to launch God's heavenly Kingdom on the earth! (Luke 6:20–21). This counterpart of God's heavenly domain could and ought to be a place where everyone shared in the bounties of life, a place where he said that no one "claimed that any of his possessions [were] his own, but . . . shared everything they had" (Acts 4:32 NIV). In his instructions on daily prayer, he asked that all of his disciples plead, "Thy kingdom come. Thy will be done in earth, as it is in heaven" (Matt. 6:10 KJV). It was a plea to promise that we would observe the principle of what John Dominic Crossan, a former priest and New Testament scholar, described as "radical egalitarianism," a term that must be understood in the context of first-century Palestine.

The Empire of Hunger and Poverty

In the Palestine of Jesus, poverty and hunger were caused by a nearly inexhaustible list of calamities and injustices. But for whatever reasons people were in need, addressing those factors was beyond the control of the vast numbers of suffering souls who could find no work; who had no education, training, or social status; or who lacked even the slightest hope of improving their situation. For others, physical and mental disabilities prevented even a modicum of an opportunity to care for themselves or to contribute to the good of others. Those who found their lives in those kinds of desperate situations were often more than destitute. They were malnourished or ravaged by disease. They lived in despicable environments not to ever be confused with a home, and they were thus denied the opportunities and choices that could have alleviated their plights. People were often crippled by their inability to even slightly achieve improvement in their personal circumstances by the smallest of measures. For

---

3. Eugene Peterson, trans., *The Message.*

the most part, they were a vast, voiceless collection of people who were totally unable to break free. In sum, the poor could not in reality fend for themselves because they were powerless, marginalized, and anonymous souls. And as Jesus observed, the poor would always be a part of that kind of society (Matt. 26:11; Mark 14:7; John 12:8).

Historians calculate that in the regions in and around Israel in AD 30 an abysmal gulf separated the wealthy from the poor. Elsewhere, we refer to those conditions as a two-tiered society. The rulers and governors of the upper tier composed about 1 percent of the population and yet owned 50 percent of the land. The priests were part of that tier, a privileged class who—along with Roman military officers, certain bureaucratic retainers, successful tax collectors, and a few fortunate merchants—owned about 15 percent of the land.[4] The remaining population was on the other side of the great divide and lived at subsistence levels. The vast majority were peasant farmers. Even lower in social standing of the lower tier were the artisans who made up about 5 percent of the population. They worked in various trades, such as stone masonry or wood working, an occupation commonly attributed to Jesus's father Joseph.[5] At the bottom of the rung were the outcasts, day laborers, slaves, and assorted hucksters and hustlers.[6]

Rabbinic writings describe bands of homeless people who roamed the countryside, so desperate for nourishment that they would stampede over one another to get at the smallest food offering. The extent of the poverty caused a second-century rabbi to callously observe that "the daughters of Israel are comely, but poverty makes them repulsive."[7] And as if to make matters worse, peasant land holdings were generally less than six acres, of which on average only 1.5 acres were cultivatable—hardly enough to support a family. To make ends meet, peasants would hire themselves out to supplement their meager incomes. In the parable of the landowner who went out early one morning to hire workers for his vineyard, Matthew tells of standing groups of unemployed workers (Matt. 20:1–16). Some lowly farmers were forced to borrow against their annual yields, with the

4. Obery M. Hendricks Jr., *The Politics of Jesus: Rediscovering the True Revolutionary Nature of Jesus' Teachings and How They Have Been Corrupted*, 72.

5. There is good evidence that Jesus may not have been a carpenter but in fact a stone mason who worked in Sepphoris, a Roman and Byzantine city in Galilee just a few miles from Nazareth.

6. John Dominic Crossan, *Jesus: A Revolutionary Biography*, 25.

7. Hendricks, *The Politics of Jesus*, 74.

next year's crop as collateral. One particularly arid year or random accident would destroy the entire family.

Taxes burdened the average person and further impoverished the masses in yet another kind of downward cycle. The empire, no matter how far from the emperor and the city of Rome, carried the burden of the annual collection of tributes and taxes on crops. After their return from Babylon, tithes for Jews were fairly limited. Priests received a small edible portion of the sacrifices made at the Temple.[8] However, as the temple cult grew, it required more and more dutiful contributions from the faithful. Josephus wrote that by the mid-first century, the aristocratic priests had become so incensed at what they perceived as lax payments of tithes and offerings, they sent their servants directly to the threshing floors to forcefully collect the tithes.[9] Eventually twelve different classes of tithes developed. When totaled, taxes of one kind or another devoured about 40 percent of a household's combined income.[10] Often the subsequent descent into poverty meant the arrival of debt collectors, who were ruthless. Debtors were threatened with imprisonment and enslavement for delinquency.

Such debt practices formed the backdrop for the parable of the unforgiving debtor (Matt. 18:23–34). In this story, Jesus told of a kingdom where a king decided to resolve his subjects' debts. As part of the process, the king generously forgave the debt of one man who owed him what translates into literally millions of today's dollars. Afterward, the man whose debts the king had forgiven in turn refused to cancel a debt of a few thousand dollars owed to him. Showing no mercy, he grabbed the second debtor by the throat and demanded payment. When the king heard of this shameful behavior, he ordered that the man he had forgiven be sold into slavery "along with his wife [and] his children, and that everything he owned [be used]—to pay the debt" owed to himself (Matt. 18:25 NLT). The parable mirrors what historians have discovered in ancient documents as an all too common practice. They cite one instance where an entire village was sold into slavery to satisfy a debt. Suicide to avoid enslavement and torture to punish the debtor were also common practices. It should not be surprising that one of the first things Jews did during the Roman

---

8. Priests had much more than the average Israelite. This added to a priestly elitism.

9. William Whiston, trans., *The Genuine Works of Flavius Josephus, the Jewish Historian*, "Antiquities," 20:181.

10. Hendricks, *The Politics of Jesus*, 64–68.

Wars that Josephus described was to seize and destroy the debt ledgers stored in the Temple.[11]

Author Obery M. Hendricks Jr. observed that "hunger, dislocation, and dispossession that resulted from indebtedness and debt default" also meant "debilitating psycho-emotional factors of abiding fear, insecurity, social alienation and seething resentment . . . [which] took their toll upon the morale of the people of Israel."[12] Economic challenges also contributed to overwhelming crime rates of the type and kind described in the parable of the good Samaritan.[13]

Once again, Jesus quoted Isaiah when he spoke of "leaders and princes" who "filled [their] barns with grain extorted from helpless people." Isaiah had demanded what Jesus then echoed. "How then dare you grind people into the dust like that!" he asked (Isa. 3:14–15 NLT).

With this depressing—and perhaps all too familiar—litany of conditions for the hungry, poor, and desolate of his day, we can more thoughtfully ask what the Gospels say Jesus did and said about this greater portion of humanity. The answer to a query of that sort is quite simple. In brief, he fed them. He knew them. He esteemed them. And finally, as the genuine messiah promised by Isaiah, he set out to reshape society into a Kingdom in which there would be no more poor in their midst.

Jesus Fed the Poor and Hungry

One of the better ways to illustrate Jesus's recognition of the very practical need for food is found in the accounts of feeding thousands of followers. On two separate occasions, Jesus responded to hunger by feeding the masses. Some Bible scholars suggest that these similar stories of miraculous feasts were actually differing accounts of the same miracle. No matter. Whether in the first instance, when he fed five thousand—a story found in all four New Testament Gospels (Matt. 14:13–21; Mark 6:31–44; Luke 9:10–17; John 6:5–15)—or in the second instance, when he fed four thousand—reported in two of the Gospels (Matt. 15:32–39; Mark 8:1–9)—Jesus's priorities were to feed them, heal them, and then to teach them about God's way of living with one another in an earthly kingdom.[14]

---

11. Ibid.

12. Ibid., 66, 70–71.

13. Ibid.

14. On both occasions, more people were present than a strict reading of the text implies. In New Testament times, counts were based on males only and did not

Known as the miracle of the loaves and the fishes, the feeding of the five thousand occurred in Matthew after Jesus had heard the news that John the Baptist had been beheaded. Getting into a boat, he was taken to a remote area on the eastern shore of the Sea of Galilee to grieve alone. The crowds heard or saw where he was going and followed him from many surrounding towns. Throngs made the nine-mile journey on foot around the northern tip of the lake to be with him.[15]

As soon as he stepped from his boat, he was mobbed by the multitudes. He recognized that many were tired, hungry, and ill. More importantly, the text says "he felt compassion" for them. So he healed their sick; then he turned to Philip and inquired where he could get bread to feed all these people. Incredulous, Philip pointed out how difficult this would be: "Even if we worked for months, we wouldn't have enough money to feed them!" (John 6:7 NLT). Simon Peter's brother, Andrew, was only slightly more optimistic. Spotting a young boy in the crowd with five barley loaves and two fishes, he said, "But what good is [that small amount of food] with this huge crowd?" (John 6:9 NLT).

Consider the nature of the available food: the loaves were likely barley bread, the least expensive kind eaten only by the poor.[16] The fishes were probably no bigger than what we know today as sardines, which had been dried or pickled to avoid spoilage.[17] Such a paltry offering was hardly enough to feed thousands.

With no viable solution in sight, Jesus told everyone to sit down (John 6:10). Then he "took the loaves, gave thanks to God, and distributed them to the people. Afterwards he did the same with the fish" (John 6:11 NLT). The people all had as much as they wanted (John 6:11–12). There was even food left over.[18] Their hunger satiated, Jesus then taught them the

---

include women and children. It can fairly be assumed that in each instance, food and spiritual sustenance were provided for crowds in excess of ten thousand people.

15. This route was familiar to the Jews, who commonly went around the northern edge of the Sea of Galilee and down the eastern side of the lake on their way to the Temple in Jerusalem during the Passover to avoid contact with the Samaritans, whom they despised.

16. William Barclay, *The New Daily Study Bible: The Gospel of John*, 202.

17. Pickled fish that swarmed in the Sea of Galilee were known all over the Roman Empire. Fresh fish, like the fish the resurrected Jesus provided his disciples on the shore of the Sea of Galilee, were a delicacy.

18. It was customary for people to leave some food as a tip, as it were, for those who served the food. See Barclay, *The Gospel of John*, 203.

principles of his gospel. Afterward, he slipped away into the hills by himself, most probably to pray and later to save the disciples as he walked on the stormy waters of the Galilee (John 6:19–20).

The next day was most likely the Sabbath. The rescued disciples and Jesus attended services at the synagogue in Capernaum. Many of the same people who had been with him the day before ran along the shore to join Jesus at the synagogue. Discerning that they were less interested in his message than they were in receiving more food, he sternly warned them that they should seek after spiritual nourishment just as persistently as they sought food to fill their stomachs.

> I tell you the truth, you want to be with me because I fed you, not because you saw the miraculous sign. . . . But you shouldn't be so concerned about perishable things like food. Spend your energy seeking the eternal life that I the Son of Man can give you. For God the Father has sent me for that very purpose. (John 6:26–27 NLT)

The crowd complained, "What should we do?" Just as God had sent manna to the children of Israel, why, they wondered, wouldn't this messiah do the same by sending them more bread without effort on their part? (John 6:28 NLT). Jesus responded, "Believe in [me], the one [God] has sent" (John 6:29 NLT). Then, in one of what William Barclay called the seven great "I Am" affirmations, Jesus declared, "I am the bread of life" (John 6:35 NLT). Then he said that if they would also partake of the spiritual nourishment he brought them, they would not be hungry again. As Jesus taught on a prior occasion, "Man shall not live by bread alone, but by every word that proceedeth out of the mouth of God" (Matt. 4:4 KJV). It seems that Jesus repeated the motif of the need for nourishment for both body and soul with the recognition that, just as in our own lives, bellies must be full so that hearts can be touched.

Jesus Included the Poor and the Hungry

By inviting the poor and the hungry to sit at his table, Jesus used eating customs and manners as yet another metaphor to illustrate the economic and social equality that should exist in the Kingdom of God. All were to be fed—rich and poor, healthy and sick. At his feast, the poor were ushered in to the seats of honor. The rich were directed to sit at the foot of the table. An appropriate example comes from the Gospel of Luke, which tells us that on one Sabbath, Jesus was dining at the home of one of the leading Pharisees. As was the custom, the uninvited poor could watch the elegant guests from outside the gates of the triclinum, or dining room, as they reclined around the low table. The poor were to be in a type of observation situation, peering rather than partaking. All the guests, as we can imagine, in turn watched Jesus "closely" (Luke 14:1 NLT). Luke tells us that at some point, Jesus noticed that all who had come to the feast were trying to take the seats of honor near the center of the table. While we might think of perhaps the most familiar image of Jesus at a table in Leonardo da Vinci's *Last Supper,* it might be better to picture Jesus and the honored guests reclining around a U-shaped table. And Jesus, making the table to stand for the Kingdom of God, was given the place of honor. He admonished those jockeying for recognition by way of table placement to "take the lowest place at the foot of the table." He said, "Those who exalt themselves will be humbled, and those who humble themselves will be exalted" (Luke 14:10–11 NLT). Then he addressed his host: "When you put on a luncheon or a banquet . . . don't invite [only] your friends, brothers, relatives, and rich neighbors. . . . Instead, invite the poor, the crippled, the lame, and the blind" (Luke 14:12–14 NLT).[19]

John Dominic Crossan explains why what he calls this "table fellowship" becomes such a powerful symbol of God's impartiality. Crossan uses the term "open commensality" to describe what he believes Jesus had in mind. We found Crossan's writing to be impactful, so it merits the inclusion of a somewhat lengthy passage. He writes:

> Think, for a moment, if beggars came to your door, of the difference between giving them some food to go, or inviting them into your kitchen with your family for a meal, or bringing them into the dining room to eat in the evening with your family, or of having them come back on Saturday night for a supper with a group of your friends. Think, again, if you were a large company's CEO, of the difference between a cocktail party in the office for all the employees, a restaurant lunch for all the middle managers, or a private dinner party for your vice presidents in your own home. Those events are not just ones of eating together, of simple table fellowship, but are what anthropologists call commensality—from *mensa,* the Latin word for 'table.' *It means the rules of tabling and eating are miniature models for the rules of association and socialization.* It means table fellowship is a map of economic discrimination, social hierarchy, and political differentiation.[20]

19. See also Matthew 22:1–13. This parable is also found in the Gospel of Thomas, a noncanonical work completely preserved in a papyrus Coptic manuscript discovered in 1945 at Nag Hammadi, Egypt.

20. Crossan, *Jesus: A Revolutionary Biography,* 68; emphasis in original.

There is hardly a more powerful image for us all. In God's earthly king-dom, the poor and the hungry will no longer watch from a distance at the feast of eternal life. The host will not offer mere table scraps to the cat-egorically destitute who are consigned to sit, like poor Lazarus in another parable of the neglectful rich man. Lazarus sat beneath his master's table to catch the scraps dropped by the wealthy. By rearranging the order of dining Jesus taught us what it means to be included. He showed that he would establish a community where people feast "without using a table as a min-iature map of society's vertical discriminations and lateral separations."[21]

The Book of Revelation sounds the same theme. In the third chapter, it describes how Jesus will knock at our doors. We will invite him in to "sup" with us. He will then reciprocate by bidding everyone to "sit with [him on his] throne," or share in everything that he is heir to (Rev. 3:20–21 NLT). Crossan writes that "open commensality is the symbol and embodiment of radical egalitarianism, of an absolute equality of people that denies . . . the necessity of any hierarchy among them."[22]

Jesus Valued the Offerings of the Poor and the Hungry

When it comes to philanthropy and compassion, Jesus understood the relative worth of a charitable gift. He recognized that in God's eyes, the inherent value of a pittance from a poor person is the same as the huge sum of gold from a wealthy person, provided the donor has a sin-cere heart. Jesus commented on this when he observed a widow make her contribution on the Temple Mount. He tenderly spoke about the woman who gave all she had. In Jesus's mind, the widow's small gift represented far more than a much larger donation from a wealthy person whose mo-tives were impure.

---

21. Ibid., 69.

22. Ibid., 71. Like Crossan, Joseph Smith had the same keen insight and followed the example of Jesus by literally putting it into practice. What Crossan calls "open commensality," Joseph calls a "feast after the order of the Son of God"—a meal to which the poor, hungry, halt, and maim were invited. The history of the LDS Church records that Joseph sponsored and attended a "sumptuous feast . . . after the order of the Son of God." The "lame, the halt, and the blind were invited, according to the instructions of the Savior." He said that his heart was "made glad" and that this was a "foretaste of those joys" that we will all experience in heaven. Joseph Smith, et al., *History of the Church*, 2:362–63.

Jesus observed this poor widow at the end of a contentious day of arguments with the Pharisees and the Sadducees. He had been cross-examined on his views ranging from paying taxes to the Romans to Jewish marriage practices. He criticized the "teachers of . . . religious law" for parading around in expensive robes and sitting in the seats of honor in the synagogue while at the same time shamelessly cheating widows out of their property (Mark 12:40). The crowds who witnessed this confrontation "listened to him with great delight" (Mark 12:37 NLT).

Wearied, Jesus made his way from the Court of the Gentiles to the Court of the Women, where he watched the crowds drop their religious donations into collection boxes called *trumpets* because of their shape— narrow at the top and wider at the foot to prevent someone from reaching in and attempting to withdraw fistfuls of money. In total there were thirteen so-called trumpets to collect money for temple expenses such as wood to burn sacrifices and incense to cover the smell of burning flesh. [23] Each trumpet was designated for different expenditures.[24]

No doubt Jesus watched the wealthy wait until all eyes were upon them and then parade across the courtyard to drop large amounts money into the trumpets (Mark 12:41). At some point he saw a widow (who would have been by definition among the poorest of the poor in ancient Israel's culture) unobtrusively drop two small coins called *mites* into one of the trumpets.[25] The coins—actually called *leptons* in Jesus's day—were the smallest Roman coins in use. They were worth next to nothing. Jesus commented to his disciples about the widow's inconspicuous contribution, saying, "I tell you the truth, this poor widow has given more than all the others who are making contributions" (Mark 12:43 NLT). Why? Because God judges a gift not by how much is given but by how much is held back. "For [the rich] gave a tiny part of their surplus, but she, poor as she is, has given everything she had to live on" (Mark 12:44 NLT).

---

23. The incense was a mixture of aromatic herbs burned twice daily on the golden altar in the temple—*ketoret* in Hebrew, from a root meaning "to smoke"(see Exodus 30:34).

24. William Barclay, *The New Daily Study Bible: The Gospel of Mark*, 351–53; see also William Barclay, *The New Daily Study Bible: The Gospel of Luke*, 301–2.

25. The mite was a coin available at the time the King James Bible was translated. The denomination was known in the Netherlands and was a very small coin. By 1611, production had stopped but many were still in circulation.

The Solution

Jesus's ultimate solution to end poverty and hunger went far beyond charitable giving. It involved reordering society into the Kingdom of God and a type of communal living where there would be no poverty. "All the believers were united in heart and mind. And they felt that what they owned was not their own, so they shared everything they had" (Acts 4:32 NLT). As a result, "there were no needy people among them, because those who owned land or houses would sell them and bring the money to the apostles to give to those in need" (Acts 4:34–35 NLT). That was the pattern Jesus admonished the disciples to follow when he made a post-resurrection appearance in the Americas: "And they had all things common among them; therefore there were not rich and poor, bond and free" (4 Ne. 1:3).

Jesus's apostles and first-generation Christians implemented communal-living orders, and "there were no needy people among them" (Acts 4:34 NLT). Luke's Gospel tells of Ananias and his wife, Sapphira, who were asked to sell *all* they had and donate it to the Church for the benefit of everyone. Nothing was to be withheld! We are told in a disturbing story that Peter, as a leader of the new church and Kingdom of God, met with Ananias and Sapphira separately to receive the consecrated cash proceeds from the sale of their property. Ananias misled Peter by not telling him that he had secretly held back some of the money for his personal use. When Peter discovered that Ananias was not telling the truth, he said, "You lied to the Holy Spirit, and you kept some of the money for yourself" (Acts 5:3 NLT). At that very moment Ananias collapsed, dead on the floor.

Then Luke writes that about three hours later, Peter met with Ananias's wife, who had not been informed of her husband's demise. Peter asked her if the amount of money she gave to the community represented all of the proceeds from the sale of their property. She also prevaricated. Peter responded, "How could the two of you even think of conspiring to test the Spirit of the Lord like this?" (Acts 5:9 NLT). Instantly, like her husband, she fell to the floor, dead! The brethren then carried her out and buried her next to her husband. When the rest of the members heard about their deaths, terrible "fear gripped the entire church and everyone else who heard what had happened" (Acts 5:11 NLT). We can surmise that Luke's purpose for including this surprising incident was to advise us against greed and illustrate our obligation to care for others.

Jesus and first-generation Christians who followed him realized that permanently solving poverty involved more than changing hearts and asking for donations. A genuine solution "demanded sweeping comprehensive changes in the political, social, and economic structures."[26] Vast differences in financial resources and the subsequent privileges wealth brought about had to be eliminated. The gulf between rich and poor could not continue. Such radical change meant that a comprehensive revolution in the "distribution of authority and power, goods and resources" was essential if "all people—particularly 'the least of these,' our brethren, as Jesus called them—might have lives free of political repression, enforced hunger and poverty, and undue insecurity."[27]

Within a few centuries, the communal-living orders of first-generation Christians were absorbed once more into the more general, prevailing economic systems. There were some exceptions. To this day, various monastic orders and other small groups of Christians live together in communal-living situations, sharing everything. The communities of believers initiated by the resurrected Lord in the Americas lasted hundreds of years, while those set up by Joseph Smith in Kirtland, Ohio, and Jackson County, Missouri, lasted only decades.

For the most part, the vast majority of true Christian disciples have been content to be a great deal more practical and give what they could through charitable organizations. Protestant Christianity during the nineteenth and twentieth centuries made conscientious efforts to apply Christian ethics to problems such as economic inequality, poverty, racial tensions, child labor practices, poor schools, and war. So-called "social gospel" advocates have continued to focus on the problems associated with poverty and social disparity. Although the movement peaked in the early part of the twentieth century, many of its ideas played an important role during the civil rights movement of the 1960s in the United States.

Today, Christian social principles continue to motivate millions throughout the world who fight poverty, hunger, and disease. Joint efforts by various nondenominational organizations to alleviate the ills of the world are prevalent. LDS Humanitarian Services and its Catholic counterpart are two of many highly organized groups whose stated objective is to relieve suffering for people of all nationalities and religions. The LDS Church often works with Catholic Relief Services to provide help to victims of famine and other natural disasters. One example of the Church's effort to feed the hungry is the Atmit Program, which produces a specialized porridge for malnourished children and others who have lost the

26. Hendricks, *The Politics of Jesus*, 7–8.
27. Ibid., 7–8.

ability to digest regular food. However, none of the mainstream Catholic, Eastern Orthodox, or Protestant groups, including the Mormons, have even begun to implement the living arrangements that can eradicate poverty on the scale Jesus envisioned.

Jesus, Judgment, and the Poor, Hungry, and Destitute

At the end of Jesus's ministry, his priorities had not shifted from those he announced by way of reading the Isaiah text as he stood on the *bimah* in Nazareth. Prior to his betrayal, Jesus spoke about the Final Judgment. He reminded those who heard him then, as well as those who hear him today, that when our lives are weighed in the balance, we will be judged not on what we know or on how many church meetings we attended. Rather, we will be judged on the basis of how well we loved our neighbors, and how well we fed the hungry, clothed the naked, cared for the sick, and visited those in need (Matt. 25:31–46). Love in action was and is the crux of the matter. Do we care deeply enough about all God's children to do something about the most basic needs of our brothers and sisters?

Returning to Isaiah, we are reminded that God asks each of us: "When you come to worship me, who asked you to parade through my courts with all your ceremony? Stop bringing me meaningless gifts; the incense of your offerings disgusts me! . . . I want no more pious meetings. . . . Learn to do good. Seek justice. Help the oppressed. Defend the cause of orphans. Fight for the rights of widows" (Isa. 1:12–13, 17 NLT).

chapter 5

Jesus and the wealthy

In this chapter we want to illustrate that in the days of Jesus's ministry and the early church, pride, self-importance, suffering, and wealth were loyal traveling companions. In addition, after some careful study of the Gospels, we'll argue that the texts quite conclusively indicate that Jesus told parables to warn that those who enjoyed the comfort of money and education too often found enormous satisfaction from undue and relentless admiration of their own achievements and possessions. In the stories, the wealthy convinced themselves that they were more important or better than others because of what they owned. Furthermore, whatever Jesus had to say about wealthy people, it applied to only a few individuals in his day, making their selfishness all the more offensive. John Dominic Crossan has observed the same. He writes that in the Palestine of Jesus's day there was an "abysmal gulf" between the rich and the poor.[1] The rulers and governors comprised about 1 percent of the population, yet they controlled virtually all of the excess capital and wealth. Only a fortunate few were wedded to this small circle of the privileged (bureaucrats and retainers, priests, military generals), and a great divide separated the rich from the rest of the population—many if not most of whom lived in abject poverty.

Although the rich formed a sliver of Palestinian society, they invariably came under scrutiny by Jesus in reverse proportion to their numbers. In stories about farmers with too many barns as well as encounters with people like the haughty man called Dives, he expressed his disapproval. The rich, he said, were susceptible to serious individual temptations. First and foremost, he said they simply failed to notice human suffering. He reproached them for being prideful. Moreover, he pointed out that many had no time for God. And he said that the love of wealth made the rich greedy and selfish. For these reasons most were unfit for the Kingdom of God——a Kingdom where all members would share what they had with each other.

---

1. John Dominic Crossan, *Jesus: A Revolutionary Biography*, 23–26.

The Example of Herod

Herod the Great, king of Judea, epitomized what was so wrong with so many of the rich and powerful of his day. In the end, he was devoid of genuine wealth. Born in 73 BC, Rome appointed Herod their titular client king of Judea at the age of 36. He reigned for just over 40 years until his death in AD 4. He claimed to be a practicing Jew of Arab origin, but pious Jews rightly questioned his religious orthodoxy. Judea prospered under his early reign, mostly because his building program was one of the most ambitious in the ancient world. It primed the economy of the wealthy and lined and re-lined their pockets. He built fortresses, palaces, harbors, aqueducts, and theaters literally on the backs of the poor. His most impressive project was the expansion of the Second Temple in Jerusalem. Thousands upon thousands of pilgrims who came to Jerusalem to celebrate the calendar year's religious festivals must have been dazzled by his new Temple on Mount Zion.

He also used his wealth to maintain his debauchery, cruelty, and power, which were legendary. He was promiscuously unfaithful to his first wife, Dorus. Then he banished her so he could marry the Hasmonean princess, Mariamne. The Hasmoneans were the heirs to the absolutely powerful Maccabean line of high priests. He arranged the marriage in order to manipulate and intimidate the religious leadership and local Roman authority.[2] Later he had Mariamne's sons executed along with his own eldest son, fearing that they were rivals to his throne. He then became disenchanted with Mariamne and finally had her executed as well. It was commonly said, "It [is] better to be Herod's pig than his son."[3] Matthew tells us that when Herod believed that a baby had been born in Bethlehem who might become a contender to his throne, in a horrible fit of rage and paranoia he ordered the murder of all the male children two years old and younger in that village (Matt. 2:16–18).

Ultimately, Herod fell prey to mental illness, becoming only more dangerously unstable and physically debilitated. He suffered worm-infested sores all over his body. His final illness, sometimes referred to as Herods's Evil (Fournier's gangrene), involved putrefaction of the perineum—possibly related to syphilis. Other evidence suggests that he also suffered from kidney disease and bipolar disorder. He died not long after an unsuccessful suicide attempt. His self-serving exploits, heartless butchery,

---

2. Hasmonean priests controlled the Temple.

3. Stephen M. Wylen, *The Jews in the Time of Jesus*, 72.

and despicable use of his ill-gotten wealth and its attendant power stand out as an appalling example of excess.

The Sin of Neglecting the Poor

The story Jesus told about a beggar and a rich man's banquet table in Luke's Gospel is our first example of the sin of neglecting the poor. The protagonist of the story, Lazarus, was penniless. The antagonist, a rich man referred to by early tradition as Dives (simply the Latin word for rich), lived in luxury. Each day, Lazarus, who was covered with sores, lay at Dives's gate in hopes of eating a few scraps of bread that might be thrown his way. As Lazarus lay there, diseased and starving, dogs licked his open sores. Ultimately, Lazarus died and "was carried by the angels to sit beside Abraham." Thereafter, Dives also died and found himself tormented in hell (Luke 16:20–23 NLT).

Next, Jesus told of a scene in the afterlife. Dives saw Lazarus far away, sitting across a great divide that separated the righteous from the wicked.[4] Dives shouted: "Father Abraham, have some pity! Send Lazarus over here to dip the tip of his finger in water and cool my tongue. I am in anguish in these flames." Abraham rebuffed him, saying, "Son, remember that during your lifetime you had everything you wanted, and Lazarus had nothing. So now he is here being comforted, and you are in anguish" (Luke 16:23–25 NLT).

Some additional historical details corroborate Jesus's characterization of Dives as a truly indolent, self-indulgent rich man. When the wealthy of the Roman world ate a meal, they would not sit in chairs or eat with knives, forks, and napkins. Rather, they would recline on pillows on the floor, leaning on one elbow with their legs outstretched, pointing away from the low table. They ate with their hands. Because napkins were unknown, they would clean their hands on hunks of bread and discard the greasy pieces on the ground for the poor, like Lazarus, to grovel after.[5] Another clue that Dives was a glutton is the use of the Greek word for "feasted" in the Amplified Bible (Luke 16:19 AMP). It is not a word that describes an ordinary meal but a sumptuous assortment of gourmet foods.[6] Finally, Jesus commented that Dives wore purple robes only the rich could afford, which was consistent with Dives's habits and lifestyle.

---

4. See also Luke 16:26 NLT and Doctrine and Covenants 138.
5. William Barclay, *The New Daily Study Bible: The Gospel of Luke*, 245.
6. Ibid., 245.

Purple dye was exorbitantly expensive because it had to be painstakingly extracted from sea snails. It was sought after because it did not fade but brightened under the glare of the desert sun.

Why then was Dives in hell? It certainly was not because he was spiteful or mean-spirited toward Lazarus. He did not cast him out or object to him picking up the crumbs from his table. The problem was that Dives was indifferent. Lazarus was simply part of the landscape. As William Barclay writes,

> The sin of Dives was that he could look on the world's suffering and need and feel no answering sword of grief and pity pierce his heart; he looked at a fellow human being, hungry and in pain, and did nothing about it. His was the punishment of the man who never noticed.[7]

Not noticing, or self-absorption that went as far as narcissism, is the disease that often plagues the wealthy. It is also what inhibits all of us from rushing forward to "lift up the hands which hang down" and strengthen "the feeble knees" (Heb. 12:12 KJV). As Daniel Goleman, a well-known psychologist, said, "A prerequisite to empathy is simply paying attention to the person in pain . . . which in turn can lead to understanding, concern and, if the circumstances are right, compassionate action."[8] Noticing the plight of others helps us keep the golden rule to "do to others whatever you would like them to do to you" (Matt. 7:12 NLT).

James, the brother of Jesus, who is traditionally believed to have written the Epistle of James, spoke about wealth in much the same way as Jesus. Parts of his letter sound much like a commentary on the Dives and Lazarus story. James chastened the wealthy for their needless accumulation of wealth and pleaded with them to notice and to listen to the cries of the poor:

> Look here, you rich people, weep and groan with anguish because of all the terrible troubles ahead of you. Your wealth is rotting away, and your fine clothes are moth-eaten rags. Your gold and silver have become worthless. The very wealth you were counting on will eat away your flesh in hell like fire. This treasure you have accumulated will stand as evidence against you on the day of judgment.
>
> For *listen! Hear the cries* of the field workers whom you have cheated of their pay. The wages you held back cry out against you. The cries of the reapers have reached the ears of the Lord Almighty.

---

7. Ibid., 245–46.
8. Daniel Goleman, "Rich People Just Care Less."

You have spent your years on earth in luxury, satisfying your every whim. Now your hearts are nice and fat, ready for the slaughter.

You have condemned and killed good people who had no power to defend themselves against you. (James 5:1–6 NLT; emphasis added)

The Sin of Worldly Neglect

Jesus's outlook on how wealth can interfere with a person's time and inclination to pursue spiritual values is illustrated in two parables from Luke's Gospel: first we consider one referred to as the farmer scattering seed, and second, we consider another one called the wedding feast or banquet. We believe the point of both is that incessant managing of one's wealth becomes selfishly time-consuming and supplants time spent on the things of God.

In the parable of the farmer scattering seed, Jesus compares a seed to God's word, which either takes root and flourishes or does not. The point of the story is to illustrate which temptations and life situations inhibit spiritual growth. Jesus uses a seed to represent the word of God. In one of his scenarios, he talks about a seed that fell among thorns and perished. The thorns have been interpreted as material concerns and worldly possessions that consume all the farmer's time, in this case to excess. They sap his energy and inhibit him from increasing his faith. Jesus explained that the seeds that fell among the thorns represent the unworthy cares and riches of this life that crowd out the good works that should consume the farmer. And so his faith never grows into maturity (Luke 8:13 NLT).

The parable of the wedding feast or banquet is even more explicit about the worldly possessions that place barriers between the wealthy guests and their place in the Kingdom of God. Jesus used a wedding celebration as a vivid and effective allegory. In it the king's servants were literally sent out to personally invite guests to a party, as was the custom in Jesus's day. According to the parable, all the invitees "began making excuses. One said, 'I have just bought a field and must inspect it. Please excuse me.' Another said, 'I have just bought five pairs of oxen, and I want to try them out. Please excuse me'" (Luke 14:18–19 NLT). Another said, 'I just got married, so I can't come'" (Luke 14:20 NLT). Note that all the excuses were about attending to possessions, perhaps including the new wife.

The same parable is found in the noncanonical Gospel of Thomas,[9] which adds more to the list of obstacles that keep some people of means

9. The Gospel of Thomas was discovered near Nag Hammadi, Egypt, in December 1945. It was one of a number of writings referred to as the Nag

from accepting God's message. "I have bills for some merchants. They are coming to me this evening. . . . Excuse me from dinner," one said (Thomas 64:3). Finally, another wealthy man complained: "I have bought a village. Since I am going to collect the rent, I will not be able to come. Excuse me" (Thomas 64:10).

At this point in both stories a disheartened messenger returned to report to his master that only a few had accepted the invitation to the wedding festivities. His master was "angry." He changed the guest list. In place of inviting the rich, he sent messengers out to invite the lowest of society's outcasts. "Go quickly into the streets and alleys of the city and invite the poor, the crippled, the blind, and the lame" (Luke 14:21 NLT). But even then, there was still room for more. So the master said, "Go out into the country lanes and behind the hedges and urge anyone you find to come, so that the house will be full" (Luke 14:23 NLT). At the end of the parable, he said that all the places at the feast were filled, a warning directed at the wealthy: "For none of those I *first invited* will get even the smallest taste of what I had prepared for them" (Luke 14:24 NLT; emphasis added).

The Sins of Self-Importance and Hoarding Wealth

We so often advise that a man can eat only one loaf of bread at a time. Thus, obsessively protecting more than that is hoarding and wasteful. It is a sin. (We tried to find a more appropriate word for that particular offense but "hoarding" is the one we chose to use because it means more than protection of wealth and much more than simply increasing it.) Jesus taught that "[i]f you have two shirts, . . . give one to the poor. If you have food, share it with those who are hungry" (Luke 3:11 NLT).

When a rich young man came to him with this question: "Teacher, what good deed must I do to have eternal life?" Jesus answered, "Live the Ten Commandments. You must not murder. You must not commit adultery. You must not steal. You must not testify falsely. Honor your father and mother. Love your neighbor as yourself" (Matt. 19:16, 18–19 NLT). The rich man told Jesus that he had obeyed all of these religious laws throughout his life.

Satisfied, Jesus invited this good man to join the Kingdom of God by giving all he possessed to the poor. "If you want to be perfect, go sell all

---

Hammadi library. It comprises a wide range of material, including excerpts from *Plato's Republic* and a gospel by Philip, one of Jesus's disciples.

your possessions and give the money to the poor, and you will have treasure in heaven. Then come, follow me." But "when the young man heard this, he went away sad, for he had many possessions" (Matt. 19:21–22 NLT). This wealthy young man had more than he could possibly use, but he could not say in his heart, "It is more blessed to give than to receive" (Acts 20:35 KJV). Because he was unwilling to part with his excess, his condemnation was self-inflicted. He was unfit, at least temporarily, for the Kingdom of God.

Luke speaks of the same sin. In the twelfth chapter of his Gospel, Jesus told of a farmer who had stockpiled his bumper crop. "What should I do?" the farmer asked himself. "I don't have room for all my crops" (Luke 12:16–17 NLT). In a stunning illustration of the sin of hoarding one's wealth, the farmer decided that rather than sharing his excess with others, he would pull down his barns only to build more and bigger ones so that he could protect even more of his belongings. "I'll sit back . . . [I] have enough stored away for years to come. . . . Now take it easy! Eat, drink, and be merry!" (Luke 12:19 NLT). Jesus called the farmer a fool and explained that this man was going to "die this very night." Then, Jesus asked, "Who will get everything [he] worked for?" (Luke 12:20 NLT).

Jesus explained that such selfish behavior makes it impossible to have a truly gratifying or complete "relationship with God" (Luke 12:21 NLT) because greed is inconsistent with loving one's neighbor or with being the generous keeper of one's brother. Ken Stern, the former CEO of National Public Radio, addressed the problem: "Personal drive to accumulate wealth may be [and is statistically proven to be] inconsistent with the idea of community support."[10] And when the community is the Kingdom of God, we can be assured that "personal drive to accumulate wealth" is utterly inconsistent with the Father's plan unless its purpose is to bless the community generally.

Amassing wealth for its own sake alone by building extra barns is the opposite of what Jesus taught, but using one's wealth for the benefit of others is precisely what we must do with what God has given us. It is ironic that the widow's two tiny mites, the entirety of her estate that she offered to others, was worth not even half of the smallest Roman denomination. Yet it was more purely given than anything the conspicuously affluent elite gave at the Temple on the day she dropped her offering into the trumpet receptacle (Mark 12:41–44; Luke 21:1–4).

10. Ken Stern, "Why the Rich Don't Give to Charity."

But we should be clear. Jesus did not condemn wealth in and of itself. Rather, he expected those who made or inherited their wealth honestly—those who, like the righteous wealthy young man, had possessions, goods, and services that might be appropriated to indulge only themselves—to turn away from any selfish accumulation. Jesus called for a more equal distribution of wealth and opportunities to benefit as many as possible. Barclay expressed the idea this way: "If people look on their possessions as given to them for nothing but their own comfort and convenience, those possessions are a chain which must be broken; if they look on their possessions as a means to helping others, those possessions are a crown."[11]

A Camel through the Eye of a Needle

After the rich young man refused Jesus's invitation to give all he had to the poor, Jesus and his disciples discussed how difficult it was for such an individual to enter the Kingdom of God. The young man was an ethical person. He lived an honorable life. He was honest. He was undoubtedly faithful to his wife and family. He cared for his parents. He told Jesus so. Yet he was not ready to take the final step—to consecrate his wealth and himself to the Christian community. Living the Ten Commandments had not had its intended effect to deepen his love enough for others that he was willing to freely share. He had not grasped that "the essence of eternal life is not a carefully calculated keeping of the commandments and the rules and the regulations." Nor did he understand that "eternal life is based on an attitude of loving and sacrificial generosity to other people."[12] When the rich young man's character was put to the test, he flinched. He was controlled by the things of this world and would find it just as nearly impossible to divest himself of his possessions as a camel that tried to "pass through the eye of a needle."[13]

We should take a moment here to observe that many students and scholars of the Gospels have considered the full import of these verses about the camel and the needle. Some have suggested that Jesus's camel metaphor should *not* be taken to mean that the wealthy are excluded from the Kingdom of Heaven. Rather, it simply illustrates what really difficult things the wealthy must do before they can enter. Accordingly, the camel

---

11. William Barclay, *The New Daily Study Bible: The Gospel of Matthew*, 251.

12. Ibid.

13. First-generation Christians lived in communal orders (Acts 4:32–35; 5:1–11).

metaphor was meant to bring to mind what happened when a camel, loaded with goods, was led to enter a walled city after the gates had been closed and secured at night. For those travelers who still needed to enter, it has been said that there was a low, narrow gate tangentially connected to the larger one that was used during the day to accommodate the late trade and traffic. When the gates were locked, a guard was posted to make sure that all entering the city under cover of darkness had good intentions. If the guard was satisfied that no ill will was intended, he would open the smaller gate, which had an opening that was only big enough to allow a large man to hardly pass upright. It has been said that this opening was sometimes referred to as the "needle's eye." If a wealthy traveler with a camel loaded with goods presented himself, it was difficult, if not impossible, for the camel to fit through this small gate without its load, let alone with it. To enter, the camel would have to be stripped of everything the beast was carrying. The camel would then be forced down on its knees to humbly crawl through the gate into the city. It was a fitting analogy in light of Jesus's teachings on wealth, the hoarding of it, and entrance into God's Kingdom.

A second interpretation of this story, one that does not entirely exclude the wealthy, is consistent with the way Jesus treated the wealthy men and women who followed him. Remember, Nicodemus, Joseph of Arimathea, Zacchaeus, and a group of wealthy women were all devoted disciples who supported Jesus and in return were loved and included by him. Nicodemus was a member of the Sanhedrin and a Pharisee. He is mentioned three times in the Gospel of John: first, when he visited Jesus one night to listen to his teachings (John 3:1–21); second, when he interposed a legal objection when the temple guards attempted to arrest Jesus during the Feast of Tabernacles (John 7:45–51); and third, when he assisted Joseph of Arimathea to prepare Jesus's body for burial (John 19:39–42).

Joseph of Arimathea was also a wealthy member of the Sanhedrin (Matt. 27:57; Luke 23:50) as well as a secret disciple of Jesus (John 19:38). He and Nicodemus were friends, and together they dressed Jesus's dead body with fine linen, myrrh,[14] and aloe[15] (Mark 15:46; John 19:39–42).

---

14. Myrrh was a dried resin made from a small thorny shrub that grows in rocky terrain. The shrub's resin is a waxy and brittle substance that can be clear or opaque and varies in color depending upon how old it is. Myrrh is sometimes referred to as the balm of Gilead and is so valuable that in weight, it has been equal to the value of gold.

15. Aloe comes from a flowering succulent plant and is the source of aloe vera gel, believed to have healing properties.

Such items were expensive and far beyond the financial resources of all but the wealthy.

Zacchaeus was an affluent Jewish tax collector who was converted by Jesus himself in Jericho. He repented of his sins and shed his possessions after making amends with those he had cheated. Luke also reported that a group of wealthy women traveled with Jesus and contributed "from their own resources to support Jesus and his disciples" (Luke 8:3 NLT).[16]

It should be noted, however, that other scholars disagree about the possibility of wealthy persons gaining heaven's reward. David E. Garland makes the case that Jesus meant what he said. It is virtually impossible for the wealthy to be saved. Furthermore, he writes that there is no historical evidence for a gate in Jerusalem being called or referred to as the "eye of a needle." Even though walled cities had smaller gates beside or built into a larger gate, they were used for foot traffic only and not larger animals. In addition, Garland says the story of a camel literally crawling through a small gate called the "eye of a needle" as an explanation for what Jesus meant to say can be traced back only to the fifteenth century or possibly the ninth century.[17] Garland claims that it is, therefore, an after-the-fact explanation intended to tone down what Jesus really meant.

Regardless of how difficult Jesus believed it was for a rich man to enter the Kingdom of God, the camel metaphor raises an important issue. How can those who have plenty possibly make the claim that they are following the law and the prophets if they give nothing or only a small portion of what they have to those around them who are in dire need?

In the apocryphal Gospel of Hebrews there is an account that goes to the heart of the matter. It tells the story of the rich young man, but from a slightly different point of view. In this story the rich man said to Jesus, "Master, what good thing must I do really to live?" Jesus responded, "Man, obey the law and the prophets." The young man said, "I have done so." Jesus then told him to go and sell all that he had and distribute it to the poor.

> The rich man began to scratch his head because he did not like this command. The Lord said to him, "Why do you say that you have obeyed the law and the prophets? For it is written in the law, 'You must love your neighbor as yourself,' and look [at] you—there are many brothers of yours, sons of

---

16. These women undoubtedly came from wealthy Jewish or Roman households where the females had some independent means and ability to help financially, and were attracted to Christianity by Jesus's liberal views on the standing of women in society.

17. Leon Morris, *The Gospel According to Matthew*, 493.

Abraham, who are dying of hunger, and your house is full of many good things, and not one single thing goes out of it to them." And he turned and said to Simon, his disciple, who was sitting beside him, "Simon, son of Jonas, it is easier for a camel to go through the eye of a needle than for a rich man to enter the kingdom of heaven."[18]

The rich man from Hebrews who Jesus said could not enter heaven was an utterly selfish individual and gave nothing away. "His real God was comfort, and what he really worshipped were his own possessions and his wealth."[19] In such a case a rich man could not follow Jesus's admonition to become his disciple unless he sincerely repented.

However, within a nanosecond before Jesus's invitation to the young man to "come and follow me," Mark writes, "Jesus felt genuine love for [this man]" (Mark 10:21 NLT). Father James Martin, in a memoir on his pilgrimage to the Holy Land in 2014, writes about his encounter with the text while on the supposed spot where Jesus told the story of the rich young man:

> Jesus "loved him"? Where did that come from? I had heard this Gospel story dozens of times. How had I missed that line? . . . Those three words . . . altered the familiar story and thus altered how I saw Jesus. No longer was it the exacting Jesus demanding perfection; it was the loving Jesus offering freedom. Now I [and we] could hear him utter those words with infinite compassion for the man.[20]

Father Martin goes on to say that the epiphany about the young man and his wealth, together with Jesus's unencumbered affection for him despite his selfishness, changed the way he, Father Martin, saw Jesus's commands. He also observes that later in the story,

> Jesus explicitly offers a promise of abundance: for everyone who leaves behind something, as the rich young man was called to do [as we enter the Kingdom of God], he or she will receive "a hundredfold."

Father Martin writes with a tone of gratitude, "More abundance!"[21] Once again, Jesus tenders us a priceless gift.

Later in the story, Jesus offers the same message to his disciples that Father Martin understood at that moment in Israel. They had pressed him to answer the question of how hard it was for a rich man to get into heav-

---

18. Barclay, *The Gospel of Luke*, 228.

19. Ibid., 228–29.

20. James Martin, *Jesus: a Pilgrimage*, 271.

21. Ibid.

en. Jesus said, "I tell you the truth, it is very hard for a rich person to enter the Kingdom of Heaven" (Matt. 19:23 NLT). Then he told them about the camel and the needle's eye. At this, his disciples were astounded. "Then who in the world can be saved?" they asked. Jesus became pensive and "looked at them intently." He said, "Humanly speaking, it is impossible. But with God everything is possible" (Matt. 19:25–26 NLT). Nothing, not even the sin of accumulating but then keeping wealth to oneself, was out of the question for God to forgive.

The Worth of a Soul

Finally, in the Gospel of Matthew, Jesus summed up the relative worth of wealth in comparison to the worth of a soul. He queried: "What good will it be for a man if he gains the whole world, yet forfeits his soul? Or what can a man give in exchange for his soul?" (Matt. 16:26 NIV). For Jesus, the redemption of a single human being far outweighed the wealth and comforts of this life. Jesus understood that wealth more often than not could be an impediment to spiritual progress. All the wealth of the world was transitory and fleeting, while the life of the immortal soul was an enduring treasure. "Lay not up for yourselves treasure upon earth, where moth and rust doth corrupt, and where thieves break through and steal" (Matt. 6:19 KJV). "Sell your possessions and give to those in need. This will store up treasure for you in heaven! And the purses of heaven never get old or develop holes. Your treasure will be safe; no thief can steal it and no moth can destroy it" (Luke 12:33 NLT).

In the context of his times, Jesus's reference to storing up treasures in heaven where "moth and rust" could not destroy them and where thieves could not "break through and steal" them was a particularly powerful comparison that impressed upon the minds of those who heard his message of how pointless it was to trust in and hoard treasure (Matt. 6:19–21; Luke 12:33–34).[22] In Palestine, "moth and rust" were broad terms connected to any form of wealth. Moths were understood to refer to the destruction of a rich person's fine fabrics and clothing that in Jesus's day were a major investment. The word "rust" (*brosis* in Greek) referred to oxidized metals but may also have been a reference to rodents that consumed supplies of

---

22. A more comprehensive usage of "moth and rust" is suggested in the Amplified Bible: "Do not gather and heap up and store for yourselves treasures on earth, where moth and rust and *worm* consume and destroy" (Matt. 6:19; emphasis added).

grain. Once a store of grain was polluted, it was worthless. Finally, the reference to thieves breaking through was quite a literal one that suggested the common method of entry for thieves. The walls of homes were made of baked clay, and burglars could enter by simply digging through the wall. A man's wealth was hard to secure and was subject to the uncertainties of life.

It is stunningly apparent that when it comes to securing our treasure, things have not changed since Jesus's day. For any of us who rely on money to safeguard our lives, that kind of security can be gone in an instant. The "moth and rust" of losing our employment, of recessions or depressions, of a financial crash in the stock market, of a depreciated housing market, or of the sudden onset of sickness, disease, and accompanying mounting medical bills all loom over us. Ultimately, the only genuine security is the quiet faith that the Lord Jesus Christ brings us the ultimate assurance of eternal life.

The early Christian church "always lovingly cared for the poor, the sick, the distressed, the helpless and those for whom no one else cares."[23] Under the reign of the Roman Emperor Decius, the Christian laity suffered terrible persecution. This era marked the first universal and organized oppression of Christians. Believers were slaughtered. The Roman authorities broke into Christian churches to loot their treasure. On one occasion the Roman prefect demanded of a deacon named Laurentius, "Show me your treasures at once." Laurentius pointed to "the widows and orphans who were being fed, the sick who were being nursed, the poor whose needs were being supplied. 'These, he said, 'are the treasure of the Church.'"[24] We will not be saved by wealth, but rather we will be saved by what we will discover to be the promised reward for kindness to and pure philanthropy for others, what Father Martin calls with considerable surprise and longing—"Abundance!"

23. Barclay, *The Gospel of Matthew*, 279.
24. Ibid.

chapter 6

jesus and the sinner

Both Matthew and Luke recorded what Jesus offered as a template for effective, sincere communication with his Father. It has come to be known as the Lord's Prayer, or in the Eastern Orthodox tradition, simply as the Our Father—a reference to the salutation in the first line.[1]

Matthew included the prayer as part of the celebrated Sermon on the Mount. Jesus delivered that beloved homily in the early part of his ministry when crowds had begun to follow him everywhere because of his powers of healing. Matthew's account of the Sermon says that Jesus "sat down" as he began to teach the large gathering of disciples as well as detractors, likely at the bottom of a natural amphitheater-shaped hillside on the northwest shore near Capernaum, on the Sea of Galilee. In one passage of the Sermon, Jesus said that those who followed him should not "do good" just to be observed by and rewarded with the praise of others. Rather, kindness without regard for public attention should be their law. And neither should true disciples make public demonstrations of their prayers in order to garner the same sort of praise. They should instead go to their "closets," pray in secret, and avoid rattling on with overlong prayers, as did the pagans who demanded attention in the public setting. Finally, Jesus's truly converted disciples should use the Our Father template. Here is Matthew's version of that prayer:

> Our Father which art in heaven, Hallowed be thy name.
> Thy kingdom come. Thy will be done in earth, as it is in heaven.
> Give us this day our daily bread.

---

1. The final line of the prayer, which begins "For thine," is commonly referred to as the Doxology. It was not part of the original text in either of Matthew's or Luke's accounts. The practice of ending a prayer with such an avowal of God's glory was, however, a fairly routine practice. (See, for example, 1 Chron. 29:10–13.) The Doxology appeared at the end of the Lord's Prayer as early as the first century in the Didache (the teachings of the Twelve Apostles). Jerome, the fifth-century translator of the Greek Bible into Latin or Vulgate, wrote that the Doxology was part of the Mass. See William Saunders, "Who Added the Doxology?"

And forgive us our debts, as we forgive our debtors.
     And lead us not into temptation, but deliver us from evil: For thine is
the kingdom, and the power, and the glory, for ever. Amen.
     (Matt. 6:9–13 KJV; emphasis added)

We should note that in the prayer quoted above from the King James Bible, Jesus prayed about sin metaphorically. He compared the sins we ask to be forgiven of to being indebted to God; we "owe" something to him as payment for his benevolence. In the King James Bible the word "debts" is what we ask to have canceled by the Father, who will in turn forgive or cancel those debts to the extent that we forgive others who owe us. The Latin phrase *quid pro quo*—meaning something that is given to you or done for you in return for something you have given to or done for someone else – is appropriate here. It seems to refer to the conditions of the covenant relationship between God and the person offering the prayer.

Luke's account of the prayer comes to us in a more intimate context. He wrote that "one day Jesus was praying in a certain place. When he finished, one of his disciples said to him, 'Lord, teach us to pray, just as John taught his disciples'" (Luke 11:1 NIV). In this personal setting, Luke's version of the Lord's Prayer differs from Matthew's in several ways. It is only half as long, and it uses no metaphors that, although literarily beautiful, may confuse the issue of sin and forgiveness.

Luke's rendition of Jesus's template for prayer (a mere thirty-four words) is more direct. It places sin and God's cognizance of our indebtedness to him in frank yet stark focus. And our attention turns not only to the simplicity of the transaction between the sinner's sovereign and the rest of mankind but also to the grandeur of Jesus's teachings concerning three important ideas: first, the ancient covenant and Oral Laws that precisely defined all manner of sinful thoughts, attitudes, allegiances, and behaviors for first-century Jews; second, the new promise from Jesus concerning redemption from the effects of the litany of those sins; and third, the conditions upon which that redemption is claimed.

We will look at each of those ideas in turn, but in the context of Israel in Jesus's day. Look first, however, through the lens of the line emphasized below in Luke's version of the prayer, and understand the truly revolutionary nature of Jesus's teachings. He said to the disciples:

When you pray, say:
Father,[2] hallowed be your name, your kingdom come.[3]
Give us each day our daily bread.
Forgive us our sins, for we also forgive everyone who sins against us.
And lead us not into temptation.
(Luke 11:2–4 NIV; emphasis added)

Sin Defined for the Covenant People of Israel

The problem of sin is at the heart of Christianity. As Marcus Borg writes, sin is the "central issue in our life with God." Simply put, he says, "We have sinned and need forgiveness."[4] For the ancient people of the covenant, however, understanding what was forbidden or sinful was perhaps even more fundamental.

From a modern perspective, something wrong or "sinful" in a sociocultural context is any act that violates a society's moral rules or any behavior considered forbidden by that society. Generally, the moral code of a group is an agreed-upon set of behaviors that make it possible for men and women to live peacefully together in communities. Thus, something wrong in a civil context might be defined as violation of a society's moral expectations, which revolve around the related ideas of family, sexual conduct, fairness, country, honor, duty, and loyalty—lofty values as well as practical, day-to-day taboos.

It seems that anthropologists, social scientists, political scientists, and philosophers have all had a go at defining sin. Our Google search on the Internet yields 80,600,000 results in 0.55 seconds, with entries from scholars in think tanks to . . . well, one can only imagine. One particularly interesting anthropological explanation of sin begins with the question of why civilizations unite around a common set of values, the violation of which is considered forbidden or sinful. For example, some observers believe that individuals apply distinct sets of moral rules to people depending upon their membership in an in-group (those entitled to be treated by the same rules, often because they belong to the same culture or race) or an out-group (those *not* entitled to be treated by the same rules). A num-

---

2. Some translations say, "Our Father in heaven."

3. Some translations say, ". . . come. May your will be done on earth as it is in heaven."

4. Marcus J. Borg, *Speaking Christian: Why Christian Words Have Lost Their Meaning and Power—And How They Can Be Restored,* 143.

ber of anthropologists hold that the in-group/out-group division evolved to enhance survival. Political scientists Gary R. Johnson and V. S. Falger postulate that nationalism is a form of this in-group/out-group mentality.[5] Group exclusivity and survival may also help explain why some persecuted religious groups coalesce around behaviors considered to be infractions of the norm that challenge the beliefs of the prevalent community. The practice of polygamy by the Mormons during the latter part of the nineteenth century is but one case in point.

From a perspective of ancient religious practice, the issue of what constitutes sin is deceptively simpler. Ancient peoples generally believed in a code or laws that originated from divine beings who governed by covenant relationships. Somewhere in the society's distant past they announced what was moral and immoral based on what offended or pleased them. Gods pronounced the terms and benefits of the covenant relationships as well as the punishments for violating those terms. One of the most ancient examples of such a moral code is the stele, or marker stone, commissioned around 1754 BC by Hammurabi, the sixth Babylonian king of the First Babylonian Dynasty. At the top of the stele is a bas-relief showing two figures. On the left, the smaller figure of King Hammurabi stands before the patron god of Babylon, Shamash (the god of justice), who is seated on his throne and wearing a stately crown consisting of four sets of bull's horns. His size (nearly double that of Hammurabi), his crown, as well as other symbols of his power tell us the order of the Babylonian universe. Shamash, as suzerain alone, hands the law code directly to Hammurabi, who humbly does as his patron directs. Hammurabi, the earthly king and priest, is Shamash's sole representative, interpreter, and enforcer in the empire. Hammurabi's code, consisting of 282 laws with ascending punishments, is typical of the Ancient Near East's eye-for-an-eye (*lex talionis*) ethic. The laws cover such things as contracts, family relationships, acceptable sexual behavior, divorce, and military matters. The code is a transactional one—accepted as well as prohibited behaviors are defined; the violation of the enumerated behaviors is considered sin not only against the community and individuals but also against the will of Babylon's patron god. Punishment follows.

We recognize the same structure for God's commands offered in a kind of covenant relationship in other sacred texts such as the Qur'an for Muslims, the Shruti (Sanskrit for "What Is Heard") for Hindus and, of course, the

5. Jonathan Haidt and Jesse Graham, "When Morality Opposes Justice: Conservatives Have Moral Intuitions that Liberals May Not Recognize," 98.

Torah and the Prophets for Jews, together with the New Testament for Christians. God-generated notions of sin often include more than behaviors. They focus on thoughts, motivations, and feelings. But however and whenever sin is defined, it is always considered harmful, selfish, shameful, and alienating from the divine being who has proffered the laws.

The Law

Like Hammurabi's law code, Jews in Jesus's day defined sin as breaking the commandants dictated to Moses by Yahweh (Hebrew: יהוה [YHWH], traditionally translated as "the LORD" or "Jehovah" in the King James Bible). We know it was Yahweh who wrote the code for covenant Israel in the ten directives, the Decalogue, on stone tablets on Mount Sinai. They included instructions on how to worship this one God, direction to keep the Sabbath day holy, and an absolute imperative to honor one's parents. The code includes prohibitions against blasphemy, idolatry, murder, theft, false witness, dishonesty, and adultery. These Ten Commandments are found twice in the Hebrew Bible—once in Exodus and then reiterated in Deuteronomy.

The Decalogue was the prime directive, but other more specific directives came from five books in the Hebrew canon known as the Pentateuch. These books (originally transmitted orally) were titled after the first words in the texts. They are the foundational texts of Western civilization familiar to us all. Genesis, Exodus, Leviticus, Numbers, and Deuteronomy contain at least another 613 interdictions referred to as the Mitzvah. Taken together, the Decalogue and the Mitzvah were and still are at the core of Israelite law, ethics, and practices. The Mitzvah addresses subjects ranging from dietary laws to animal husbandry. While 248 of the 613 commands were positive, 365 were negative.

A short list of sins called the *Yehareg V'al Ya' avor* was considered so important that "one should let himself be killed rather than violate" the list. Chapter 18 of Leviticus lists murder, idolatry, and forbidden sexual relations—incest, bestiality, and homosexuality. Although many of the 613 laws should not or cannot be observed today because they pertain to animal sacrifice or other out-of-date social taboos, and although scholars debate the dates of their origins, in the time of Jesus, all 613 were considered of equal importance. Much of life for a devout Jew was spent in guaranteeing daily observation and obedience to the laws in order not to offend Yahweh.

Another aspect of Israelite sinfulness revolved around the notion of *ritual cleanliness,* an idea that is perhaps counterintuitive for those living in the twenty-first century. In fact, there is no word in English that completely expresses the concept of ritual cleanliness. The Bible uses the terms "clean" and "unclean," although physical hygiene is not the issue. The words *pure* and *impure* also fall short and do not adequately convey what Jews had in mind, because immoral or intrinsically bad behavior was also not at issue. Rather, the idea of ritual cleanliness centered on who and what "was suitable to enter the sacred precincts of the Temple to approach the divine."[6]

What made a person ritually impure is the subject of author and scholar Stephen M. Wylen's book, *The Jews in the Time of Jesus.* He has compiled a short list that includes, among other things, certain foods, contact with carcasses, genital emissions for both men and women, and contact with people with a list of skin diseases which must all be avoided. Wylen explains that when a person became impure, the primary mode of removing the impurity was the *mikvah,* or full immersion in *living,* or unpiped water. Furthermore, special rituals and animal sacrifices during a full week of purification were necessary in some instances. In other words, acts or behaviors that seem morally neutral to us barred people in the context of ancient Jewish religious culture from full participation in their most sacred rituals.

The Pharisees emphasized ritual cleanliness in everyday life in addition to temple observance, and therefore their days were filled with dozens upon dozens of rituals and practices designed to keep them ritually pure in the sight of God. Those rituals included special hand-washings before meals, abstinence from certain foods, restrictions on what Pharisees could touch or what persons they could associate with. Gentiles, tax collectors, lepers, and menstruating women were all out-of-bounds. Consequently, for the devout followers of Judaism, sin involved far more than what we think of as moral turpitude.

Layered over the Ten Commandments, the Mitzvah's 613 commandments and the rules of ritual purity were the prescriptions of what was known as the Oral Law. Jews believed that at the time Moses received the Ten Commandments on Sinai, he also was given an oral tradition that was handed down through the scholarly religious leaders of each generation. The Oral Law, or unwritten instructions, was at the center of religious observance in Jesus's day, and the Oral Law was considered as binding as any written text.

---

6. Stephen M. Wylen, *The Jews in the Time of Jesus,* 88–89.

Certain differences existed in the Oral Law depending on the rabbi, but the scribes and Pharisees each scrupulously adhered to their particular version of it. The Oral Law explained exactly how a person put into practice the more general principles set out in the Hebrew canon, especially the Decalogue. For example, the command to keep the Sabbath day holy became a complex set of rules. Jews refrained from all work on the Sabbath (from sundown on Friday until sundown on Saturday). They could not carry certain items, light fires, or fight (except to defend themselves). Pharisees could not walk more than two thousand paces. Lamps had to be lit on Friday before sundown. A false tooth or a wig had to be removed lest it cause the user of it to work by carrying extra weight. A sick person could not be healed on the Sabbath but only kept alive in a kind of stasis until the next day.

Keeping track of the canon law must have been exhausting. Seeking forgiveness for offenses was equally onerous. Leviticus specifies the necessary sacrifices for what were called the "sin offering" and the "guilt offering" (Lev. 4:1–35; 5–7 NIV). Each required physical presence at the Temple in Jerusalem as well as the sacrifice of an animal deemed pure. The ritual spilling of the blood of the animal was, according to Levitical direction, pleasing to Yahweh, who required the sacrifice as compensation for the sin that offended him as well as a token of contrition for the person making the sacrifice. The rituals were complicated and expensive. Using Matthew's metaphor in his version of the Lord's Prayer, the spiritual debt owed to Yahweh, incurred for infractions great or small, was heavy and could be relieved only by exacting rituals.

The New Promise from Jesus Concerning Sin

While the ultra-religious scribes and Pharisees in Jesus's day looked to the Decalogue, the Mitzvah, and the Oral Law as a sort of comprehensive catalog of possible sins, Jesus rejected the list-of-commandments approach to sin. The Gospels present a Jesus who was openly critical of this mode of religiosity. He observed and taught others to live the Ten Commandments, but he openly criticized and even ignored many of the oral rules and regulations that grew up around the core commandments. He dined with sinners, ignored well-established Sabbath day rules, and did not ritually wash his hands before eating. He touched unclean objects and people, including lepers, dead bodies, and menstruating women. He rejected religious legalities.

Jesus's contradictory approach to what was sinful began with the two great commandments—love of God and love of neighbor. They are reflected in his prayer template because the plea for forgiveness involved empathy for others' sins and imperfections. He said that "[o]n these two commandments hang all the law and the prophets" (Matt. 22:37–40 KJV). He reasoned that what made our behavior right or wrong, good or bad, sinful or exculpatory, depended upon the answers to a set of questions. First, he asked, did a particular thought, behavior, or deed demonstrate love of God? Second, did a particular thought, behavior, or deed demonstrate love (and hence forgiveness) for individuals? Jesus taught that if our thoughts and behaviors are kindhearted and loving—that is, if they lift, comfort, encourage, forgive, and support others in compassionate and virtuous ways—then God approves. Anything less than this constitutes sin.

This emphasis on loving others cannot be self-absorbing. It is a way of being that includes consideration of others and, as Jesus taught, should even extend to embracing our enemies (Matt. 5:42–44). Jesus's personal example confirms this way of living. He reached out to the outcast, the sick, and the disconsolate. Jesus summed up the core of true religion when he said: "Do to others whatever you would like them to do to you. This is the essence of all that is taught in the law [Torah] and the prophets" (Matt. 7:12 NLT).

The Gospels tell us that Jesus believed that religions that focused on upright conduct based on strict compliance with a list of dos and don'ts are asking us to be self-centered and self-absorbed. His emphasis was and is on individual behavior that if taken to its extreme promotes an unpleasant kind of narcissism. Those who have mastered only a specific lists of dos and don'ts tend to become judgmental and critical of those who have not. Jesus realized that a religion that cultivates a list of outward behaviors (distinctive ways of dressing, speaking, and behaving) quickly produces self-righteous adherents. The sanctimonious religious elite set themselves apart from the sinful and less privileged. The rules and regulations they adhered to became offensive to others and placed unnecessary barriers between God and his children. Such conduct violated the second great command to love one's neighbor.

Marcus Borg identifies another reason it is so fundamentally wrong to focus on our own deeds alone rather than on love of God and neighbor. Doing so is a way of "puffing oneself up to inordinate size. . . . It means making oneself the center of the universe and the center of one's concern" and it is a form of idolatry.[7]

---

7. Borg, *Speaking Christian,* 148.

It is a matter of lordship. It is a matter of either loving and serving God with all our heart, soul, might, mind, and strength, or loving something else (Matt. 22:37; Mark 12:30; Luke 10:27; Deut. 6:5; D&C 4:2; 59:5). The questions Borg asked are, "Who is your lord," and is he "the center of your allegiance?" If the center of your allegiance is *yourself*, *your* religious exactitude, *your* own personal comfort and pleasure, *your* politics, *your* profession, *your* hobbies, *your* bank account—something other than God and neighbor—then you cannot convincingly call yourself a Christian.[8] In the final analysis, it is what we decide to love that really counts.

The Conditions for Redemption

In the context of Jesus defining sin as any thought, behavior, or deed that does not demonstrate love for others, repentance takes on a different meaning. It is more than simply *not* doing something that is specified in a code to be wrong—violations of the Mitzvah, rules of ritual cleanliness, and the Oral Law. It is about a *change of heart*. It is about becoming the kind of person who genuinely desires to bless the lives of others by becoming more generous, loving, and compassionate. It is an attitude that turns one away from destructive behaviors, harsh words, disparaging voices, and vicious contention.[9] It is an attitude that—recall the line in the prayer—forgives the sins of others. As Jesus said, "It is the thought-life that defiles you. For from within, out of a person's heart, come evil thoughts" (Mark 7:20–22 NLT).

In fact, without this change of heart, repentance is pointless, because we return to our old sinful behaviors. Once again, as Borg points out, when personal selfishness is the problem, forgiveness is an inadequate remedy. We may forgive a person for being stubbornly selfish and therefore caught in sin, and that person can feel forgiven. But a "person brutally or miserably afflicted by self-centeredness . . . [is] still a prisoner of *hubris*" and will undoubtedly be a repeat offender.[10] Paul expressed the same sentiment: "For the kind of sorrow God wants us to experience *leads us away from sin* and results in salvation. There's no regret for that kind of sorrow. But worldly sorrow, which lacks repentance, results in spiritual death" (2 Cor. 7:10 NLT;

---

8. Ibid., 150.

9. See also 3 Nephi 11:29: "For verily, verily I say unto you, he that hath the spirit of contention is not of me, but is of the devil, who is the father of contention, and he stirreth up the hearts of men to contend with anger, one with another."

10. Borg, *Speaking Christian,* 149.

emphasis added). In other words, insincere serial repentance for the same bad behavior does not reflect heartfelt change.

Jesus's view of repentance, therefore, involved more than absolution for our indebtedness to Yahweh created by violation of the law; it also required a permanent change of direction and behaviors that originated in the heart. This idea is consistent with the way the word *repentance* is used in the biblical text. In the Old Testament, it means "to turn" or "to return" to God, as the case may be.[11] It refers to Israel's experience of exile in Babylon and means to steadfastly "embark on a journey of return to God—a journey that is also with God."[12] In the New Testament, the more ancient meaning was retained. It meant to faithfully embark on the "way of the Lord," by being baptized into the community of Jesus and experiencing a change of heart that brought about a change in behavior (Prov. 10:29 NLT; Matt. 7:13–14; Acts 2:28).

This change of heart is evidence that a committed disciple sees the world from a uniquely Christ-like point of view, through a different set of glasses. In fact, one of the connotations for the word *repent* in the New Testament is that one's actions "go beyond the mind that we have."[13] Borg elucidates: "The mind that we have is the mind acquired by being socialized in our particular place and time."[14] We see things from the vantage point of our own culture based upon what we have learned. Therefore, to "go beyond the mind" means that we begin to see things in a new way—"a way shaped by God as known decisively in Jesus" that changes our values and the way we conduct ourselves.[15]

Jesus's Attack on the Sinful Practices of the Scribes and Pharisees

Putting love of God and neighbor first challenged the way the scribes and Pharisees observed their religious laws, rules, and regulations. Jesus warned them that living the commandments in ways that harmed others was unacceptable to God. For instance, when Jesus was teaching and was confronted in Galilee by the Pharisees for not washing his hands so as to avoid ritual impurity, Jesus severely reprimanded them for skillfully

---

11. Ibid., 158.
12. Ibid.
13. Borg, *Speaking Christian*, 159.
14. Ibid.
15. Ibid.

sidestepping the Fifth Commandment to honor father and mother (Mark 7:9). He said that some pious Jews refused to help their parents in need of basic sustenance by claiming that they had no funds available to them because all their excess property had been pledged to God. Such religiously encumbered property was called *Corban*[16] (Mark 7:11 KJV). We spoke about Corban in a previous chapter. Recall that the word described a particularly pernicious practice of making a gift specifically dedicated to God and set apart from all ordinary purposes only to be reclaimed by the giver at his discretion. In Jesus's mind, "any regulation which prevented anyone from giving help where help was needed was nothing less than a contradiction of the law of God."[17]

Jesus disclosed how he felt about Corban-like practices that may soothe our consciences by invoking the name of God for something that was obviously wrong. He quoted Isaiah: "You hypocrites! Isaiah was right when he prophesied about you, for he wrote, 'These people honor me with their lips, but their hearts are far away. Their worship is a farce, for they replace God's commands with their own man-made teachings'"— namely Corban, parts of the Mitzvah, ritual cleanliness, and the Oral Law (Mark 7:6 NLT).

It was on this occasion that he castigated dietary restrictions required to maintain the ritual purity enumerated in Leviticus: "You may eat any animal [which had been heretofore prohibited]" (Lev. 11:3–4 NLT).

Jesus said that the practical effect of irrational purity laws was to direct attention away from the inner man and direct it towards love and forgiveness of others. The Pharisees fixed attention instead on outward observances. In a single sentence he did away with religious eating restrictions: "[H]e declared that every kind of healthy food was acceptable in God's eyes" (Mark 7:19 NLT). His disciples were confused. "Don't you understand either?" Jesus exclaimed. "Can't you see that what food you put into your body won't defile you?" (Mark 7:18 NLT). "Food doesn't go into your heart, but only passes through the stomach and then goes into the sewer" (Mark 7:19 NLT).

> It is the thought-life that defiles you. For from within, out of a person's heart, come evil thoughts, sexual immorality, theft, murder, adultery, greed, wickedness, deceit, eagerness for lustful pleasure, envy, slander, pride, and foolishness. All these vile things come from within; they are what defile you and make you unacceptable to God. (Mark 7:20–23 NLT)

---

16. William Barclay, *The New Daily Study Bible: The Gospel of Mark,* 196.
17. Ibid., 197.

Jesus's teachings represented a radical shift in the dogma defining what was therefore sinful. In fact, they contradicted the core of how an orthodox Jew of his day thought he must conduct his life.

Paul also spoke about the supremacy of the law of love when he said, "If you love your neighbor, you will fulfill all the requirements of God's law." Explaining further that the commandments were meant to be an expression of love toward others, he said:

> For the commandments against adultery and murder and stealing and coveting—and any other commandment—are all summed up in this one commandment "Love your neighbor as yourself." Love does no wrong to anyone, so love satisfies all of God's requirements. (Rom. 13:8–10 NLT)

Jesus's Response to Those Who Sinned

Jesus's response to individuals who sinned was invariably compassionate. He was sympathetic to those who, for whatever reason, yielded to life's temptations. He demonstrated his approach to sin when the Pharisees brought a woman accused of adultery to him to be judged pursuant to the Law of Moses. "They put her in front of the crowd charging her with adultery" (John 8:3 NLT), a capital offense in the Old Testament as well as in Jesus's day, although some scholars have suggested that this penalty was rarely if ever carried out. But the law was without equivocation: "If a man commits adultery with another man's wife, both the man and the woman must be put to death" (Lev. 20:10 NLT). Depending upon the circumstances, the guilty were executed either by stoning or strangulation (Deut. 22:13–24).[18]

It was with this severe penalty in mind that some of the scribes and Pharisees brought the accused woman to Jesus on the Temple Mount and pressed him to agree that she should be stoned (John 8:3). They knew that Jesus had a reputation for being compassionate and forgiving, and if they could provoke him, they might be able to "trap him into saying something they could use against him" (John 8:6 NLT).

Barclay explained Jesus's dilemma:

> If he said that the woman ought to be stoned to death, two things followed. First, he would lose the name he had gained for love and for mercy and would never again would be called the friend of sinners. Second, he would come into collision with the Roman law, for the Jews had no power to pass or carry out the death sentence on anyone. If he said that the woman should

---

18. William Barclay, *The New Daily Study Bible: The Gospel of John*, 2:2.

be pardoned, it could immediately be said that he was teaching men to break the Law of Moses, and that he was condoning, and even encouraging [people] to commit, adultery.[19]

However, before the death penalty for adultery could be carried out, a kind of Jewish due process required that at least two witnesses catch the couple in "the very act" of illicit sexual contact. "'Teacher,' they said . . . 'this woman was caught in *the very act* of adultery'" (John 8:4 NLT; emphasis added). Pressing their point further, they reminded Jesus that if he refused to agree that this woman should be executed, he would be in disagreement with Moses the Lawgiver. "The law of Moses says to stone her. What do you say?" the scribes and Pharisees queried (John 8:5 NLT).

Jesus responded: "All right, stone her. But let those who have never sinned throw the first stones!" (John 8:7 NLT). At this point Jesus stooped down and wrote with his finger on the ground for a second time. The woman's accusers "slipped away one by one beginning with the oldest, until only Jesus was left in the middle of the crowd with the woman" (John 8:9 NLT).

The Armenian New Testament adds a verse not in the King James Bible that explains why the woman's accusers left.[20] In this account, as Jesus wrote in the dust on the ground, he disclosed for all to see the sins of the men who accused the woman of adultery. "He himself [Jesus], bowing his head, was writing with his finger on the earth to declare their [the woman's accusers'] sins; and they were seeing their several sins on the stones."[21]

Although this part of the story is not recorded in the King James Bible, the Greek words used to describe what kind of writing Jesus was doing on the dusty ground implies what is missing. The Greek word used broadly to refer to writing anything down is *graphei*.[22] The Greek word used to accuse someone in writing is *katagraphein*—to write down a record *against someone*. The King James uses the latter word to describe what was happening.

At this point in the story, the woman's accusers had gone and Jesus found himself and the woman in the center of a gawking crowd come to see the spectacle of the condemned and shamed woman receiving justice. Jesus asked her: "Where are your accusers? Didn't even one of them con-

---

19. Ibid.

20. Saint Mesrob is responsible for an early fifth-century translation of the Bible known as the Armenian Bible, which traces its roots back to about AD 411 and was completed about AD 434.

21. Barclay, *The Gospel of John*, 2:3.

22. Ibid.

demn you?" After she answered him that no one condemned her, he said, "Neither do I. Go and sin no more" (John 8:10–11 NLT).

The contrast between Jesus and the scribes and Pharisees here is glaring. The scribes and Pharisees were grim investigators, the moral watchdogs of the community, seeking justice and exacting punishment. They saw this poor woman as a pawn in a plot to ensnare Jesus. What authority they had they used to judge and condemn.

Jesus, on the other hand, did not join in the public censure of this woman. Rather, he was interested in reclaiming a child of God. He did not condemn her as an irredeemable sinner, but simply asked her to change and had confidence that she could. "Go and sin no more," Jesus said. His compassion for her to do better reflected his love for her and his belief in her ultimate goodness. He expressed sympathy. He used his mantle of authority to encourage rather than to condemn her.

Often in Jesus's ministry he pointed out that he had not come to doom the world. Rather, he came to redeem it. He said, "I have come to save the world and not to judge it" (John 12:47 NLT). And, "Ye judge after the flesh; I judge no man" (John 8:15 KJV). He expected his disciples to do likewise. "Stop judging others, and you will not be judged" (Matt. 7:1 NLT). Furthermore, he asked rhetorically,

> And why worry about a speck in your friend's eye when you have a log in your own? How can you think of saying, "Let me help you get rid of that speck in your eye," when you can't see past the log in your own eye? Hypocrite! First get rid of the log from your own eye; then perhaps you will see well enough to deal with the speck in your friend's eye. (Matt. 7:3–5 NLT).

Throughout his ministry, Jesus would come under condemnation for his willingness to forgive and associate with sinners. In fact, Mark wrote that

> Levi invited Jesus and his disciples to be his dinner guests, along with his fellow tax collectors and many other notorious sinners. (There were many people of this kind among the crowds that followed Jesus.) But when some of the teachers of religious law . . . saw him eating with people like that, they said to his disciples, "Why does he eat with such scum?" When Jesus heard this, he told them, "Healthy people don't need a doctor—sick people do. I have come to call sinners, not those who think they are already good enough" (Mark 2:15–17 NLT).

Jesus the Messiah, and Sin and Redemption

At first, Jesus's disciples fully expected him to fit the popular expectation of the role of a messiah—to be some kind of Jewish king from the Davidic line who would overthrow the Roman government, re-enthrone Israel, and usher in a Messianic age of universal peace and brotherhood on the earth without crime, war, or poverty. Nevertheless, this was not the kind of messiah Jesus intended to be. After his death, when the hopes that Jesus would have dethroned the Romans were dashed, his followers came to realize that the days for millennial peace would come at some time in the future, after his Second Coming. But during the meridian of time, Jesus had come for a different purpose, and that was to teach people how to love each other and to reconcile humankind with God. He said he had come "to give his life a ransom for many" (Mark 10:45 KJV). He came to vanquish sin and its companion death.

There are many ways of explaining how his suffering, death, and ultimately his resurrection redeemed mankind from sin and why his redemption was efficacious, but that is not our purpose here. Suffice it to say that there are more theories on this subject than could possibly be discussed in a book this size. It is enough to say that the early Christians came to believe that Isaiah was speaking about Jesus of Nazareth when he said, "and he was numbered with the transgressors; and he bare the sin of many, and made intercession for the transgressors" (Isa. 53:12 KJV). John summed up Jesus's concern for the sinner when he said, "Behold the Lamb of God, which taketh away the sin of the world" (John 1:29 KJV).

We conclude this chapter by considering how Jesus taught us to overcome the effects of sin and violence directed at us by others. Once again, he taught us by his example. When sins, atrocities, and violence were committed against Jesus, how he responded tells us the answer. He did as we are instructed to do in the Lord's Prayer. He forgave. He returned good for evil. He could have responded in kind and used his marvelous powers to destroy, but he did not. In not retaliating, he absorbed the wrongs that were directed at him. In the final moments of his life, as if to acknowledge the complexities of mortals' culpability, he asked the Father to "forgive these people, because they don't know what they are doing" (Luke 23:34 NLT).

As N. T. Wright has pointed out, by his example he showed us how to stop the cycle of violence and hurt.

> You have heard that the Law of Moses says, "If an eye is injured, injure the eye of the person who did it. If a tooth gets knocked out, knock out the

tooth of the person who did it." But I say don't resist an evil person! If you are slapped on the right cheek, turn the other, too. (Matt. 5:38–40 NLT).

His method was remarkably simple: "Don't resist evil." By this he did not mean that we should allow evil in the guise of cultural mores or even as blatant wickedness to persist. He meant, rather, that we, each of us who profess discipleship, should merely oppose evil with good.[23] That is how we can overcome our own sins and the world's sins.

---

23. In other words, it is wrong to use violent force to advance objectives. Jesus meant that the end does not justify the means.

chapter 7

jesus and the sick and Afflicted

The litany of afflictions in our day is small compared to that of first-century Palestine of Jesus's day. In his time, every type of disease was rampant in an environment that lacked even the basics of modern healthcare and urban planning. Antibiotics were nonexistent. More often than not, the causes or correct diagnoses of disease were not well understood. The most serious went untreated, only to lead the sufferer to his or her death. Often, ancient remedies made it more unlikely that patients would survive. Bloodletting, for example, was a common practice generally supposed to cure stagnated blood in the extremities that caused many or most sicknesses. To effect a cure, physicians expelled the "bad" blood from the body to restore what the ancients called the "humoral balance." Indeed, the Talmud even recommended a specific day of the week and days of the month for bloodletting. Similar rules are found in Early Christian writings. The practice was not abandoned until well into the second half of the nineteenth century.

The Connection between Sin, Sickness, and Affliction

In the modern era we tend to look for underlying pathogenic causes and genetic dispositions to explain why people get sick. At the time of Jesus, however, the most common explanation for physical illness was relatively simple—sin. Whether as a consequence of an act or as a punishment for some infraction of God's law, sin caused leprosy, blindness, fevers, and untimely death. Rabbi Ami put it this way: "There is no death without sin, and no pains without some transgression."[1]

The men and women of Jesus's day simply worked on the assumption that where there was misery of any sort, there must also be greater or lesser sins involved.[2] And as we wrote in the previous chapter on Jesus's treatment of sinners, there were literally hundreds of ways one might sin.

---

1. William Barclay, *The New Daily Study Bible: The Gospel of Matthew*, 1:277.
2. William Barclay, *The New Daily Study Bible: The Gospel of John*, 2:37.

The list that Moses received from God, together with the Oral Traditions, was an extensive litany of how, when, and with whom one could purposefully or even inadvertently offend God. In addition, there were scribes and priests whose job descriptions included policing society and vociferously pointing out the cause-and-effect nature of the human condition with reference to sin.

"In addition to the idea that sin was the source of suffering and disease, there was a belief that no sickness could be cured until the underlying cause—the sin—was expurgated.[3] For this reason, Rabbi Alexander said, "The sick arises not from sickness, until his sins are forgiven."[4] Rabbi Chija ben Abba explained, "No sick person is cured from sickness, until all his sins are forgiven him."[5] And Rabbi Alexandrai taught, "No man gets up from his sickness till God has forgiven all his sins."[6] Consequently, when Jesus healed the sick, he often uttered a simultaneous acknowledgement that the cure pardoned the sin. Physical healing and forgiveness of sin were opposite sides of the same coin.

The connection between sin, suffering, and sickness—a staple idea in the culture of the Palestine of Jesus—has its roots in the more ancient narratives of the Old Testament. In fact, Genesis begins the story of Adam and Eve and their descendants' sojourn in the lone and dreary world with that very cause-and-effect relationship. When God confronts the couple with questions about their disobedience, their confessions are followed by God's denunciations and punishments. The connection could not be clearer! He says that "because" Eve sinned, he will link her disobedience to "pain" that he will "sharpen" in pregnancy and childbirth. And Adam, whose work will become heavy and long, will "suffer" his whole life through the curse, that he must "*struggle* to scratch a living" from the "cursed" ground (Gen. 3:13–19 NLT; emphasis added).

Likewise, it is hard to find a more direct connection between even vicarious sin and suffering than the plagues visited upon the Egyptians as punishment for Pharaoh's broken promises. As Moses led the Israelites out of the land of Egypt, God sent a decree to the newly freed slaves that if they would "listen carefully to the voice of the Lord your God and do what is right in [my] sight, obeying [my] commands . . . then I

3. Barclay, *The Gospel of Matthew*, 1:277.

4. Ibid.

5. Ibid.

6. William Barclay, *And He Had Compassion: Signs and Wonders*, 73; see also Brad H. Young, *Jesus the Jewish Theologian*, 41.

will not make you suffer any of the diseases I sent on the Egyptians" (Ex. 15:26 NLT). Another example concerns the five offerings described in Leviticus 1 through 7 (burnt, meal, peace, sin, and trespass). They were each performed as either requests for supernatural protections, appeals for miraculous deliverances, or thanks for those deliverances from conscious or inadvertent sins.

Next, we need only read the twisted syllogisms of Job's supposed friends as they each in their turn visited the man whom God had allowed Satan to tempt in a sort of wager concerning Job's righteousness. Eliphaz asked, "Think now, *who that was innocent ever perished?* Or where *were the upright cut off?* As I have seen, those who plow iniquity and sow trouble reap the same" (Job 4:7–8 ESV; emphasis added). Bildad, his second visitor, expressed the identical claim: "See, *God will not reject a blameless person* nor take the hand of evildoers" (Job 8:20 ESV; emphasis added). And the third so-called friend, Zophar, reprises the refrain in the eleventh chapter. A final Old Testament reference comes from King David, who in one of the earlier Psalms, wrote, "Have mercy on me. Heal me, for I have sinned against you" (Ps. 41:4 NLT). Later he sang that the Lord "forgives all my sins and heals all my diseases" (Ps. 103:3 NLT).

Mental illnesses, as opposed to diseases, were explained somewhat differently in Old and New Testament contexts. The most common rationalization for them was the omnipresence of evil spirits. Malevolent spiritual beings hovered about everywhere, especially in the wilderness or in cemeteries. It was said that a person could not stick a pin into the air without pricking one. Consequently, simple, inadvertent, and everyday contact with them was unavoidable and therefore, ex post facto, the cause of a deranged mind. When Jews observed various psychoses, including wild thrashing movements, loss of awareness, dissociative disturbance, multiple personalities, senseless speech patterns, or untamed behaviors, they believed that evil spirits had entered the body and taken control.

Like the causes of physical illnesses, it was assumed that individual transgressions made it easier for such spirits to overwhelm an otherwise healthy individual. Disembodied evil spirits were believed to be wicked people who had died and now longed to be intertwined with corporeal bodies. The text in Genesis even tells us that they were connected with the sons of God who came to earth and begat offspring with the daughters of men (Gen. 6:1–8).[7] Their progeny were supposed to be the unclean spirits who haunted the air.[8]

Jesus rejected the cultural assumptions of his day about the causes of sickness and mental afflictions. Jesus did not teach that sin or evil spirits *invariably* caused disease, physical disabilities, and mental illness.[9] Certainly, he would have admitted, as we all do, that sins and bad behaviors can be the source of physical and psychological illness. The Gospels clearly justify a claim that identified what afflicted men's minds as "evil spirits" (Matt. 8:28–34).[10] However, unlike his contemporaries, Jesus did not teach that there was an absolute causal link between sin and sickness, between possession by evil spirits and mental illness.

Perhaps the most pointed example of what Jesus believed about the connection between sin and afflictions is found in the ninth chapter of John. As Jesus walked with his disciples in Jerusalem, he saw a man who had been blind from birth. His disciples asked, "Why was this man born blind?" As we would expect, they immediately assumed that this man's physical disability was "because of his own sin" or "his parents' sins" (John 9:1–2 NLT).

How could his blindness be connected to sin if he had been sightless from birth? The answer is relatively simple: Jews had devised an explanation even for birth defects. A fetus could sin, they said, while in the womb. An imaginary conversation between a man called Antonius and the Rabbi Judah the Patriarch makes the point. Antonius asks the Rabbi, "From what time does the evil influence bear sway over a man, from the formation of the embryo in the womb or from the moment of birth?" The Rabbi is said to have answered with confidence, "From the formation of the embryo."[11] Antonius then goes on to convince Rabbi Judah that he is wrong, but such an argument for prenatal sin was taken seriously.

---

7. In some modern translations of Genesis 6:4 the word "Nephilite" from the Hebrew *nepilim* is used in place of the word "giant." In this context a Nephilite is an evil spirit that has mated with a human and produced evil offspring that perpetuated the wickedness that brought about God's judgment in the form of a flood. See David Noel Freedman, ed., *The Anchor Bible Dictionary*, s.v. "Nephilite."

8. William Barclay, *The New Daily Study Bible: 1 Timothy*, 104.

9. This is not to say, however, that Jesus rejected the idea that there was a devil and evil spirits who could afflict men and women. His experience with Satan when he was tempted in the wilderness is evidence of this (Matt. 4:1–11).

10. Jesus acknowledged that evil spirits possessed bodies when he healed the demon-possessed man on the western shore of the Sea of Galilee in the region of Gadarenes (Matt. 8:28–34).

11. Barclay, *The Gospel of John*, 2:37–38.

Yet another explanation for birth defects was based on the Jewish belief in a premortal existence. The soul of a man could sin prenatally and thus be afflicted with physical defects at birth.[12] A final way to explain congenital birth defects was to blame them on the sins of the parents. Exodus explains that God would literally "lay the sins of the parents upon their children; the entire family is [thus] affected—even children in the third and fourth generations of those who reject me" (Ex. 20:5; 34:7; Num. 14:18 NLT).

So, with those premortal, in utero, and parental connections to sin in mind, let us return to the disciples' query about the cause of the blindness of the man they encountered on the streets of Jerusalem. Jesus answered their question by saying, "It was not because of his sins or his parents' sins." Rather, he declared that this "happened so the power of God could be seen in him" (John 9:3 NLT). Then, by means of a mud and spittle poultice that Jesus applied to the man's eyes, and with instructions that he rinse it off in the Pool of Siloam just south of the entrance to the Temple Mount, Jesus gave the man his sight (John 9:6–7). Can we even imagine the feelings of the awestruck man? Of his parents? Of the disciples? Or of anyone close by who witnessed the miracle? John wrote that the incident quickly came to the attention of the ever-watchful Pharisees, who interrogated the man's parents as to their sins and the truthfulness of their son's claim to have been healed.

Jesus recognized in the man born blind the idea that sin at any stage of a man's life, or his parents' lives, was not the invariable and only cause of sickness and suffering. Jesus's response to the bad or malicious acts of others and to the accidents and natural disasters illustrates a corollary idea we might call the cause-and-effect nature of sin. Once again in Jerusalem, Jesus was asked about an actual event. The Roman prefect Pilate had recently ordered the executions of Galileans as they were offering sacrifices at the Temple (Luke 13:1). The provoking circumstances had involved a controversy over Pilate's decision to renovate the local water supply. Pilate had proposed to finance the project with temple money dedicated to God. While the need for a more efficient water system was apparent, Pilate's proposal that dedicated holy funds be used for a water project infuriated the elders. Some Galileans, generally thought to be easily impassioned political rabble-rousers, protested. Pilate had sent his soldiers to mingle among the demonstrators, "wearing cloaks over their battle dress for dis-

---

12. Ibid.

guise." The Gospel of Luke recounts that "they were instructed to carry cudgels rather than swords. At a given signal they were to fall on the mob and disperse them."[13] Tragically, the soldiers exceeded their command to break up the gathering without resorting to deadly force. They "dealt with the mob with a violence far beyond their instructions and a considerable number of people lost their lives."[14]

Knowing that his listeners connected sin with suffering, Jesus asked, "Do you think those Galileans were worse sinners than all the other people from Galilee [so that they died while others were spared]? Is that why they suffered?" We can easily picture each person in the crowd nodding in agreement. "Not at all!" Jesus said. "And you will also perish … unless you repent of your sins and turn to God" (Luke 13:2–3 NLT).

On this side of superstition we can infer from Jesus's rhetorical question and his answer that this calamity came about for reasons entirely unrelated to any so-called transgressions of the victims, either individually or collectively. He seemed to say that had those questioning him about this confrontation with the Roman soldiers been unlucky enough to be on the Temple Mount themselves, they too would have suffered the same fate.

Not satisfied with his answer, someone in the crowd pressed Jesus to explain further. As an answer, he reminded the crowd of another tragedy. Eighteen people had died when the tower in Siloam fell on them. So, "were they the worst sinners in Jerusalem?" Jesus asked. Then he answered his own question: "No, and I tell you again that unless you repent, you will perish too" (Luke 13:4–5 NLT).

We might now recall the questions asked and answered by Eliphaz in the story of Job. "Does the innocent person perish? When has the upright person been destroyed? My experience shows," he declared, "that those who plan trouble and cultivate evil will harvest the same" (Job 4:7–8 NLT). For Jesus, however, physical disabilities, disease, and the suffering associated with accidents and natural disasters were not necessarily directly tied to the sins of those who suffered or lost their lives. He said, God "maketh his sun to rise on the evil and on the good, and sendeth rain on the just and on the unjust," (Matt. 5:45 KJV). Likewise, evil was not necessarily the cause of catastrophes. Terrible things can happen to extraordinarily righteous people. Conversely, wonderful things can happen to utterly despicable people.

---

13. William Barclay, *The Gospel of Luke*, 173.
14. Ibid.

The Miracles of Healing

Jesus healed the sick against the backdrop of a society that believed sin and evil spirits caused sickness, mental illness, and random adverse events. By all accounts, the well-witnessed events of restoration of health for the sick and afflicted were the most famed parts of Jesus's ministry. They were what impressed his friends—and rankled his enemies—the most. Those who saw Jesus give sight to the blind, return hearing to the deaf, remove the blight of disease from the leper, and cause the lame and the halt to walk normally again were amazed. And without question, it was the miracle of bringing the dead back to life that caused people to be astounded and therefore compelled to worship him. Crowds followed him everywhere, yearning to be restored to health. They came from places throughout the entire area, "carrying sick people on mats to wherever they heard he was" (Mark 6:55 NLT).

Mark writes that "[w]herever he went—in villages, cities, or the countryside—they brought the sick out to the market places. They begged him to let the sick touch even the fringe of his robe, *and all who touched him were healed*" (Mark 6:56 NLT; emphasis added; see also 4:23–25). As more and more were healed, news of his miracles "swept through the entire countryside" (Matt. 9:26 NLT) so that when Jesus entered a village or town, the numbers soon became so large that Jesus instructed his disciples to have a boat ready so the "crowd would not crush him" (Mark 3:9 NLT). Interest in his ministry was intense and largely came about because he "had healed many people . . . so all the sick people eagerly pushed forward to touch him" (Mark 3:10 NLT; see also Luke 6:19).

We know that even those who were only marginally aware of Jesus mentioned his wondrous powers. Josephus, the Jewish historian and Roman apologist, described a Jewish sect led by James the Just, whom he identified as the brother of Jesus. His history includes sections on John the Baptist, the high priest Annas, Pontius Pilate, and Jesus the Messiah. In his *Testimonium Flavianum,* part of his *Antiquities of the Jews,*[15] Josephus wrote about Jesus as a teacher and miracle worker who attracted a large following even after his death.[16] As New Testament scholars Gerd Theissen and

15. Josephus, *Antiquities of the Jews*, 18.63–64.

16. Some scholars question whether Josephus wrote this passage and believe this paragraph to be a later addition.

Annette Merz conclude, Jesus's "miracles are attested in so many old strata of tradition that there is no doubt about their historical background."[17]

Even Jesus's detractors realized that his powers were breathtaking and undeniable. Because so many people witnessed his marvels, detractors and disciples alike were forced to admit that the healings, the miracles, and the exorcisms really happened, though some tried to explain them away by claiming that the source of his extraordinary powers was the devil, not God.

At the synagogue in Capernaum, upon finding a man with a deformed hand and after a discussion with the Pharisees about whether it was lawful to heal on the Sabbath, Jesus "restored" the man's hand so it was "just like the other one!" (Matt. 12:13 NLT). Soon after that healing, Matthew included an account of a demon-possessed mute and blind man who was brought to Jesus. "He healed the man so that he could both speak and see" (Matt. 12:22 NLT). Dumbfounded, jealous, and skeptical, the Pharisees and scribes searched for an explanation: "It is only by Beelzebul, the prince of demons," they said, "that this fellow drives out demons." (Matt. 12:24 NIV).

Jesus responded that "any kingdom divided by civil war is doomed. A town or family splintered by feuding will fall apart. And if Satan is casting out Satan, he is divided and fighting against himself. His own kingdom will not survive." He then assured those who were listening that he was casting out demons by "the Spirit of God" (Matt. 12:28 KJV).

Here we pause to observe something unexpected: Jesus's detractors never claimed that his miracles had not happened or that he had tricked them. They could only say that his powers came from the Prince of Darkness or Beezubul.

And what of those whose bodies and minds were healed, those who had been restored to physical comfort and peace of mind? Often they began to worship Jesus as the messiah. So after he had restored sight to the blind man, Jesus found him and asked, "Do you believe in the Son of Man?" The man answered, "Who is he, sir? I want to believe in him." Then Jesus said, "You have seen him and he is speaking to you!" Without any hesitation, the newly sighted man said, "Yes, Lord, I believe!" And then he "worshipped Jesus" (John 9:35–38 NLT).

When Jesus healed the leper, "everyone was gripped with great wonder and they praised God, exclaiming, 'We have seen amazing things today!'" (Luke 5:26 NLT).

---

17. Gerd Theissen and Annette Merz, *The Historical Jesus: A Comprehensive Guide*, 281.

The Unique Nature of Jesus's Healings

Jesus surpassed all other healers, but he lived in a world of reports and rumors of others who achieved astonishing cures. People expected miracles, or they explained incomprehensible events by attributing them to miracles. It was a common belief in the Ancient Near East and in ancient Egypt that temples were places where the gods would heal the infirm.[18] The sick were often reported to have been healed at the Temple. There were even reports from time to time of healers raising people from the dead. What is remarkable for us about Jesus, however, was that his healings and miracles received such notoriety in such a competitive healing environment. People seem to have been convinced that Jesus's miracles were not only astonishing and extraordinary but unique.

Typical of Jesus's "competition" was a healer named Elezar. He used conjurations, a ring, and a root to drive out demons.[19] People believed that if Elezar could unerringly perform his ritual, then healing would follow. Any misstep in the liturgical script (a wrong pronunciation, omission of a word or phrase, or even an odd pause) negated a positive outcome. The emphasis, therefore, was on the exact recitation of words, sentences, and paragraphs, and the precise execution of certain magical rituals and incantations to heal the sick.

Cato the Elder, a Roman statesman who lived in the second and third century BC, described a chant that could cure a dislocated limb:

> Take a green reed, about four or five feet long, split it down the middle, and have two men hold it against their hips. Begin to chant: *motas vaeta daries dardares astataries dissnapiter.* Continue until the two halves of the reed come together. Wave an iron knife over the reed. When the haves have joined and are touching one another, take the reed in your hand and cut it on the right and on the left. Fasten it to the dislocation or fracture, which will then heal. Continue to chant every day: *huat hauat, ista pista sista dannabo dannaustra.* Or: *huat haut haut istasis taris ardannabou dannaustra."*[20]

If the healing did not occur, then it could be assumed that the healer had missed a step and must start again.

We may then ask what was unique about the work of Jesus's healing miracles? One fairly obvious element is what is missing from the accounts

---

18. Barclay, *And He Had Compassion,* 7–10.

19. Theissen and Merz, *The Historical Jesus,* 292.

20. Gary M. Burge, Lynn H. Cohick, and Gene L. Green, *The New Testament in Antiquity,* 102–3.

of his miracles rather than what is included. Jesus neither used nor was impressed by formulaic white magic like Cato's chant. In most cases he skipped rote rituals altogether. He healed a leper by the touch of his hand (Matt. 8:1–4). He touched Peter's mother-in-law, and her fever left her. He healed the Roman officer's young servant by simply saying, "[I]t has happened" (Matt. 8:13 NLT). Jesus's modus operandi was straightforward, spontaneous, and not the by-product of complex and belabored rituals. His healing miracles were not formulaic, and they were well beyond the horizon of what people expected.[21]

In addition to the lack of a set ritual, a second feature of Jesus's miracles is that he taught that the key ingredients were the faith of the afflicted person and the power vested in him by his Father. So when two blind men came to him, asking that he have mercy on them, he said, "*Believe* ye that I am able to do this?" They answered, "Yea, Lord." Then, as he touched the blind men's eyes, he said, "According *to your faith* be it unto you" (Matt. 9:28–29 KJV; emphasis added).

When Jesus was entering Jericho, another blind beggar sat at the side of the road. "Jesus, Son of David, have mercy on me!" the beggar shouted. "Be quiet!" the people yelled. The man only yelled louder. When Jesus heard him, he stopped and ordered that the man be brought to him. He asked, "What do you want me to do for you?" Came the response: "I want to see!" Jesus then simply said, "All right, receive your sight! *Your faith has healed you*" (Luke 18:35–42 NLT; emphasis added).

In situations where there was less faith, Jesus's miracles were scarce. For example, in his hometown of Nazareth, Jesus "did only a few miracles there because of their unbelief." He observed, "A prophet is not without honor, save in his own country, and in his own house" (Matt. 13:58, 57 KJV). When faith was not present, the balance in the equation was insufficient. Jesus was more restrained and unwilling to heal the sick and perform miracles.[22]

Consider a final observation on what distinguished Jesus's healings from those by others. His healings were based on the belief that he was doing the will of his Father in Heaven. There was an acknowledgment on his part that his extraordinary power (and permission to use it) came from one greater and separate than himself. When the rich young man approached and called him "Good Master," Jesus's self-effacing response was, "Why callest thou me good? There is none good but one, that is,

---

21. Theissen and Merz, *The Historical Jesus,* 294.
22. Ibid., 293.

God" (Matt. 19:16–17 KJV). He recognized that he was subservient to his Father. "I can of mine own self do nothing. . . . I seek not mine own will, but the will of the Father which hath sent me" (John 5:30 KJV).

When Jesus came to the tomb of Lazarus, he sought his Father's permission before calling a revivified Lazarus from his tomb (John 11:41). He performed the ultimate miracle. When he cried loudly, "Roll the stone aside" (John 11:39 NLT), Martha protested, "Lord, by this time he stinketh: for he hath been dead four days" (John 11:39 KJV). Then, at Jesus's command, Lazarus rose from the damp slab and walked from his tomb. Jesus acknowledged his Father. "[T]hank you for hearing me. You always hear me, but I said it out loud for the sake of all these people standing here, so they will believe you sent me" (John 11:41 NLT).

Finally, Jesus's healings, unlike the work of the magicians who roamed the streets in ancient Palestine, were not self-aggrandizing. He was not interested in impressing the crowds with his personal prowess, or with having a mastery of chants and the healing arts to enhance his reputation. After he had performed a healing or a miracle, Jesus often was heard to say, "See thou tell no man" (Matt. 8:4; 16:20; Mark 7:36; 8:30; Luke 5:14; 9:21 KJV).

The Meaning of Healing Miracles

The Jesus movement came at a time of intense and most often superstitious belief in miracles.[23] Supernatural manifestations were then a kind of proof certain that Jesus was the authentic messiah. In part, these miracles also accounted for the powerful interest in his ministry and the numbers of people, like ancient groupies, who followed him from one location to another. What a show it must have been to witness such extraordinary marvels and sensational acts. In addition to the honest-to-goodness theatricality of the healings and miracles, those who were his hecklers and detractors must have provided additional atmospherics. Finally, for a population that was deeply rooted in an overwhelming belief in the possibility of miraculous cures for the sick and afflicted but also that firmly believed in the connection between transgression and illness, Jesus's miracles were evidence of the confidence they could and did vest in his authority to absolve the sins of those he healed.

Jesus's celebrity and his ability to work miracles always preceded him. And in the context of political as well as spiritual expectations concerning

---

23. Ibid., 290.

a savior, his miracles were verification that he was powerful enough to not only overthrow the empire but also to inaugurate the new Davidic kingdom. But Jesus did not overthrow the Jewish or Roman oppressors. Notwithstanding, he walked out of his tomb with a renewed body. And when he did, his followers understood that he was the messiah, though not the one they had been looking for in vain.

The seventeenth and eighteenth centuries brought to European sensibilities a belief in man's ability to prefer both reason over emotion and the exaltation of the individual. In addition, philosophers wrote to reject conventional religious performance as empty traditions while amending the definition of the miraculous. Many took the position that rather than being reasons to believe in Jesus as the promised, eternal, living Messiah, accounts of his "so-called" miracles were reasons not to believe. Those who lived in the age of science, with its stress on empirical laws of cause-and-effect, had diminished confidence in the miraculous. Theologians tended to doubt the reliability of miracles and looked for more logical explanations for events labeled metaphysical. Rationalist theologians attempted to make miracles plausible. As early as the mid-eighteenth century, German biblical scholar Karl Friedrich Bahrdt said he did not doubt the miracles in the Bible but gave various reasoned descriptions for them. Jesus walking on water, he said, was to be explained by the presence of precisely ordered logs floating in the shallow waters of the Sea of Galilee. Ironically, such an explanation is as incredible as simply accepting that Jesus did indeed walk on water unaided. Others said that the miracle of the loaves and fishes was only an account of people sharing what they already had for the good of the group.

In the milieu of the early nineteenth-century America, the well-educated and upper classes of society began to question miracles. Thomas Jefferson was a prominent advocate of a scientific approach to religion. He edited his own version of the New Testament and used a razor to excise any references to the supernatural in his personal Bible. Thomas Paine agreed with Jefferson that "all the tales of miracles, with which the Old and New Testament are filled are fit only for impostors to preach and fools to believe."[24] Similar views discounting the miraculous increased in societies that valued the scientific method. On the other hand, the lower, less literate classes remained enthusiastic participants in white magic and took pride in using peep stones and divining rods.

---

24. Moncure Daniel Conway, ed., *The Writings of Thomas Paine*, 4:289.

It should not be surprising, then, that many Christian denominations, including Mormons, felt and still feel comfortable with an explanation of the miraculous as simply another more perfect dimension of the cosmos. God is, after all, subservient to the eternal laws of the universe. Dr. John A. Widtsoe, a renowned Mormon scientist, theologian, and church leader at the turn of the twentieth century, said, "A miracle is simply that which we cannot understand, and at which we marvel."[25] Dr. James E. Talmage, a scientist, church leader, and contemporary of Widtsoe, expressed the same idea: "Miracles are commonly regarded as supernatural occurrences, taking place in opposition to the laws of nature. Such a conception is plainly erroneous, for the laws of nature are inviolable." He continued, "However, as human understanding of these laws is at best but imperfect, events strictly in accordance with natural law may appear contrary thereto. The entire constitution of nature is founded on system and order."[26] The idea that miracles cannot violate the natural law is not an entirely new one. In rabbinic Judaism, Talmudic scholars agreed. In their view, when the walls of Jericho came tumbling down, it was not because God directly caused it. Rather, God knew that there would be an earthquake at that place and time so that the city would fall at the exact instance that Joshua's priests blew their horns.

In the twentieth century and beyond, theologians continue to run the gamut of belief—from literal to symbolic to decently skeptical interpretations of the miracles in the Gospels. John Polkinghorne, a theoretical physicist and Anglican priest born in 1930, explained miraculous events in the Gospels as a "new regime of physical experience."[27] John Dominic Crossan, a contemporary historical Jesus scholar, has also written about Jesus's miracles; he offers in *Jesus: A Revolutionary Biography* several compelling interpretations of their empirical reality and social purpose in a "first-century Mediterranean Jewish environment."[28] He argues that there is a "process by which a tradition [of miraculous healings has] changed from its *original situation* in the life of Jesus through its *oral transmission*" to the final canonical form.[29] "Miracles" such as the healing of a leper who was ritually unclean made him symbolically eligible for re-inclusion

---

25. John A. Widtsoe, *Rational Theology as Taught by the Church of Jesus Christ of Latter-day Saints*, 158.

26. James E. Talmage, *The Articles of Faith*, 220.

27. John Polkinghorne, *Faith, Science and Understanding*, 59.

28. John Dominic Crossan, *Jesus: A Revolutionary Biography*, 77.

29. Ibid.

in Jewish society; he became a symbol of "social-boundary protection" in "a society whose leadership [was] intensely concerned with the danger of being absorbed" by the more powerful Rome.[30] "[B]ecause of symbolic contamination," the leprous and unclean person threatened "in microcosm the very identity, integrity, and security of society at large."[31] If symbolic, Crossan argues, then events involving Jesus's compassion and pity for those who were pronounced unclean might, in the process of their transmission, have become magnified into miracles. He elaborates that in our modern societies a cure is likewise the most desirable outcome for disease, "but in its absence, we can still heal the illness by refusing to ostracize those who have it, by empathizing with their anguish and by enveloping their sufferings with both respect and love."[32] It appears that for Crossan, at least, the miraculous healings of the sick in the Gospels are likely elaborations of past real events, but are nonetheless terribly important for us all as lessons in how we ought to love and care for our neighbors.

N. T. Wright disagrees with Crossan with considerable energy. He writes that Jesus would not have attracted huge crowds wherever he went if he was just some "soul doctor." Rather, Jesus challenged the existing power structure as he went about literally "transforming their lives."[33] And Jesus's most extraordinary miracle—bringing Lazarus back from death's cold chambers—is so much more than a call for social reformation, says Wright. Jesus was a genuine healer.

As we write about Crossan and Wright, we can agree with Crossan's conclusion that Jesus's healing miracles provide vitally important lessons for every Christian. We therefore endorse with whole hearts that when Jesus healed the man who had waited for decades at the pools of Bethesda, for example, that event was in every measurable and incalculable way evidence of his infinite love, and therefore symbolic of his wish to have the ritually unclean and undesirable return to social inclusiveness. But notice that as we take to heart Crossan's view of the symbolic meaning of his healing the man at the pools, we also agree with Wright. We see that the symbolic meaning of the event is an equal partner to the belief of its literal reality. Finally, we cite Matthew, who tells us of Jesus's purpose in healing the sick and afflicted. His gospel tells us that "when he saw the crowds, he

30. Ibid., 78.
31. Ibid., 79.
32. Ibid., 81.
33. N. T. Wright, *Simply Jesus: A New Vision of Who He Was, What He Did, and Why He Matters*, 58.

had compassion on them, because they were harassed and helpless" (Matt. 9:36 NIV). And again, when he "went ashore and saw a great throng of people, He had compassion (pity and deep sympathy) for them and cured their sick" (Matt. 14:14 AMPC). He had compassion for them!

In many faith communities, marvelous healings and other miracles are part of the experience of being disciples of Jesus. Believers, therefore, are not overly concerned with the mechanics of how these wonders happen. It is enough to simply experience them. But whether students of the Gospels believe in miracles or not, such events are vitally important to an investigation of the historical Jesus. William Neil, author of numerous books on the Bible as history, said, "If the Gospel records are not to be dismissed as wholly fraudulent, we have to reckon with someone who had this unique power."[34] As a conclusion to a chapter on healing, we write as believers in Jesus as the promised Messiah. We choose to believe in both the literal existence of healing miracles as well as their symbolic power. And we quote William Barclay: "[A healing miracle was] one of the most powerful ways that Jesus defeated pain and suffering. It revealed his compassion or pity—a pity and compassion that ran to the depth of Jesus' being. Jesus's miracles were and are a sign that God cares and that he can make his care effective."[35]

---

34. William Neil, *The Rediscovery of the Bible*, 205.
35. Barclay, *And He Had Compassion*, 81.

chapter 8

jesus and the lost

If we are to consider Jesus and his treatment of an assortment of individuals who have been branded simply as "the lost," perhaps we first ought to think about several Biblical references for that label and exactly who might be included among them. In other words, we need to have a general understanding of what it meant to be called "lost" in his day.

Of the thirty or so times English translations of the Old Testament refer to the idea of loss, nearly all are literal. For example, Genesis speaks about Hagar and her son, Ishmael, after Abraham cast them out. She "wandered on [aimlessly] and lost her way in the wilderness" (Gen. 21:14 AMPC). At age seventeen, Joseph, the beloved firstborn son of Jacob and Rachel, likewise wandered and became lost to his father (Gen. 37). Of course we know that the brothers counterfeited his death and sold him to a caravan on its way to Egypt, and as a result he again became lost to his entire family. Exodus 22 refers to dispute-resolution procedures arising over ownership of an "ox, donkey, sheep, article of clothing, or any lost property" (Ex. 22:9 NLT). And the sixth chapter of Leviticus lays out directions about how a convicted thief must restore to its rightful owner that which was lost by theft (Lev. 6:4). Other Old Testament books refer to lost garments, lost land, lost horses and chariots, and more lost donkeys.

It is, however, the poetry of the psalms and passages of Isaiah that begin to speak about loss in metaphorical rather than literal terms. Psalm 18:45 speaks of "foreigners who lose heart," which obviously does not refer to immigrants who misplaced the muscle that pumps blood throughout their bodies; rather the phrase refers to those who become melancholy or discouraged. Likewise, in the Psalms, King David laments the fact that he has "wandered away like a lost sheep" (Ps. 119:176 NLT). Isaiah writes a soaring prophetic conversation between the Lord and Zion as the personification of his covenant with Israel, whose children are lost both physically and spiritually (Isa. 49:20–21). Many Christian denominations believe in the literal gathering of Israel and in the restoration of the lost Ten Tribes who were carried away from their homes as part of the conquering army's displacement strategies (A of F 10). This passage, however, is also decidedly metaphoric because it casts Israel as a parent whose children are lost in the sense of turning from their covenant heritage and responsibilities.

The references to loss and the lost in the four Gospels are fairly sparse. They all refer to an individual who has spiritually, perhaps even morally, lost their way, with one exception in John that first mentions literal loss when claiming that no crumbs were lost in the miracle of the loaves and the fishes (John 6:12). Matthew's references to loss come in the context of salt and savor (Matt. 5:13), the "lost sheep of Israel" (Matt. 10:6; 15:24 NIV), and Jesus's declaration that he had "come to save that which is lost" (Matt. 18:11 KJV). Mark's single reference is a duplicate of Matthew's reference to salt that has lost its "saltiness" (Mark 9:50). In the remaining uses of the metaphor of loss in John's Gospel, we read of Jesus's declaration, similar to Matthew's report, that he had lost none of the children the Father gave him (John 17:12; 18:9). Finally, in the Gospel of Luke, Jesus said that Zacchaeus, the commissioner of taxes in Jericho, had found salvation and was therefore no longer lost (Luke 19:9–11).

The Bay of Parables

It is in the fifteenth chapter of Luke, however, that we read perhaps the three most deeply impactful parables in all the Gospels. At face value, each is first about the literal loss of something valuable.

Beloved Church of Scotland minister and Bible scholar William Barclay, whose BBC weekly radio broadcasts have been published and re-published as daily Bible study lessons, explained that the three parables come with a sense of ascending importance concerning, as their titles suggest, the lost sheep, then the lost coin, and finally the lost son who we most often call the prodigal son. Nevertheless, it is the consistent, unfailing reactions of the shepherd, the woman, and the father (to both of his sons), as well as friends and relatives, that bring together the message of our chapter on Jesus and those who are lost and then found.

It seems fairly obvious that the lost individuals referred to in the title of our chapter are not those in Jesus's day who may have found themselves to be literally disoriented strangers in the crowded streets of Jerusalem in need of a physical direction. Neither does the word *lost*, used as an adjective in the titles of the three parables of the fifteenth chapter of Luke, describe the likes of an Old Testament donkey, a chariot, or a horse that is out of the vicinity of its owner in ancient Judea, in the illegal possession of another, or otherwise *unfound.* Clearly, the allegorical meanings of lost persons or things in these richly evocative stories and our chapter are the states of minds or chosen set of dissolute, profligate, or irresponsible behaviors that create a sense of alienation from someone, something, or some way of living. However, the more consequential message of the parables is without question the subsequent elation of the shepherd, the woman, and, most importantly, the forgiving father at the discovery and return of the lost. In that sense, we could venture to re-title all three parables by characterizing the finders: The Attentive Shepherd, The Thankful Woman, The Merciful Father.

In his *Jesus, A Pilgrimage,* Father James Martin writes about these and other parables. He and a fellow pilgrim to the Holy Land searched for one of the places Father Martin most wanted to see when they arrived at the Sea of Galilee. He knew it as the Bay of Parables, a place near "the shoreline [that] is a naturally occurring amphitheater, where people would have been able to sit comfortably to listen to Jesus; moreover, the unique acoustics of the site made it easier for the large crowd to hear [him]."[1]

Using directions from a Benedictine monk working in a gift shop at Tabgha, Father Martin found himself at the edge of the lake, gazing "on the blue-green water sparkling under the sun." He found that it was easy to picture Jesus sitting at the base of the amphitheater teaching his followers. He saw "rocky ground, fertile ground, stony ground, and even a thorn bush." He asks: "Does that sound familiar?"[2] At that moment he saw the very stuff of the parable of the sower and The Way found in the three Synoptic Gospels (Matt. 13:1–23; Mark 4:1–20; Luke 8:1–15).

It was also at this site that Jesus taught his listeners—gently, effectively—by means of the brilliant images of his parables, images so familiar to those who heard him teach. He taught them how to find The Way through his gospel. Walter Brueggemann writes about Jesus's methods: "The deep places in our lives—places of resistance and embrace—are not ultimately reached by instruction. Those places of resistance and embrace are reached only by stories, by images, [by] metaphors, and [by] phrases that line out *the* world differently, apart from our fear and hurt."[3]

So on the northern end of the Sea of Galilee, near the site now known as Tabgha, three of the Gospels tell us that Jesus narrated first an extraordinary parable that dealt with a process for finding a road when we

---

1. James Martin, *Jesus: A Pilgrimage,* loc. 356–57, Kindle.
2. Ibid., 357.
3. Walter Brueggemann, *Finally Comes the Poet,* 109–10; emphasis in original.

lose connection with The Way through deception, inadvertence, lack of knowledge, lack of interest, competing interests, and sin.[4]

In the parable of the sower, Jesus anticipated the obstacles that would prevent people from entering or remaining in his Father's Kingdom. Matthew's record says that as Jesus "was sitting beside the sea. . . . such crowds gathered about Him that He got into a boat and remained sitting there, while all the throng stood on the shore. He told them many things in parables, saying, "Listen carefully" (Matt. 13:1–13 AMPC).

But that was not the end of his message at the Bay of Parables. Jesus demonstrated an undaunted commitment to go after, find, and reclaim those who were missing. In that light, we tell each of the three parables about loss and recovery in some detail to add context to the powerful stories, because through them we understand the effort required of each of us to find not only other lost souls but also ourselves.

The Attentive Shepherd

In the parable of the lost sheep, Jesus compared a wandering lamb to an individual who imperceptibly and unintentionally drifted away from God. Interpreted, the parable is about someone who traveled into potentially dangerous circumstances through lack of attention; or, as in the parable about the sower, it describes someone who "does not understand *and* grasp" Jesus's message (Matt. 13:19 AMP; emphasis added).

A certain shepherd, Jesus said, owned one hundred sheep. One of the shepherd's lambs wandered off. He left the ninety-nine to search for it. Once he found the lost sheep, the shepherd "joyfully" carried it "home on his shoulders" (Luke 15:5 NLT). Upon his return to the sheepfold, he invited other shepherds (who probably shared the responsibilities of the fold) to celebrate the lamb's return as well. Jesus concluded his story by saying that "there is more joy in heaven over one lost sinner who repents

---

4. Russian author Leo Tolstoy, a convert to The Way in later life, explained what happened to cause his conversion. He said that the professed orthodoxy barely resembled what Jesus actually taught in the four Gospels, and various "religious doctrine, accepted on trust and supported by external [social, cultural, institutional] pressure, thaws away gradually under the influence of knowledge and experience of life which conflict with it, and a man very often lives on, imagining that he still holds intact the religious doctrine imparted to him in childhood whereas in fact not a trace of it remains." Leo Tolstoy, *The Complete Works of Leo Tolstoy: Confessions,* loc. 2558, Kindle.

and returns to God than over ninety-nine others who are righteous and haven't strayed away!" (Luke 15:7 NLT).

Jesus's comparison of a person who has become lost to a missing sheep was a metaphor everyone in his day could have readily related to. Most people understood that sheep were not always attentive, and if they ambled away from the shepherd and the herd, fatal consequences could follow. A lamb could easily starve to death, become dangerously dehydrated, or be attacked by a wild animal. If the lamb panicked, it could career off a cliff in the rugged countryside and be fatally injured.

In his book *A Shepherd Looks at Psalm 23*, W. Phillip Keller describes additional potentially dire consequences of a lamb becoming separated from the fold. He explains that sheep are indiscriminate eaters and will feed on poisonous weeds. They are also vulnerable to changes in the weather. They must be checked regularly for cuts, abrasions, insect bites, and parasites. When flies buzz around their eyes, they have been known to beat their heads on trees or rocks until they die by their own brute wounds. Sometimes flies lay eggs in a sheep's eyes and cause blindness. And, of course, their greatest enemies are roving predators that slaughter them.[5] Without the constant watchfulness of an attentive shepherd, any lone member of the flock is in serious peril.

Using this parable, Jesus illustrated the kind of caring relationship members of his community should have with each other and especially with those who wander from the fold. He wanted his followers to be conscious and thoughtful of the needs of others, just as a shepherd was alert to the needs of his flock. Keller points out that it was well known that shepherds intermingled their flocks in one place at nightfall. The shepherd recognized every lamb and named each one. In the morning, a shepherd would divide his sheep from the other shepherds' flocks by the sound of his voice. Calling them by name, he would lead them to places where they could safely graze. If one or two started to stray, the shepherd might use his slingshot to edge them back into the fold. He would never drive them, as is customary in the West, where dogs are trained to nip at the back of a sheep's hooves. Rather, the shepherd would gently lead them out to pasture for nourishment.

During the day, shepherds were known to protect their sheep from assaults. Each shepherd possessed a staff and a rod. The shepherd used his hooked staff, or crook, to snag the neck of a stray sheep and pull the ani-

---

5. John MacArthur, *The MacArthur New Testament Commentary: Matthew 8–15*.

mal in the right direction. His rod was a stout stick three or four feet long with a ball on the end about the size of an orange. The shepherd would use it as a weapon to drive off wild beasts and marauders. At night, when each animal entered the sheepfold, the shepherd looked to see if any of his lambs had been injured during the day or was sick, giving special care to those in need. He would affix his rod in a horizontal position across the opening of the fold and require each animal to pass under it so he could carefully examine each one, making certain that it was healthy and strong (Ezek. 20:37 KJV). The fold was often made of piled rocks with thorns along the top or a grotto or other enclosures to protect the sheep from wild animals or thieves. The shepherd himself would sleep at the fold's entrance to protect the entire flock. If the shepherd noticed a missing lamb before retiring for the night, he would expertly track the sheep even for miles to find his animal.

The message of this first parable, then, is twofold. First, Jesus wanted us to understand that we should guard defenseless members of God's Kingdom by caring for his children as a shepherd cares for his sheep. We should lead the way, protecting the young and defenseless, knowing each member of the flock, lovingly nurturing and succoring every person, and inquiring after individual needs. Second, we should be watchful and know when a "lamb" has wandered. We should expertly seek out a lost soul even if it takes us into a menacing wilderness. When we find a lost brother or sister, we should carry them back on our shoulders as it were to safety. Most importantly, at home again, we should wholeheartedly rejoice, forgive, and accept "that which was lost" into our association with no reservations (Matt. 18:11; Luke 19:10 KJV).

When Jesus told this story, the scribes and Pharisees who heard it were offended by the subtext and grumbled at his comparisons. They despised shepherds and everything about them. To use them as an example of what a person should do to care for others was deeply offensive. Shepherds were low on the "scale of religious order."[6] They ignored the Oral Law in large part because as a practical matter they could not observe long hours of prayer or follow the rituals of hand washings before eating or the purity law for handling blood of injured animals. They were by definition unclean. Their lives spent in the fields tending sheep made such religious demands impossible.

---

6. William Barclay, *And Jesus Said: A Handbook on the Parables of Jesus,* 177–80.

The teachers of religious law and the Pharisees, on the other hand, would have preferred that Jesus tell a story about a man of religious rectitude to occupy the center of the story—someone like themselves. But Jesus understood that men like the scribes and Pharisees did not model what he had in mind. They did not go after lost souls but rather criticized them for leaving. If a sinful brother or sister wanted to come back into the fold, they erected religious roadblocks. The offender must prove that he had changed by participating in vacuous prayers, multiple hand washings, and careful eating habits. Jesus loathed such self-righteousness. His shepherd-like concern did not focus on retribution. Instead, Jesus offered compassion, forgiveness, and joy at return—carrying the inadvertent sinner on his shoulders back into the fold.

Neither did the attending scribes and Pharisees overlook the fact that Jesus referred to himself as the good shepherd. He preferred this title to that of Rabbi.[7] "I am the good shepherd: the good shepherd giveth his life for the sheep" (John 10:11 KJV). This designation was intended to describe the kind of leader Jesus was in contrast to the orthodox leaders of his day. It was his way of drawing people into closer proximity to him as an intimate helper. It was his way of shortening the distance between himself and those most in need, and by extension between God and humankind, echoing the twenty-third Psalm: "The Lord is my shepherd; I have everything I need. He lets me rest in green meadows; he leads me beside peaceful streams. He renews my strength. . . . Surely [his] goodness and unfailing love will pursue me all the days of my life and I will live in the house of the Lord forever" (Ps. 23:1–3, 6 NLT).

The Thankful Woman

The parable of the lost coin is about a woman who misplaced one of ten silver coins attached to a necklace. In a way, the parable examines the reverse of the attentive shepherd and his sheep. In the story of the lost sheep, it is the lamb that aimlessly and unintentionally wandered away from the flock. In the story of the coin, however, it is the owner's lack of attentiveness that brought about the loss.

As Jesus told the story, a woman lost a special coin. Distraught, she did everything she could in a frantic search to find it. She lit a lamp and

---

7. See Matthew 9:36 KJV: "But when he saw the multitudes, he was moved with compassion on them, because they fainted, and were scattered abroad, as sheep having no shepherd."

searched in every nook and cranny of her home. Finally, in despair, she combed through the rushes on the floor until she found it (Luke 15:8 NLT). Like the shepherd who found the sheep, when the woman recovered it, she celebrated. She called "in her friends and neighbors and [said], 'Rejoice with me because I have found my lost coin'" (Luke 15:9 NLT). Jesus interpreted the parable for us. Search diligently for lost souls, he said, because "there is joy in the presence of God's angels when even one sinner repents" (Luke 15:10 NLT).

The urgency to find the lost coin is more dramatic when we understand the coin's value. It was likely a drachma, worth about a day's wages in ancient Palestine. Marriage customs of the day held that where means allowed, a Jewish girl conscientiously saved until she had ten drachmas strung together and worn as a necklace or headdress. The ornament was her exclusive property alone and could not even be ransomed to pay her husband's personal debt. Without it she could not be married. And once married, like a ring, it signified her status and therefore had more than sentimental or even economic value.[8]

The difficulty of searching for a coin on the floor of a typical home at the time should not be overlooked. Even though a coin might be lost in a confined area (houses were small and cramped), lack of light would make it difficult to find small objects. Most homes had only small circular windows approximately eighteen inches across that let in little light. The hardened dirt floors were covered with dried reeds and rushes, in which small objects might never be recovered. The broom the woman would have used to sweep the floor in search of the coin would be made of palm branches. Unlike modern brooms, it was a rather inadequate instrument, ill-suited for the task at hand. Undoubtedly, she used the broom to beat the floor's rushes to dislodge the coin from its hiding place rather than to sweep the floor.[9] Once again the message is clear. Lost souls are worth the greatest effort that might be required to recover them. We must search for them and then rejoice with others when they are found.

The Merciful Father

In the parable we know as The Prodigal Son, the loss is most egregious for both the son who goes missing and the father (and we must assume mother) of that child. Jesus's parables of the lost sheep that wandered with-

---

8. Barclay, *And Jesus Said*, 179–80.
9. Ibid., 180–84.

out culpability, the inert coin that was lost by chance, and now the lost son who consciously decided to live a life of deliberate depravity, emphasized the escalating importance of kinds of loss. In this last parable, the son intentionally marches off the path into forbidden territory, rejecting his loved ones, his heritage, and his faith. The details of the story bring us to the conclusion that whatever occurred, the son was at fault. He had asked for an early inheritance. He committed the sins by exploiting that inheritance. When he eventually came to realize that he could not sink lower and that his sins were very serious, he knew he would not be welcomed back at the same status in the family without the imposition of significant penalties.

Unlike the parables of the shepherd and the woman, this story is not about the lengths to which a father might go to find his son. In fact, we may perhaps assume he knew where his son was and possibly even what he was doing. But on this point the text offers no comment. We can imagine, however, that this father felt terrible grief over the loss of a child. But the story is, after all, about the willingness of a heartbroken father to welcome back a humiliated son who chooses at last to come home. It is also a story about the older brother who could not find it possible to re-admit his younger sibling to the family and the household.

The plot of this parable needs only a small amount of context. The younger son who demanded his share of his father's estate before his father died would not have been unknown in Jesus's milieu. Although not common, it was a practice that was actually possible in ancient Palestine. A father could distribute his estate while living, especially if he "wished to retire from the actual management of affairs."[10] So, flush with unearned prosperity, the young man packed his belongings and "moved to a distant land, and there he wasted all his money in wild living" (Luke 15:13 NLT). As his older brother was quick to point out, he not only squandered all his inheritance, but he also spent much of it on prostitutes (Luke 15:30).

After his money was exhausted, "a great famine swept over the land, and he began to starve" (Luke 15:14 NLT). Desperate, he hired on with a local farmer who "sent him into his fields to feed the pigs," something abhorrent to any Jew, who were not allowed to eat pork (Luke 15:15 NLT). The son became so hungry that even the pods he fed to the swine looked good to him. In abject misery, he decided to humbly return home to determine if his father would accept him back as the lowest of servants, a mere slave not even worthy to live in his father's house (Luke 15:16–19).

---

10. William Barclay, *The Gospel of Luke,* 242.

The last of the three parables about loss then turned to the father's response to his lost son's return and also, by contrast, the older brother's response. The father, catching only a glimpse of his younger son from "a long way off," was "filled with compassion." He gathered up the skirts of his robes and "ran to his son, embraced him, and kissed him" (Luke 15:20 NLT). We can easily visualize the scene. Rembrandt painted the moment for us. He pictured the fetid, ragged son with no shoes on his foul feet as the son knelt to bury his shaved and filthy head in his father's stomach. In the painting the father's covered head is turned down toward his son, his arms embracing his son's shoulders. Thereafter, the father called for a feast in his wayward son's honor; a fatted calf was killed and roasted. "We had to celebrate this happy day," his father said. "For [my son] was dead and has come back to life! He was lost but now he is found!" (Luke 15:32 NLT).

Before the celebration, the merciful father fully restored all of his returning son's rights and privileges. He was bathed and dressed in fine linens. The father then gave him his best robe (a symbol of honor), a signet ring (a symbol of authority to stand in the place of the father and transact business), and shoes (a symbol of full acceptance in the family as opposed to the position of a family slave, "for children of the family wore shoes and slaves did not").[11]

Be that as it may, the oldest son was resentful. "All these years I've slaved for you," he complained, "and never once refused to do a single thing you told me to. In all that time you never gave me one young goat for a feast with my friends. Yet when this son of yours comes back after squandering your money on prostitutes, you celebrate by killing the fattened calf!" (Luke 15:29–30 NLT). Certainly, the older son wanted his father to exact penance for his younger brother's sins.

As the scribes and Pharisees listened to Jesus tell this story, we can easily imagine that the sympathies of some were with the *righteous* older son who had never strayed in the first place. Their natural tendency would have been to begrudge the compassion offered to the sinful younger brother. If he wanted to reconnect with his family, then it should have been without fanfare and never with the restoration of privileges. It was only fair. He must be punished for his indebtedness. As far as the keepers of the Law were concerned, the story had the wrong ending.

---

11. Ibid., 243.

The Meaning of Being "Found"

The parables in the fifteenth chapter of the Gospel of Luke are stories of increasing sophistication and nuance. All three have elements of tragedy and loss, of grief at losing some prized thing or individual. And all three have as a sort of third act denouement, the exquisite joy when the lost is returned.[12] Each one emphasizes different aspects of loss and finding. However, the underlying commonality is that all that is lost, no matter the how or the why of becoming absent, is worth reclaiming and is cherished in the sight of the owner. For Jesus there are no "hopeless souls."[13] All of us are worth scouring the earth for and being welcomed home to God.

In Islam, Jesus is recognized as a prophet who was "gentle and mild in word and conduct."[14] In that faith tradition, we chose a final story about Jesus. It illustrates his perspective on finding and seeking out the missing, even the vilest of sinners, like the younger son in Luke's parable. In the Islamic story, we read that one day Jesus came upon a crowd gathered around a "dead scavenger dog; everyone voicing disgust." His disciples are reported to have said, "How noisome (foul) is the smell of this dog." But "said Jesus: (on him be peace) 'How beautiful is the shine of his white teeth'" as if he wanted to rebuke them for [verbally] abusing the dog. . . . [They are only to speak of the lost and] of what God created save at its best."[15] The creature and all of humanity were worth worlds in the eyes of the Master.

A thirteenth-century poet called Nizami Ganjavi (Jalal-ud-Din) told the same story but in traditional *masnavi* rhyming couplets. It is appropriately known as "The Eye of Charity." It begins

> The Messiah's feet, which forever shows us the world,
>> into a small bazaar they journeyed one day where unfurled
> Before him a scene of a wolf-dog lying upon the road . . .
>> like Joseph leaving the well, its soul had left its load.

"Sightseers" came to gape and stare at the dog's body like "vultures at carrion." They called it "disgusting to the brain." One in the crowd "held his nose;" a woman "shut her eyes and looked away." They "threw abuse" at the poor beast.

> "A detestable creature!" "It defiles the earth and air!"
>> "Its eyes are blurred!" "Its ears are filthy!" "Ribs are bare!"

---

12. Ibid.
13. Ibid., 264.
14. Samuel M. Zwemer, ed. *The Moslem World*, 149.
15. Ibid.

Then Jesus came to the scene and "went straight to the meaning":

> "Inside His [the Sultan's] palace many engravings one can find
>   but pearls as white as this wolf's teeth . . . ah, one of a kind!"

The final couplets in Paul Smith's translation are particularly poignant and appropriate to close a chapter about Jesus finding and loving those who are lost:

> The abusive crowd fell silent and ashamed like one
>   rebuked by an insight and wisdom greater than their own.
> There is never one of His creatures that so abused can be . . .
>   without something fine inside, that a loving eye can see.[16]

---

16. Nizami Ganjavi (Jalal-ud-Din), *Nizami: Selected Poems*, loc. 296–97, Kindle.

chapter 9

jesus and the outcasts

The word "outcast" (or rather, *outcasten* in Middle English) first appears in a thirteenth-century book titled *Ancrene Riwle. Outcasten* was related to the Old Icelandic word *kata,* which meant "to throw." The word was first seen in English literature during the sixteenth century and is generally applied to a person who has been ostracized—even forcibly evicted (thrown out) from society.

The common, modern-day use of "outcast" refers to any person or group systematically excluded from another social, political, economic, or religious group. Such collections of individuals are often despised and ignored. Most of us uncomfortably avoid contact with those deemed to be outsiders—we avert our eyes, we abhor their smell, and we deride their clothing. We condemn or mock their insanities and loathe their addictions. We often fear their religious practices. We may just as often judge their customs, rituals, morals, and even their gods. Outcasts are often held responsible for some of the more serious ills of society. We often ignorantly blame them for creating their situations, even to the point of claiming that they bring their rather desperate situations upon themselves.

Fear and ignorance fuel these feelings toward those on the outskirts of society, and countering resentment may develop when the divide between the outcasts and the rest of society widens, leading to grievance that frequently begets violence. In extreme circumstances, those who befriend or extend sympathy to those considered to be outsiders become unpopular or even become outcasts themselves.

It is strange indeed that we can assert with some confidence that today's outcasts in most cases fit easily into the same broad categories as the unclean and the outcasts in New Testament times. In the twenty-first-century United States, the list of outcast groups might include illegal immigrants, refugees, African-Americans, Muslims, Hispanics, women, LGBTQ persons, the homeless, and the mentally incapacitated. In Jesus's day, although the ethnicities or religions may have been different, the list is painfully similar, but with some interesting twists. Jews ostracized Gentiles and

Samaritans. Romans lived apart from Jews, whose devotions they despised. Women were treated as indentured servants or worse. Day laborers and the poor were ignored. Bands of destitute, sick, and infirm people roamed the countryside or begged in city streets. Slaves were exploited as dispensable and impersonal tools. Although, as Martin Luther King Jr. said (quoting the ninteenth-century American minister Theodore Parker), "The arc of the moral universe is long" and "bends toward justice," the outcasts of society were then and are now continuously with us.

Romans, Pagans, and Other Gentiles as Outcasts

There was an irony of role reversals in first-century Palestine. Jews outside that tiny piece of real estate on the Roman Empire's eastern shores of the Mediterranean were despised by the greater Roman states. But inside the country and among the covenant people of Israel, it was the Roman occupiers, pantheists all, who were unclean. For Jews, the Romans were God's outcasts. The vast conglomeration of non-Jews, labeled Gentiles (from the Latin *gentilis,* meaning a foreign clan or tribe that was simply anything other than Jewish), were the outcasts. They were the ones hardly worthy of association, let alone the blessings of Abraham. Gentiles were by their very nature unclean and unworthy.

The Apostle Paul summed up his general feelings about Gentiles when explaining his attitude *before* his conversion: "Live no longer as the *ungodly* do, for they are hopelessly confused. Their closed minds are full of darkness; they are far away from the life of God because they have shut their minds and hardened their hearts against them. They *don't care anymore about right and wrong,* and they have given themselves over to *immoral ways.* Their lives are filled with all kinds of *impurity and greed*" (Eph. 4:17–19 NLT; emphasis added).

If Paul, the apostle to the Gentiles, at one time felt this way, it may be easy to understand how other conservative Jews like Peter found it so extraordinarily difficult to eat with Gentile converts *even after* God had made it clear to him in a vision that the Gentiles were not unclean (Acts 10:9–16).

The rituals and architecture of Hebrew temple worship in Jerusalem are perhaps at this point a fitting metaphor for the way the Jews separated themselves from the rest of humankind, whom they considered castoffs from God's presence. On the Temple Mount, a low but clear barrier surrounded the Courts of the Women and the Priests as well as the Temple itself from the larger Court of the Gentiles, or non-Jews. And to make the code of clean-versus-unclean even more unequivocal, a stone stele was placed on the low parapet at each of the thirteen entrances to the Temple's inner courts—the areas specifically reserved only for Jews. This permanent signage warned in both Greek and Latin that "no foreigner is to enter within the forecourt and the balustrade around the sanctuary. Whoever is caught will have himself to blame for his subsequent death."[1] Such particular and pointed restrictions for those considered as clean for temple worship constituted only one of many social and religious boundaries that separated Jews from the rest of the unworthy world.

The conviction that Jews were set apart as God's superior people made outcasts of all Gentiles. The Jewish prohibition of associating with Gentiles, infidels, and idolaters had its roots in the all-too-familiar story of the Israelite descendants of Abraham, Isaac, and Jacob—and their exodus out of Egypt. While traveling through the wilderness, Moses declared to them, "For you are a holy [as in set apart from all others] people, who belong to the Lord [Yahweh] your God. Of all the people on earth, the Lord [Yahweh] has chosen you to be his own special treasure" (Deut. 7:6 NLT). To prove it, Yahweh entered into a singular covenant with them and granted them unique blessings. The most positive interpretation of this special relationship with God was that the children of Abraham through Isaac and Jacob were set apart for a specific mission that included blessing the nations of the earth by exemplifying God's goodness and by exercising exclusive priesthood powers (Gen. 15; Abr. 1:1–4).

In the *Interpreter's Bible* commentary, the introduction to the Book of Jonah claims that because of the extreme hardships the people of Israel had endured, their confidence in their special status as God's helpers became a sense of superiority and a desire for revenge. It goes on to describe how this minor prophet Jonah was an example of post-exilic Israel. In the years that followed their trials, "there grew up in Israel a spirit of bitterness and vengefulness toward other lands."[2] Israel had endured so much at the hands of their enemies that "there was little inclination to keep alive the vision of Israel as God's servant through whom redemptive truth would one day reach all men."[3] The task for Jonah (and other Old Testament prophets, as well as for Jesus) was "to awaken once again in the people the love God had for *all* people"[4] and to remind Jews that God made all

---

1. Douglas R. Edwards, "Court of the Gentiles," 2:963.
2. *Interpreter's Bible*, 6:872.
3. Ibid.
4. Ibid.; emphasis added.

men and women in "his own image" (Gen. 1:27 KJV). Instead, Jonah initially refused to engage the people of Nineveh and hope for their repentance. Rather than try to help them, Jonah stood as evidence that the Jews' "most passionate desire was that God's wrath should utterly consume all of Israel's enemies."[5]

Jesus's disciples believed him to be the promised messiah who had come to save those who were God's covenant people. But the context of that belief created a situation in which it was simply taken for granted by Jesus's followers that this message of salvation was exclusively for the house of Israel. Thus his disciples assumed that they were to avoid the Gentiles and the Samaritans and only go to the people of Israel. Jesus expanded their mission to include everyone (Matt. 24:14).

Yet early on, Jesus had already begun to broaden the scope of his message. For example, after his encounter and conversation with the Samaritan woman at Jacob's Well, he approved of her taking the message to her local village. Then, Jesus traveled there himself and appealed to other Samaritans to receive his teachings and follow him (John 4:39–41). Likewise, on the other side of the Sea of Galilee, Jesus healed a man possessed of devils. He commanded the man to go and tell the Gentiles who lived in the ten pagan cities on the east side of the Jordan, known as Decapolis, of his marvelous cure at Jesus's hands (Mark 5:15–20 NLV). On another occasion, after Jesus had healed the young servant of a Roman officer, he said, "I tell you the truth, I haven't seen faith like this in all Israel!" (Matt. 8:10 NLV). Then he prophesied that "many Gentiles will come from all over the world— from east and west—and sit down with Abraham, Isaac, and Jacob at the feast in the Kingdom of Heaven"[6] (Matt. 8:11 NLV).

Even though Jesus seemed to "redefine the boundaries of Israel's election,"[7] and despite the fact that he demonstrated an openness to extend salvation to the Gentiles, the Jewish apostles resisted such a generous scope for his work. As mentioned earlier, Peter needed a vision repeated three times to convince him that the gospel should be extended to the Gentiles. "God has shown me that I should never think of anyone as impure," he declared afterward (Acts 10:28 NLT). Unlike the other apostles,

---

5. Ibid.

6. Whether Jesus intended to include Gentiles is a matter of dispute among modern scholars. David Strauss and Ernst Renan believe that Jesus was initiating a universal religion of love in contrast to Jewish xenophobia. Adolf von Harnack, Max Meinertz, and Maurice Goguel do not. See Michael F. Bird, "Gentiles," 214.

7. Ibid.

Paul was chief among those who understood that he had a special commission to "be a light of the Gentiles . . . [and] to bring salvation to the furthest corners of the earth" (Acts 13:46–47 NLT).

Once Peter was persuaded, missionaries went to Samaria, where Philip preached (Acts 8:5). When the apostles in Jerusalem heard of Philip's success among the "outcasts," Peter and John joined him (Acts 8:14). Philip converted and baptized a eunuch, a court official for the queen of Ethiopia (Acts 8:26–39). Over the span of two decades, Paul founded several churches among the Gentiles in Asia Minor and Europe so that by the time he was martyred, he had spread the Christian message throughout the Roman Empire and beyond.

Outcasts within the House of Israel

Whereas Jews generally saw Romans, Gentiles, and virtually every other outsider as those who would be cast out of God's presence, some within the ranks of the *chosen* were likewise despised and excluded. In fact, on the scale of Jewish antipathy, some internal segments of Jewish society were even more repugnant than the Gentiles—such as prostitutes, tax collectors, lepers, and various others according to Torah law. When Jesus was asked why he had shared meals or table fellowship with such "filth," he said, "Healthy people don't need a doctor—sick people do. I have come not to call *those who think they are righteous*, but those who know they are sinners and need to repent" (Luke 5:30–32 NLT; emphasis added).

Jesus was criticized because he did not judge the human family harshly. He drew circles of inclusion, not exclusion. When he reflected on humanity, he made no distinctions between rich and poor, responsible and irresponsible, refined and vulgar, corrigible and incorrigible, healthy and sick. There were no outcasts, no castaways. All were redeemable.

Jesus's close association with tax collectors, especially his fellow apostle Matthew, was particularly vexing to Orthodox Jews (Mark 2:14). As far as they were concerned, Matthew was a sinner by occupation, a traitor to his own community who did the dirty work of collecting taxes for the empire. The Romans levied assessments to pay for governmental operations (military, police, building projects). They imposed customs duties on people in the form of a head tax. Levies on land, houses, slaves, ships, produce, and goods at home or in transport were included. But this was not all. Temple authorities imposed taxes to maintain the Temple. Religious authorities collected tithes on agricultural produce and an additional yearly head tax that went to support priests as well as to pay temple-related expenses.[8] Thus, this double-tiered tax structure was deeply resented. It was onerous and burdensome.

Jewish bitterness about taxes was compounded by the known graft and greed prevalent in the collection of taxes up and down the line. Roman authorities contracted with wealthy local individuals who prepaid the taxes levied by the state for a specific geographical area. Those individuals then collected the amount owed to Rome in addition to what they deemed as their own expenses—at a considerable profit. They hired co-workers called "tax farmers" to do the bulk of the labor. We do not know whether Matthew was one of these wealthy contractors or a tax farmer; regardless, everyone involved made exorbitant profits.[9] Orthodox scribes and Pharisees avoided all contact with them because the law laid down from Sinai forbade profiting from debt (Ex. 22:25; Lev. 25:36–37; Deut. 23:20). The Pharisees contrasted their piety with the evil deeds of tax collectors and criticized Jesus for being a friend to such unclean sinners (Matt. 11:19).[10] No wonder Jewish tax collectors like Matthew and those who associated with them were despised.

With this in mind, it is not difficult to understand why people resented Jesus dining at the home of Zacchaeus, a "very rich" tax collector who lived in Jericho (Luke 19:2 NLT). When Jesus walked into the city, crowds gathered round to get a glimpse of him. Zacchaeus was a short man, so he climbed into a nearby sycamore tree to see the famous healer (Luke 19:4). As Jesus walked through the city, he saw Zacchaeus and called him by name. "Quick, come down!" he said. "I must be a guest in your home today" (Luke 19:5 NLT). Zacchaeus "climbed down and took Jesus to his house in great excitement and joy. But the people were displeased. 'He has gone to be the guest of a notorious sinner,' they grumbled" (Luke 19:6–7 NLT).

At dinner, Zacchaeus was converted and was persuaded to repent. He gave half of his wealth to the poor. For those he had overcharged, he gave "them back four times as much [money as he had taken]!" (Luke 19:8 NLT). His restitution and generosity went further than was legally necessary. Only if his pilfering had been violent was it necessary to recompense the victim fourfold (Ex. 22:4). For ordinary theft, only twofold recompense was mandatory (Ex. 22:4, 7). If an offender voluntarily confessed,

---

8. Lee Martin McDonald, "Tax, Tax Collectors," 620–22.
9. Ibid.
10. Ibid., 621–22.

then the fine was the amount taken plus one-fifth (Lev. 6:5; Num. 5:7). Zacchaeus showed by his deeds that he regretted his sins.[11]

Let us consider some other examples of Jesus's inclusiveness for the ostracized. People shunned lepers at all costs for fear that contact with them would spread the disease. It was probably for this reason that religious laws and observances carefully regulated the treatment of the poor souls afflicted with leprosy. A lack of medical knowledge meant that a diagnosis did not distinguish between different types of skin diseases, so the label of leprosy included both curable and deadly skin diseases under one heading. Concern over how a skin rash or discoloration might develop into something life-threatening led to a general dread of all skin diseases, even such common ailments as psoriasis and eczema. The end result was that those with skin conditions of even small consequence withdrew or were put out of the way. If a leper was somehow cured—actual leprosy in Jesus's day was incurable—the person had to submit to a complicated religious ceremony described in Leviticus to certify that it was truly safe for the person to associate with others. [12]

The multifaceted rituals in Leviticus 14 suggest an extreme level of concern. To be certain a cure had been effectuated, a priest carefully examined the supposedly cured individual. If the person was found to be healthy and well, two birds were killed over running water. A living bird was then dipped in the blood of the dead birds, as was some cedar, crimson yarn, and hyssop. The living bird was set free. The individual then washed himself and his clothes and shaved his face. After seven days had passed, the person was reexamined. The person's head was then shaved along with the eyebrows. Sacrifices were made—two lambs without blemish and one ewe—and offered along with a measure of flour mixed with oil. If still found to be free of the skin disease, the sufferer was anointed on the tip of the right ear, the right thumb, and the right great toe with blood and oil. Upon a final and third examination by the priest, if the person's skin looked normal, they would be handed a certificate stating that the bearer was free of any leprosy and therefore ritually clean and allowed to reenter society.[13]

Dr. E. W. G. Masterman, an early-twentieth-century scholar and physician who wrote about Jewish law and disease, observed that alarm at the very thought of a bad case of leprosy grew out of the realization that "no

---

11. William Barclay, *The New Daily Study Bible: The Gospel of Luke*, 235.
12. William Barclay, *The New Daily Study Bible: The Gospel of Mark*, 50–52.
13. Ibid., 51.

other disease reduces a human being for so many years to so hideous a wreck."[14] A brief digression at this point might help us to understand why lepers were among the most wretched of outcasts.

There were three kinds of leprosy—nodular or tubercular, anesthetic, and a mixture of the two. Nodular or tubercular began with overwhelming fatigue and joint pain. Discolored patches appeared on the back. On the patches, little pink nodules formed and later turned brown. The skin thickened. The nodules concentrated in the folds of the cheek, nose, lips, and forehead. The appearance of a person's face changed beyond recognition. The nodules grew larger and larger, ulcerated, and oozed a foul discharge. The eyebrows fell out and the eyes became staring. The voice became hoarse. When sufferers breathed, they wheezed. The hands and feet also ulcerated. The course of the disease was about nine years and ended in mental decay, coma, and ultimately a terrible death.

Anesthetic leprosy was even worse. Although in the initial stages the disease behaved as described above, as time progressed the nerve trunks were affected and lost all sensation. The muscles wasted away, tendons contracted, and the hands became like claws. Chronic ulceration of the feet caused fingers, toes, and limbs to fall off.[15] There simply could be no more repugnant affliction in the ancient world, and it is understandable why Jews or anyone else for that matter would try to avoid those whose lives were ruined by the disease.

Because people believed that even inadvertent contact with a leper might spread the disease, lepers were banished to quarantine camps outside the cities. When the lepers ventured outside the camps, they were compelled to be identifiable and forced to bare their heads, wear wrent clothing, and cover their lips as they cried out a warning to those approaching: "Unclean, Unclean!" (Lev. 13:45 NLT)[16]

It is with this in mind that we observe a leper who approached Jesus. Undoubtedly, those around Jesus fled as the leper hesitantly approached the Son of God. Jesus was utterly still. The leper knelt in front of him begging to be relieved of his disease. "If you are willing, you can heal me and make me clean," he said. Jesus was "moved with compassion." So he did what must have been completely astounding to anyone observing the situation. He "reached out and touched him." In the same moment, he put his own health at risk and made himself unclean for touching a leper. Then

14. Ibid., 48.
15. Ibid., 49–50.
16. Ibid., 50.

he simply said, "Be healed!" Mark says that "instantly the leprosy disappeared, and the man was healed" (Mark 1:40–42 NLT). Compassion,
inclusion, power, and healing came together to restore vigor and health to
this man sufficient to make him part of the community once again.

Sacred prostitution, meaning sexual encounters legitimated by
association with cultic temple rituals and worship, was an integral part
of ancient Mesopotamian society associated with Canaanite and several
ancient Roman religious observances. Although Torah law did not specifically condemn cultic prostitution, ubiquitous street prostitution or "har-
lotry" in its various iterations was always defined as sinful and thus cause
for a woman to be made an outcast (Lev. 19:29; Deut. 23:18–19). Jesus
spent little time discussing sexual immorality. He abhorred immoral behaviors that weakened marital relationships—and particularly those that
harmed women (Matt. 5:27–28 NLT). Yet Jesus's relationship with prostitutes or harlots lacked overt condemnation. As with the woman caught in
adultery, he said only that sinful behavior should cease and that judgment
was to come at a later date (John 8:1–11). As seen with the tax collectors,
Jesus's empathy overcame his outright condemnation of such practices. As
a result, he included those guilty of such sins into the fold.

One of Jesus's interactions with a prostitute occurred when he was
invited to the home of a Pharisee. In the Middle East, famous rabbis like
Jesus were customarily invited to dine with the affluent and to speak about
the important religious issues of the day. It was the custom during such
an event that townspeople were free to come to the gates of the courtyard
to observe the dinner or even, like the beggar Lazarus, come to the home
of the rich man to pick up table scraps (Luke 17:19–21; John 5:39–47).
In this instance, a repentant prostitute discovered Jesus eating dinner and
"brought a beautiful alabaster jar filled with expensive perfume. Then she
knelt behind [him] at his feet, weeping. Her tears fell on his feet, and she
wiped them off with her hair. Then she kept kissing his feet and putting
perfume on them" (Luke 7:36–38 NLT). We should recall that diners
would recline on low couches with heads and shoulders angled toward the
low table and feet stretched away from the table, thus allowing the woman
to approach Jesus and the others from behind their couches and the table;
the other diners as well as Jesus may have been caught by surprise at first.
But quickly the Pharisees eating with Jesus were aghast! They vehemently
and loudly condemned her behavior as well as his. They concluded that
Jesus could not be a prophet or he would not knowingly have allowed
such a woman to touch him much less to "kiss" and "perfume" his feet

(Luke 7:39 NLT). But in response, Jesus not only allowed her attentions, but he also condemned his host in a stunning turnabout of custom and dining propriety, saying that "corrupt tax collectors and prostitutes will get into the kingdom of God before you do" (Matt. 21:31 NLT).

Jesus's willingness to associate with prostitutes, tax collectors, lepers, and a host of other outcasts was an indication of his compassionate consideration for every human being. Each encounter stands as evidence of how much he valued all of God's children and believed them to be redeemable. Furthermore, he demonstrated that he understood that some sinners were more fit for the Kingdom of God than the sanctimonious and pious Jewish leaders who were so secure in their position that they did not recognize that they were living oblivious lives contrary to the will of God by endorsing rules, regulations, and laws that excluded others. Unlike the Pharisees, who erected holiness barriers to God, Jesus did not situate emotional or religious walls between those who were shunned by the society and the ultra-religious.

Jesus's impulse for compassion surpassed the Pharisees' quest to be separate and apart from the evils of the world. Even the dregs of society—the poor, the meek, and the immoral—could be retrieved. For Jesus, compassion and inclusion defined himself and therefore his Father. Through him we know what God is like, and we see that we are to love and nurture all of our brothers and sisters regardless of their circumstances.

chapter 10

jesus and suffering

A chapter about Jesus and suffering could easily begin with any number of references to a piece of music, a classic work of literature or art, or, always, a verse of scripture. In fact, this introduction is the fourth or fifth iteration we have attempted on this topic using all of the above. Finally settled and sufficiently narrowed, however, let us begin with an image from a small fourteenth-century chapel in Padua, Italy, and verses from a twentieth-century hymn. Each work introduces the topic as only the arts can, with an economy of visual or written vocabulary that condenses our deepest feelings about a word that we use to incorporate dozens of other words. Indeed, the word *suffering* as a universal condition, or as an adjective to describe the condition, has so many possible nuanced synonyms—pain, agony, ache, hurt, grief, sorrow, torment, torture, anguish, bereavement, heartache, heartbreak, disappointment, anxiousness, worry, distress, woe, misery, travail, desolation, wretchedness, melancholy, despair, despondency, trauma, hopelessness, ailing, dejection, disconsolation, hardship, misfortune, and affliction.

The Image of Suffering

The tiny, private chapel in Padua, Italy, is known as the Arena Chapel by virtue of its proximity to an ancient Roman amphitheater in the city. The chapel was commissioned by a wealthy banker by the name of Enrico Scrovegni (who is pictured on the west wall among the saved in a setting of the Last Judgment). He is shown presenting a model of the chapel to the Virgin, perhaps as an act of penance for his sins. The artist Giotto painted the scene—as well as all of the paintings on literally every inch of the other three walls—at the turn of the fourteenth century.

One of the most famous frescos in Renaissance art is in the center of the chapel's north wall. This painting is titled *The Lamentation*. Its subject is a medieval one, not actually part of any account in the four Gospels. It is a painting of pure, abject suffering. Every single synonym we listed above applies to the twenty-seven figures who surround the body of Jesus. Ten angels in the sky wring their hands, cover their faces, contort their bodies, and open their mouths in silent agony. Two men standing below on our right look on, also in soundless grief, their faces showing solemn, desolate expressions. The only other living male is most likely John the Beloved. Standing to the left of the older men, he is younger and beardless. He flings his arms behind himself as he bends toward the lifeless form of Jesus, keening with his entire body. It is the women, however, whose suffering grips us the most—especially that of Mary, the mother of Jesus. She cradles her son in her lap, her eyes examining his lifeless face as if imploring him to stir. We know that within hours he will awaken, renewed, but for the eternal moment of the painting, pools of suffering surround her and her son as she weeps.

The Hymn

Emma Lou Thayne, a prolific Mormon author, wrote hundreds of poems before her death in 2014 at age ninety. In 1973 the LDS Church published some of her most beloved verses in the LDS hymnal. The circumstances of one poem's composition were personal, but the sentiment is universal inasmuch as we all strain to find relief from, or at least explanations for, suffering. The first two of four verses read:

> Where can I turn for peace?
> Where is my solace
> When other sources cease to make me whole?
> When with a wounded heart, anger, or malice,
> I draw myself apart,
> Searching my soul?

> Where, when my aching grows,
> Where, when I languish,
> Where, in my need to know, where can I run?
> Where is the quiet hand to calm my anguish?
> Who, who can understand?[1]

There is hardly a more appropriate pairing of image and poetry on the subject of suffering and on the model Jesus provided in the Gospels.

---

1. Emma Lou Thayne, "Where Can I Turn for Peace?"

The Nature of and Responsibility for Suffering

As is so often the case, before we can consider Jesus's genuinely radical teachings on suffering, we should first think about the religious context for them. In Chapter 7, for example, we examined the often-false assumption that Jews in Jesus's day made about the connection between sin and sickness. We noted in the Gospel of John's account of the man born blind that the rigid, rule-bound Pharisees assumed that the man—either in life or in utero—or his parents had caused his blindness by committing one or more of hundreds of specified sins. We also recalled the curses pronounced on Adam and Eve as they left Eden that illustrated the cause-and-effect relationship between sin and sickness or misfortune. God said that because they sinned, they were cursed with specific gender-based suffering.

Harold S. Kushner, a well-known contemporary American rabbi and author, can help us understand the attitudes of first-century Jews. Rabbi Kushner served as the congregational rabbi of Temple Israel of Natick in Massachusetts for more than a quarter of a century. In a thoughtful meditation on the premature death of his fourteen-year-old son, Aaron, Kushner wrote a hugely successful book on suffering and on the responsibility of God and himself in this personal tragedy. In *When Bad Things Happen to Good People*, Kushner examined the same assumptions as the so-called friends of Job. As he has continued to write and speak about the subject in subsequent years, he has said that people who read the Book of Job must accept two of three propositions about suffering that Job's friends advance. But, Kushner reasons, that means that whatever the two accepted assumptions are, a third must stand rejected. All three cannot apply simultaneously.[2]

The first is that Job's God was all-powerful, the creator of everything; he knew everything and made everything happen in this world. The second is that, unlike other gods in ancient mythologies, Job's God was always good. He was always benevolent. The last assumption is that by Job's own testimony as well as by those of all who knew him, Job was a good man. So, Kushner concludes that God, obviously, was all-powerful and that God was literally goodness in its totality. Therefore, Job must not have been good after all. But Job *was* absolutely blameless—as was Kushner's son. Kushner's attempts at understanding not only Job's suffering but also his own and his son's became an extraordinary crisis of faith.

---

2. Harold S. Kushner, *When Bad Things Happen to Good People*, 2–14.

The goodness and power of God were not in question. God was not arbitrary and capricious. And surely he knew that Kushner's son, Aaron, was as good as Job. Then, Kushner reasoned, obviously it must be that his son had died because of something bad that he as the boy's father had done—some sin he had committed that must have angered God so that God visited such suffering on the entire family. The rabbi's sins seemed to be his only way out of the crisis. But that proposition only increased his suffering by adding guilt to his other sins!

Kushner wrote that "when bad things happen to good people," we, like others who are grief-stricken, and like Job, ransack our pasts to look for offensive behavior. Finding none of a magnitude to justify his son's death, Kushner felt estranged from and abandoned by God. Instead of receiving promised blessings, he felt that God had punished him further by multiplying his wounds "without cause" (Job 9:17 KJV).

Kushner writes that such reasoning "teaches people to blame themselves. It creates guilt even where there is no basis for guilt. It makes people hate God, even as it makes them hate themselves. And most disturbing of all, it does not even fit the facts."[3] It is also a way for observers, like Job's friends and others who attempt to console the sufferer, to preserve their faith in God by shifting the blame away from God's supposed blind but *divine* retribution and placing it on the individual sufferer. It is a way of trying to preserve God's reputation. Loved ones may say what Job's wife said to him: Why don't you get this suffering over with and simply "curse God [back for breaking his part of the covenant with you] and die"? (Job 2:9 NLT). Thus, those falsely accused often trudge on, bereft of friends, family, and even God, left to themselves to deal with their plight in terrible isolation.

So it is, then, that the people in Jesus's day could make sense of a moral universe only if, as Old Testament scholar Daniel Simundson wrote, "good is rewarded and evil is punished. Most people believe that God has the power and the will to see that it will happen."[4] Therefore, we can easily discover who is "righteous" simply by looking at how blessed they are. Poverty, sickness, and suffering are signs that a person has not found favor with God.

Rabbi Kushner asserted that while so much of what we suffer in this life we bring upon ourselves by our own bad decisions and deceptions, other things like natural disasters, germs, and genetic mutations also often cause suffering. "How can anyone who recognizes the names of Auschwitz and

3. Ibid., 14.
4. Daniel J. Simundson, "Suffering," 6:221.

My Lai, or has walked the corridors of hospitals and nursing homes, dare to answer the question of the world's suffering by quoting Isaiah: 'Tell the righteous it will be well with them'?" (Isaiah 3:10 NIV).[5] What Kushner called the laws of nature and what scientists call the laws of physics govern the universe, and these laws for good or ill affect the righteous and the wicked.

Jesus Taught about Suffering and God's Intervention

As we have seen, Jesus rejected the reasoning of Job's friends and the Pharisees. He knew, long before the scientists of our day, that sickness, disease, and calamities created suffering for reasons other than sin. Jesus knew that none of us could "assume that sufferers deserve their fate. Life is too complicated for that."[6]

For example, Jesus would not admit that the Galileans killed on the Temple Mount were worse than those who had escaped (Luke 13:1–5), and he would not concede that the man blind from birth suffered because of his or his parents' sins (John 9). There is little question that Jesus rejected "an absolute doctrine of retribution which connects sin to punishment in individual cases of suffering."[7] Although sinners often suffer because of their immoral and corrupt lives, suffering also comes from many other sources as well—carelessness, accidents, the intentional acts of others, and natural disasters. Jesus said, "For [your Father in Heaven] gives his sunlight to both the evil and the good, and he sends rain on the just and the unjust alike" (Matt. 5:45 NLT).

The view that suffering may result from different causes and usually not from personal iniquity may be comforting in the abstract, but it is of little comfort to those who are in the throws of terrible suffering. It does not answer the nagging question of why an all-powerful God doesn't just step in and do something about it. It seems so unfair and inconsistent for a God who claims to love us but does not help us when we are in desperate need. This said, we must now turn our attention to the question of how Jesus teaches his followers to endure suffering.

Before thinking that an explanation of all suffering is forthcoming in this chapter, we must acknowledge that God sometimes does not intervene. Certainly God is powerful enough to relieve our sorrows. That is not the point. Despite this paradox, Jesus does not explain why God interposes

---

5. Kushner, *When Bad Things Happen*, 14.
6. Simundson, "Suffering," 6:224.
7. Ibid.

himself at times and not at others. When God does intervene, Jesus informs us by his example to rejoice and give thanks. When God does not intervene, Jesus informs us by his example to bear our grief patiently—to endure.

The joy-and-gratitude side of the equation is marvelous. There is hardly a page in the four Gospels that does not attest to God's compassion as the sick are healed and the dead are raised. "No matter what their diseases were, the touch of his hand healed every one" (Luke 4:40 NLT). And in our own lives we also experience the intervention of God, and that undeniably reassures us of God's presence in our lives—even in some seemingly insignificant matters. In this we rejoice. Then we press on.

Yet sometimes, when only a miracle will suffice, our intense desires and faithful prayers do not bring about the yearned-for result. Nor does faith consistently quiet our fears and ease our burdens. In some situations we are left bereft and abandoned. As LDS President Gordon B. Hinckley observed at the passing of his wife, "Only those who pass through this dark valley know its utter desolation." He said there are times in our lives when there "is a consuming loneliness which increases in intensity and painfully gnaws at [our] very soul."[8]

No one invariably feels God's presence, and on many occasions we are left to meet life's adversities on our own as best we can. We come to understand that God's promise that he will not leave us "comfortless" does not mean he will comfort us at all times (John 14:18 KJV). The stark reality is that Jesus never answers the question of why God chooses not to intercede.

Abraham's Unrequited Prayer

The story of Abraham's unrequited prayer usually goes unnoticed. However, it is instructive in this context. Of all people, Abraham was revered for his unusually strong faith. Yet, like all of us, he experienced the paradox of God relieving suffering on one occasion but not on another. In one such instance, Abraham fervently prayed for God to end a drought, but nothing happened after repeated and heartfelt prayers. This must have been particularly vexing because this experience was preceded by a similar miracle during which a serious drought ended without Abraham doing so much as to mention it to God.

The details of Abraham's unanswered request for God's help are found in the Book of Abraham. Abraham and his family had experienced a re-

---

8. Gordon B. Hinckley, "Funeral of Elisa Young Wirthlin."

lentless drought and famine—so severe that it eventually took the life of Abraham's brother, Haran. Without any mention of Abraham exercising his faith and prayers, we are informed that the famine abated, perhaps as consequence of natural weather patterns.

Abraham left the land of Ur of the Chaldees and went to the land of Canaan to a place called Charran, transliterated as Haran (not to be confused with Abraham's brother with the same name). At Haran, Abraham's faith was so great that he "prayed unto the Lord, and the Lord appeared unto [him]" and gave him extraordinary promises about his posterity (Abr. 2:6, 9–11). At about this time a second famine followed. Abraham approached the Lord, made an offering, "and prayed that the famine might be turned away" (Abr. 2:17). The famine continued.

Undaunted, Abraham petitioned the Lord a second time for relief and offered a sacrifice. Concerned for the welfare of himself and his family, he prayed intensely "and called on the Lord devoutly" (Abr. 2:18). In this instance, "the Lord appeared unto [him] in answer to [his] prayers" (Abr. 2:19). But the famine continued.

A third time Abraham pleaded with the Lord. This time he "built another altar . . . and called again upon the name of the Lord" (Abr. 2:20). Yet, "there was a continuation of a famine in the land" (Abr. 2:21). In fact, the situation deteriorated and "the famine became very grievous" (Abr. 2:21). At this point, the story in the Book of Abraham ends rather abruptly. No explanation is given about why Abraham's faith and prayers were not answered and why the drought persisted.

It is reasonable to suppose that faith sufficient to visit face-to-face with God on at least two occasions would be faith sufficient to cause rain to fall on the earth (Abr. 2:12). It was not. One would think that a prophet of Abraham's stature, the prophet whose name Paul held up as the epitome of faith, could importune the heavens for a little moisture. He could not. For whatever reason, Abraham found himself in much the same position we find ourselves in at times. We know that God has answered our prayers. We know that in the past we have experienced his mighty and miraculous power in our lives. But sometimes our faith simply does not bring about precious relief in the most terrible circumstances. The moisture we so fervently desire to give life to the parched earth of our own lives is not forthcoming. We are left to face our situation with resolve and as much faith as we can muster in our extremity. Psalm 46 is one to be sung when Israel suffered annihilation. One verse we so often quote may resonate here: "Be still, and know that I am God" (Ps. 46:10 KJV).

Jesus, a Man of Sorrows and Grief

It is even more sobering to consider that even the Son of God was unable to avoid adversity and suffering. Jesus pleaded that he be spared the anguish of a slow death nailed to a cross. "Oh, my Father," he said, "if it be possible, let this cup of suffering be taken away from me" (Matt. 26:39 NLT). Yet his prayer was not answered. His torment was so formidable that his Father sent an angel to strengthen him during his ordeal (Luke 22:43). It was under these circumstances that he told his disciples, "My soul is overwhelmed with sorrow to the point of death" (Mark 14:34 NIV).

Once his suffering in Gethsemane had ended, Jesus was arrested. A band of Roman soldiers and officers came to forcibly detain him. After a night spent being tortured and scourged, he was taken at daybreak before a council and tried before Pilate, the prefect of the Roman province of Judaea. He was condemned to death and crucified along with other accused political rebels.

By the time Jesus was led to the place of crucifixion, he had experienced all manner of mental and physical torture. No doubt he was utterly spent. He was so weak that a Roman soldier commandeered a man named Simon from Cyrene, North Africa, to carry the crossbeam for Jesus to Golgotha. At this place, nails were driven through his hands to securely hold the weight of his body on the cross. To deaden the pain, he was offered a drink of drugged wine by a group of wealthy women, undoubtedly followers of Jesus. He refused it.

Jesus hung on the cross for six hours. Then, as William Barclay points out, "We have what must be the most staggering sentence in the gospel record, the cry of Jesus: 'My God, my God, why have you forsaken me?'" It came at the moment when the "weight of the world's sin fell upon the heart and being of Jesus."[9] Feeling forsaken is an emotion we are all familiar with. We all feel at times that "God has forgotten us; when we are immersed in a situation beyond our understanding and feel bereft even of God. It seems . . . that is what happened to Jesus here."[10]

Yet it was in the unspeakable depths of desolation that Jesus ultimately prevailed. In his cry of abandonment (Matt. 27:46), there is hope. Peter Pokorny writes, "Only a pious Jew could recognize these words as a quotation of the sentence from Psalms 22 that in its Septuagint version

---

9. William Barclay, *The New Daily Study Bible: The Gospel of Matthew*, 2:368–69.

10. Ibid., 2:369.

may be understood as alluding to a crucifixion (v. 16), but the second part of which (vv. 22–31) expresses the joy of deliverance."[11] It foreshadowed Jesus's rescue from the irretrievable despair that came at the moment he shouted, "It is finished!" (John 19:30 KJV). Three words in English; one in Greek: *teteletai*. *Teteletai* is the victor's shout when he has completed the task and grasped the crown.[12] It was Jesus's acknowledgment that he had passed through "the uttermost abyss, and then the light broke."[13]

Our Predicament

The difficulty for all of us is the same predicament that Abraham faced when his prayers were not answered. It is the same struggle that Rabbi Kushner addressed. It is the same sense of yearning that, after comfort in the midst of suffering, Giotto painted, Emma Lou Thayne wrote, and Jesus confronted when he felt "forsaken" of God. How do we retain our faith when our prayers are not answered during times of great suffering? How can we have confidence in God when we feel abandoned by Him, when fear stalks us, or when peace eludes us? How can we maintain our belief when we have no choice but to "walk through the valley of the shadow of death" (Ps. 23:4 KJV) and feel that we are doing it on our own? How can we face these moments of adversity and emerge whole and victorious, as Jesus did?

On a personal level, all of us come face-to-face with painful failures and situations full of retribution and bitterness. Marriages dissolve. Grandparents, parents, aunts and uncles, and brothers and sisters become alienated from one another. Relationships deteriorate with employers, between members of the local church congregation, and among neighbors. People feel alienated from one another. Addictions sometimes imprison us and make it impossible to direct our energies in positive and worthwhile directions. Loved ones die. We all have our Gardens of Gethsemane.

With so much pain and suffering around us, it is no wonder that men and women, ministers and philosophers, teachers and theologians all imagine reasons for why people suffer, and yearn for ways to comfort themselves and others. Insights and explanations are sometimes soothing and sometimes not. In some instances, the more specific and convoluted the explanation for suffering, the less satisfying it is. As David Brooks has pointed out, "Taking theology beyond its limit" is not always wise.

---

11. Peter Pokorny, "Jesus' Death on the Cross," 900.

12. Barclay, *Gospel of Matthew*, 2:369.

13. Ibid., 2:369–70.

"Theology is grounding in ultimate hope, not a formula book to explain away each individual event."[14] About all that can be said is what Jesus said to Joseph Smith concerning the conditions of our mortality when Joseph was incarcerated for six months in Liberty Jail: "All these things shall give thee experience, and shall be for thy good" (D&C 122:7). "My son, peace be unto thy soul; thine adversity and thine afflictions shall be but a small moment; And then, if thou endure it well, God shall exalt thee on high" (D&C 121:7–8). "The Son of Man hath descended below them all. Art thou greater than he? Therefore, hold on thy way" (D&C 122:8–9).

Evidently, for us to become what God wants us to become, we must be placed at huge personal risk and experience sorrow to learn genuine empathy, compassion, and affection. It must be that by undergoing the consequences of our own sins and the sins of others inflicted upon us, we can become less judgmental. By struggling with our own limitations, we can become more tolerant and forgiving. By experiencing hardships, we can become more compassionate. By our own experience, we come to be more like God and understand better why it is vital to adhere to the first and second commandments: to love God and love our neighbor.

Mortality, by its very terms and conditions, is to experience what it is like to be separated from God—to live in a place where our problems are not always alleviated; to live in a world where prayers are not always answered; to live in circumstances where the Holy Ghost is not always available to comfort and succor us. That is the nature of suffering. If God wants to bring something about, he does. At other times, regardless of our pleas, he does not. Nevertheless, every so often those with faith in the Lord Jesus Christ experience inexplicable miracles in their lives. Sometimes these miracles are astounding and come at great times of need. At other times, small miracles reassure us and give us hope. Big or small, these merciful events are meant to encourage us and remind us that we are under God's watchful eye, and that ultimately a world of compassion and justice lie ahead. But for the most part, we are left to our own devices. As Paul wrote, we "work out [our] own salvation with fear and trembling" (Phil. 2:12 KJV).

Jesus: the Hope of All Mankind

During times of suffering, the only solution for mortals is to summon faith in Jesus, to "lift up [our] heads," and to rejoice (Ps. 24:7, 9 KJV).

---

14. David Brooks, "The Art of Presence."

We commit to remember this Jesus, who is "the author and finisher of our faith," who "endured the cross, despising the shame" (Heb. 12:2 KJV). We will place our trust in the promise that our "chastening" will yield "the peaceable fruit of righteousness" (Heb. 12:11 KJV).

In days to come we take comfort in the thought that we

> shall hunger no more, neither thirst anymore; neither shall the sun light on [us], nor any heat. For the Lamb which is in the midst of the throne shall feed [us], and shall lead [us] unto living fountains of waters: and God shall wipe away all tears from [our] eyes. (Rev. 7:16–17 KJV)

Emma Lou Thayne finished her exquisite hymn with these lines:

> Where, when my aching grows,
> Where, when I languish,
> Where, in my need to know, where can I run?
> Where is the quiet hand to calm my anguish?
> Who, who can understand? He, only One.
>
> He answers privately,
> Reaches my reaching
> In my Gethsemane, Savior and Friend.
> Gentle the peace he finds for my beseeching.
> Constant he is and kind, Love without end.[15]

---

15. Thayne, "Where Can I Turn."

chapter 11

jesus, violence, and the Enemy

Although he was born a Christian, it wasn't until later in his life that Leo Tolstoy (1892–1910), the renowned Russian writer, converted to Christianity. His conversion, however, was not to the Christianity advanced by the Russian Orthodox Church, which had adopted a way of looking at Jesus that Tolstoy thought differed from the Jesus of the four Gospels. His reading of the Gospels was a transformative event in his life. It took place at the end of an "exceptionally fruitful period of fiction writing in the 1860s and 1870s,"[1] during which he produced such masterworks as *War and Peace* and *Anna Karenina*.

According to his translator, Dustin Condren, Tolstoy was shaken by a

personal and spiritual crisis that effectively halted his labors as a novelist. He had fallen into despair, become preoccupied with death and found himself on the verge of suicide, navigating existence with nothing more than the nihilistic belief that he was "an accidental clutter of parts, that there was no purpose in life and that life itself is evil."[2]

Tolstoy decided to deeply study Christianity as found in the Gospels. His conversion is described in his books *My Religion: What I Believe, The Law of Love,* and *The Law of Violence.*

Tolstoy began his study of the Gospels in 1879. It became a massive project. Over the next three years he translated the four Gospels into Russian and synthesized them into one narrative. In later years he referred to this period of penetrating study as "constant, rapturous exertion of my soul." He said that he "had 'come to know the light.'"[3] His purpose had been to find what he would come to understand as the pure principles of Jesus, decide what he should do about them, and then figure out how he should live.

---

1. Leo Tolstoy, *The Gospel in Brief: The Life of Jesus,* vii.
2. Ibid.
3. Ibid., vii–viii.

Ultimately, Tolstoy was overcome by the realization that the "law of love and its recognition as a rule of conduct in all our relations with friends, enemies, [and] offenders" is the only approach that will "inevitably [bring] about the complete transformation of the existing order of things, and does this not only among Christian nations, but among all the populations of the globe."[4] Tolstoy wrote that the commands "Thou shalt not kill" and "Love your enemies" were supreme in Jesus's teachings and therefore should not admit to any exceptions. He believed that allowing exceptions to the prohibition against taking the life of another caused the prohibition to lose its force and power to change society. The doctrine of love was thus reduced to "fruitless teaching" unable to seriously modify a "mode of living that is founded on violence." He perceived that a law of love with no exceptions "abolishes the possibility of any violence."[5] By recognizing the power of Jesus's teaching about loving one's enemy—a teaching he felt Orthodox Christianity and Hebrew Biblical accounts overlooked as simply being too difficult to take seriously—Tolstoy became a disciple of Christ. He understood that Jesus's doctrine about love in its purest form teaches that war is incompatible with Christianity.

Tolstoy's account of his profound epiphany indicates that he realized a simple truth: if all men and women at all levels of society simply refused to participate in violent acts, life would be transformed in a way that no power or government on earth has ever successfully managed through intimidation of violence. Ultimately, he said, the only way to peace was to do exactly as Jesus recommended—love our enemies, whether on a personal level or on a national level. As Tolstoy understood, "There is only one way to suppress evil, and that is to return good for evil."[6]

Our struggle against evils in the world and our tendency to respond to those evils with further violence and evil have been a part of the human story beginning with Cain's murder of his brother Abel. As N. T. Wright has observed, "Murder, misery, and mayhem still continue, as they always have, . . ." He completes his thought with this comment on the devastation visited by Christians on their enemies: ". . . even [to include] Jesus's own so-called followers," who, Wright says, contributed "their fair share" over the centuries.[7] It has come to the point that if humankind ever unleashes all of its destructive powers, Einstein's prediction may very

---

4. Leo Tolstoy, *The Law of Love and the Law of Violence*, 36.

5. Ibid., 37.

6. Leo Tolstoy, *My Religion: What I Believe*, 34.

7. N. T. Wright, *Simply Jesus*, 12.

well prove correct: "I don't know what [weapons] will be used in the next world war, but the fourth will be fought with stones."[8]

The Context for Violence in the Ancient World

In Jesus's day, Roman armies subjugated whole populations living on the perimeter of the Mediterranean Sea. The empire at its peak controlled approximately 250 million square miles. Roman legions were trained and stationed everywhere to swiftly crush rebellious foes. One such rebellion involved a series of large-scale revolts by various Jewish sects and factions against their Roman oppressors. Ultimately, the wars led to the brutal end of ancient Judaism by the time the city of Jerusalem was destroyed and the Temple razed in AD 70. After that siege, Judaism never fully recovered, with worship in the synagogue and Pharisaical traditions replacing temple worship. Jews were once again being scattered across the globe.

The violent spirit of the Empire (and indeed of the ancient world as a whole) might be epitomized by the enormous popularity of contests in arenas built for the entertainment of the masses in every Roman city throughout the empire. Gladiators provided the so-called entertainment. (Both the words arena and gladiator have Latin roots: *gladius* meaning "sword" and arena from the word meaning "sandy place" designed for the practical absorption of blood spilled in the contests.) In reality, the brutality of the contests was far more extreme than the dramatizations we see in the movies. Those romanticized cinematic heroes were likely less like heroes and more like killing machines.

The Romans had other methods of intimidating the enemy, notably including crucifixion. Crucifixion was the primary form of capital punishment employed not only to dispatch the enemies of Rome but also to terrorize the local population. Josephus, a contemporary historian, used the word *crucified* to label the method of execution in which victims were attached with ropes to wooden beams fixed at right angles to each other.[9] Sometimes victims were nailed to the structures. A small seat would occasionally be affixed to the vertical post, halfway down, making it possible for the victim to offset some of the weight of his arms and feet—a practice used to prolong the agony of death rather than provide comfort to the victim.[10]

---

8. Nuclear Age Peace Foundation, on the occasion of Albert Einstein's 125th birthday.

9. Martin Hengel, *Crucifixion*, 24.

10. Ibid., 25.

The word *crucifixion* is an Anglicized version of a combination of two verbs in ancient Greek meaning "to stake" or "impale on a plank." So when Greek texts predating Roman histories used the Greek word *anastauro,* denoting a particular method of capital punishment, the context typically meant that the condemned was "skewered."[11] Herodotus, the fifth-century Greek historian, wrote that the Persians had introduced the particular practice as part of their warfare strategy. There is evidence, however, that it was found among the Indians, Assyrians, Scythians, Taurians, Celts, Seleucids, Britanni, Numidians, and Carthaginians, the last of these having perhaps transferred their knowledge of the practice to the Romans.[12] Consequently, we can wonder about the next bit of history, although we most likely will never know the answer: Exactly when did the horrific mode of execution featuring impalement on a plank become associated with a structure in the shape of a T or Christian cross? Whenever this particularly brutal act of impalement labeled as *crucifixion* entered the war vocabulary of the ancient Greeks and hence the Roman world, it seems to always have been associated with debasement and humiliation of the enemy. It was then, as it is now, viewed as a horrifically degrading way to die; and for the ancients it was justified mortification. The famous rhetorician Quintilian (AD 35–95), writing as a loyal Roman, noted that "whenever we crucify the guilty, the most crowded roads are chosen, where most people can see and be moved by this fear. For penalties relate not so much to retribution as to their exemplary effect."[13]

The Third Servile War in about 73 BC, one of the most well-known acts of rebellion and subsequent punishment, illustrates Quintilian's point. It involved the famous escaped gladiator and slave Spartacus, who led an uprising against Rome. The kinds and numbers of punishments the Roman legions meted out on the rebellious gladiator slaves are nearly incomprehensible in today's world. We draw back from the statistic not only because of the totals but also because of the intimate cruelty of the methods used to stop the insurrection. The Romans crucified six thousand captured slaves for all to see on a twenty-five-mile stretch along the Appian Way from Rome south to Capua, near Naples. Think about that on a more relatable scale: approximately every twenty-two feet, as far as the eye could see, a dying or decaying human being was impaled. In AD 70, at the fall of

---

11. Ibid., 30.

12. Ibid., 27.

13. Marcus Fabius Quintilianus, "The Major Declamations Ascribed to Quintilian," decl. 274.

Jerusalem we mentioned a moment ago, five hundred Jews were crucified, according to Josephus. He wrote that "there was not enough room for the crosses and not enough crosses for the bodies."[14]

Today, as in Roman times, justification for violence on a large scale is much the same. When the security and well-being of one nation state is threatened, preemptive or retaliatory force against the enemy is thought of as not only justified but also required. As one side challenges the other, each side blames the other. Hostile perceptions are amplified. Mutual trust evaporates. The escalation of conflict spurs the need for revenge by one side or the other. Soon, the opponents become more committed to destroying the other, the enemy, than to developing peace or designing mutually legitimate goals. Inflicting "justified" retribution becomes the primary aim. Inhumane treatment and torture frequently become an acceptable way to achieve victory and revenge. Finally, the enemy—virtually everyone on the other side—comes to be seen as incorrigible, even diabolical.

Whether the conflict is on a personal scale such as a divorce proceeding, on a political scale in the case of an election, or in a war pitting one nation against another, it is most often characterized in binary absolutes, as a struggle between freedom and tyranny, light and dark, good and evil.

In any of the conflicts we have just described above, the fight takes on mythic proportions. The physical, if not psychological, mayhem increases and spirals upward out of control as the struggle becomes more and more difficult to end. The excuse is generally the same, whether in a family, in politics, or even in a religious disagreement over doctrine. If it were not for the meanness, corruption, brutality, out-and-out wrongness, and so forth of the other side—be it a spouse, a wayward child, a political party, or an entire people—as authors Dean G. Pruitt and Sung Hee Kim have observed, "we would not have to [physically or emotionally or financially] annihilate them and treat them as less than human."[15]

So far this chapter has mostly considered violence and the enemy on a generalized macro scale. We only briefly referred to the enemy on a more intimate scale, both ancient and contemporary. Now we look at Jesus's attitudes toward his enemies and towards any and all justifications for violence on multiple levels of angry engagement, including on the very basic one-to-one human relationships.

---

14. H. Leeming and K. Leeming, *Josephus' Jewish War and Its Slavonic Version*, 518.

15. Dean G. Pruitt, Sung Hee Kim, and Jeffrey Z. Rubin, *Social Conflict: Escalation, Stalemate, and Settlement*, 96–97 104–12.

Loving and Forgiving the Enemy

In his world of cruelty and class, not to mention religious fanaticism or gender and racial bigotry—all with the empire as a sort of "green screen" backdrop—Jesus invariably rejected violence as a legitimate means to defeat his enemies. Recall that even the confrontation between Jesus and the moneychangers and sellers of sacrifices on the Temple Mount is not the exception to that claim; rather, in that case, his wrath was channeled toward the instruments of the systemic corruption. He destroyed the tables, the coffers and cages. The record does not tell us he took a life. In addition and by way of contrast, he restored the severed ear of the temple guard who had come to Gethsemane to arrest him. N. T. Wright in *Simply Jesus* explains that then as well as now, he knew that violence in turn produced "violent regimes, which are eventually toppled by further violent change." Jesus's way, he writes, was to discover "an entirely different way."[16]

Let us examine three important texts from the Gospels on the subject of the enemy and on violence.

Resisting the Enemy

One of his most well-known admonitions to his disciples was "[D]o not resist an evil person" (Matt. 5:39 NLT). The context for that caution was once again the Sermon on the Mount: "You have heard the law that says the punishment must match the injury: 'An eye for an eye, and a tooth for a tooth.' *But I say, do not resist an evil person!* If someone slaps you on the right cheek, offer the other cheek also. If you are sued in court and your shirt is taken from you, give your coat, too. If a soldier demands that you carry his gear for a mile, carry it two miles" (Matt. 5:38–41 NLT; emphasis added).

This passage of the sermon—rendered in the King James Version as, "But I say unto you, that ye resist not evil" (Matt. 5:39 KJV)—is the preface for three examples of interactions with an enemy. The first was with an *individual* in an adversarial situation. The second was with an *institution* charged with dispensing supposedly unbiased judgment between adversaries. The third was with a genuine enemy representing *an entire government* whose superiority did not depend on justice but rather on force. By these examples, Jesus escalated the question of enemy status and our responses to these kinds of disputes with an enemy. The sweep of his

---

16. N. T. Wright, *Simply Jesus: A New Vision of Who He Was, What He Did, and Why He Matters*, 149.

teaching left his disciples little room to solve the dilemma how they might respond to an enemy, especially when the key to grasping his teaching is to once again understand the etymology of the word *resist* (as in "do not resist"). The English verb "resist" comes from the Old French word *resister*, meaning "to hold out against," and further back from the Latin *resistere*, "to make a stand against, oppose; to stand back; withstand."[17]

But the New Testament Gospels were written originally in Greek, and in Greek, the word translated into English as "resist" is *anthistemi*. It and its various cognates are often used in Bible text to refer to *violent* resistance. In the Old Testament, for example, *anthistemi* invariably referred to military actions. Our go-to historian Josephus used *anthistemi* in the same way.[18] So, to remove any ambiguity about Jesus's meaning taken from its context, New Testament scholar N. T. Wright has translated the verse, "Don't use *violence* to resist evil."[19]

It becomes clear with Wright's translation that in all of the three examples Jesus used in the passage from the Sermon on the Mount, his teaching did not mean passivity. To the contrary, in each case of enemy aggression (that is, violence from an individual, violence from a system in the form of real or perceived injustice, or violence and humiliation at the hands of an entire army of imperial enforcers), he expected opposition to the perceived enemy to involve only good or righteous responses. In every case, the desire to have absolute and immediate justice or to vanquish the enemy in the end did not justify the means by which his disciples were to achieve it. In-kind resistance of the eye-for-an-eye variety was unacceptable.[20]

---

17. Online Etymological Dictionary, s.v. "resist."

18. Preston Sprinkle, *Fight: A Christian Case for Nonviolence*, 134.

19. N. T. Wright, *The Kingdom New Testament: A Contemporary Translation*, 9; emphasis added.

20. Joseph Smith's inspired words penned in Liberty Jail on March 20, 1839, give expression to this same sentiment. They came at a time when the Latter-day Saints were experiencing violent and intense persecution. Joseph and several other Church leaders were confined for six months in a tiny, cold, dark dungeon. All the men were ill and depressed. In response to Joseph's pleas for relief, the Lord reminded him that the use of "power," or for that matter, "influence can or ought to be maintained . . . only by persuasion, by long-suffering, by gentleness and meekness, and by love unfeigned" (D&C 121:41; emphasis added). The language condemns the use of force as morally wrong by stating that power "ought"—meaning a duty or moral obligation—not be used. This passage also teaches that in the long run, compulsion cannot and will not bring about desired results, and is in the end self-defeating.

As N.T. Wright explains, the "old justice" of the Hebrew Bible was intended to "prevent revenge from running away with itself. Better an eye for an eye and a tooth for a tooth than an escalating feud."[21] Jesus, on the other hand, went a step further. He taught that there should be no vengeance at all, a teaching that revealed God's "deepest nature" as "overflowing love."[22] And he illustrated the kind of provocative resistance he had in mind with the three examples, each requiring some contextual information.

First, in Matthew 5:39 Jesus referred to a slap on the right cheek. In a face to face confrontation, it was assumed that to be struck on the right cheek meant being hit with the back of the aggressor's right hand. As Wright points out, in the context of Jesus's culture, "[t]hat's not just violence, but an insult: it implies that you're an inferior, perhaps a slave, a child, or (in that world, and sometimes even today) a woman."[23] Offering the other cheek opens oneself for an open-palmed slap and "implies: hit me again if you like, but now as an equal, not an inferior."[24]

His second example (Matt. 5:40) was the environment of a law court where a wealthy adversary might sue an inferior. It would have been nearly impossible to prevail. So voluntarily giving one's cloak after the enemy had already taken a shirt in a "world where most people only wore those two garments, [would] shame him with your impoverished nakedness" and vividly illustrated the heartlessness of the rich taking from the poor.[25]

Jesus's final example involved forcing a civilian to carry military equipment for a mile. The hypothetical reads, "If a man in authority makes you go one mile . . ." (Matt. 5:41, 42 NEB). In Jesus's day this was an order provided for in the law. However, it was also strictly forbidden to ask a civilian to go more than a mile. By continuing to walk after the initial mile, the civilian "turn[ed] the tables" on the soldier and would put him at risk if his commanding officer found out. As Wright sums up: "[T]he news that there is a different way to be human, a way which doesn't plot revenge, which doesn't join the armed resistance movement . . . but wins God's kind of victory over violence and injustice" was socially challenging while at the same time socially transforming.[26]

---

21. N. T. Wright, *Matthew: Part I*, 51.
22. Ibid.
23. Ibid., 52.
24. Ibid.
25. Ibid.
26. Ibid.

Loving the Enemy

The second text deals with Jesus's teachings about our mental and emotional state of mind when we think about or deal with our enemies—both real and imagined. The passage is once again from the Sermon on the Mount (Matt. 5:21–26).

Here, Jesus began his admonition about controlling one's anger in the context of his declaration that he had come to fulfill every bit of the Law, which in this context is a reference to the Decalogue (Matt. 5:17–19). He told those who were listening that the ancestors' prohibition against murder remained in place. But in the very next sentence, he made the leap from the commission of murder, and the judgment that must surely follow, to the motivations of the murderer. He said that even threshold behaviors like "call someone an idiot" or "curse someone"—which come from anger and could escalate to the intensity necessary to murder one's enemy—"are subject to judgment!" (Matt. 5:22 NLT). And although the King James Version includes the phrase "angry with his brother *without a cause*" (Matt. 5:22; emphasis added), modern translations do not contain this exculpatory language. It is a phrase that is not found in the earliest manuscripts. Rather, it was most likely inserted into the later texts by those trying to soften what Jesus actually taught.[27]

That being said, seeing Jesus's approach as solely a ban on emotions that propels us to violence against our enemy goes only half the distance. His teaching involved affirmative efforts to unequivocally love our enemies, a course of conduct that goes far beyond the moral and intellectual position of tolerance or begrudging standoffs of most people and all nations and states. We must be "reconciled" (Matt. 5:24). What follows in chapter 5 of Matthew are six passages that begin with "Ye have heard," a reference to the strict scribal interpretations of Law (Matt. 5:21, 27, 31, 33, 38, 43 NLT).

A Perfect Love

In the last passage beginning with that phrase, Jesus taught the second part of his admonition regarding the enemy. These are verses that provoke

---

27. The Book of Mormon rendition of the Sermon on the Mount concurs with the earliest Greek versions of the four Gospels and also leaves out the phrase "without a cause" (3 Ne. 12:22). Clearly, intense anger felt toward another is good for none of us, especially if it is combined with aggression and violence.

penetrating self-examination. They clarify his and his Father's guiding principle concerning how those who enter his Father's Kingdom on earth must learn to behave when confronted by the enemy, no matter the level. We repeat what Jesus said: "Ye have heard that it hath been said, Thou shalt love thy neighbour, and hate thine enemy. But I say unto you, *Love your enemies, bless them* that curse you, *do good to them* that hate you, and *pray for them* which despitefully use you" (Matt. 5:43–44 KJV; emphasis added).

Not only did Jesus teach those transforming behaviors, but he also personified those attitudes during his ministry. Two examples, among many, illustrate the point. At his trial, shortly before his condemnation, Pilate asked if he was interposing himself between Rome and the Jews by claiming he was "the King of the Jews." Jesus replied that if this were the case, "my followers would fight to keep me from being handed over to the Jewish leaders." Jesus then refused to incite that kind of violence. Instead, he explained that his "kingdom is not of this world" (John 18:36 NLT). And prior to this moment, when Jesus was arrested and taken into custody, he responded with benevolence toward his enemies in Gethsemane. The temple guards carried clubs and swords as they entered the friend's garden sanctuary to arrest him. After they had surrounded him, Peter drew a sword and slashed off the ear of one of the mob, a servant. Jesus immediately restored the servant's ear and said to Peter, "Put away your sword. . . . Those who use the sword will die by the sword"[28] (Matt. 26:52 NLT).

In sum, Jesus opposed violence toward his enemies, including the kind of aggression where the powerful handily dispensed with the weak— a kind of survival of the fittest. He taught that violence and force were an illegitimate means to an end. Because aggression and hostility were inconsistent with the law of love, he explained how we should reach out and bless our enemies. For Jesus, love was the highest consideration. It was a standard toward which all men and women must aspire.

Love of neighbor—and love of enemy—was not just one virtue among many that Jesus taught in the Sermon on the Mount; love was the supreme and only virtue after which all good character traits followed. It was the prevailing principle. Jesus said, "The entire law and all the demands of the prophets are based on" the command to love God and your "neighbor as

---

28. Jesus's ban on violence was unwavering. Earlier in his ministry, when he was on his way to a Samaritan village that was not disposed to welcome him, his disciples asked him to call down "fire from heaven to burn them up." Jesus turned and rebuked them (Luke 9:52–55 NLT).

yourself" (Matt. 22:40 NLT). He said, "By this shall all men know that ye are my disciples, if ye have love one to another" (John 13:35 KJV).

Jesus concluded his remarks on loving our enemies by reminding his disciples that if we love only those who love us, "what reward can you expect? Surely the tax-gatherers do as much as that. And if you greet only your brothers, what is there extraordinary about that? Even the heathen do as much" (Matt. 5:47 NEB). Jesus then invited his followers to become as God is, "whose goodness knows no bounds" (Matt. 5:48 NEB). That kind of perfection Jesus was speaking about in the context of Matthew 5 is certainly not referring to the "goodness" or perfection envisioned by the Pharisees, which was a way of being holy that required adherents to live by a long list of outward commandments—every "jot and tittle" of the Torah, the 613 commandments in the Mizvot, the Oral Law, and the purification rituals. Rather, the perfection, the goodness Jesus sought was a perfect love that radiated out to include all humanity. Luke captured the true emphasis of the command to be "perfect" in his mini-rendition of the sermon on the mount. He changed the couplet, as it is rendered in the King James Translation from "But you are to be perfect, even as your father in heaven is perfect" to "You must be compassionate, just as your father is compassionate" (Luke 6:36 NLT). Luke's version captured the essence of Jesus. It was by loving everyone that his disciples would "truly be acting as children of the Most High, for he is kind to those who are unthankful and wicked" (Luke 6:35 NLT).

The Good Samaritan

The last passage we now consider in this chapter on Jesus and the enemy is actually one of the most beloved parables in all the Gospels. We know the story well. It began with a lawyer asking Jesus to define his "neighbor," and in response Jesus tells the parable of the Good Samaritan. In this chapter, however, rather than the neighbor, we will focus on the supposed enemy in the parable who would have been easily identified not only by the lawyer but also by those who listened in on the dialogue.

One day an expert on the religious law tested Jesus and asked, "Teacher, what should I do to receive eternal life?" (Luke 10:25 NLT). Jesus responded by asking his inquisitor a question: "What does the law of Moses say? How do you read it?" (Luke 10:26 NLT). The man then gave the correct answer: "'You must love the Lord your God with all your heart, all your soul, all your strength, and all your mind.' And, 'Love your

neighbor as yourself.' 'Right!' Jesus told him. 'Do this and you will live'"
(Luke 10:27–28 NLT).

It was a flawless answer. Orthodox Jews carried the command to "love
God" with them in their phylacteries (*tefillin*), a set of tiny boxes that contained parchment scrolls with the most important verses of the Torah copied on them in the smallest readable script (Deut. 11:13). The arm-*tefillin*
was strapped on a man's upper arm, and the head-*tefillin* was secured just
above the forehead. The command to "love your neighbor as yourself" was
not specified in the *tefillin*; it was, however considered authoritative and
written in the Leviticus holiness code of personal conduct (Lev. 19:18).

Despite the lawyer's perfect answer, Jesus's response was too abbrevi-
ated and did not satisfy the inquisitor. The questioner had something more
in mind than a two-sentence answer. He wanted to expose Jesus's too-broad
interpretation of who qualified as a "neighbor." This man clearly knew that
Jesus's use of the word "neighbor" included one's enemy, a view at odds
with what the scribes and Pharisees taught. Jesus said: "Ye have heard that
it hath been said, Thou shalt love thy neighbour, and hate thine enemy. But
I say unto you, Love your enemies, bless them that curse you, do good to
them that hate you, and pray for them which despitefully use you" (Matt.
5:43–44 KJV). The teachers of religious law, on the other hand, limited
their definition of "neighbor" to members of their own group. William
Barclay observes that Jews, "at worst and their narrowest, . . . confined the
word *neighbor* to their *fellow Jews*." For example, some said it was illegal
to help a Gentile woman in her "sorest time" of childbirth, because "that
would only [bring] another Gentile into the world."[29] It is probable that
Jesus's examiner was trying to stir up controversy by drawing out the full
implications of what Jesus meant when he said to "love thy neighbour."

To be forthcoming and to more fully answer his interrogator, Jesus
told him the now-familiar story: A Jewish man was traveling along the
twenty-mile stretch of road that led from Jerusalem to Jericho.[30] The narrow road descended 3,600 feet from the heights of the City of Jerusalem

---

29. William Barclay, *The New Daily Study Bible: The Acts of the Apostles*, 80.

30. The New Living Translation identifies the traveler who was accosted as
a Jew. Most translations do not identify him, and a strict reading of the Greek
does not allow for this conclusion. However, it is reasonable to assume that this
individual was Jewish. He was traveling from Jerusalem, where the vast majority
of people were Jewish. The Greek reads "anthropos tis," or a "certain man." The
use of this term is broad and includes any person, mankind, the human race,
enemy, child, friend, human, men, and women.

(2,300 feet above sea level) to the depths of Jericho (1,300 feet below sea level). Rocky passages obscured a traveler's view of what lay ahead behind the curves along the steep roadway, the perfect places for thieves to surprise and rob an unwary traveler. St. Jerome (c. AD 347–420) referred to it as "The Red Way" or "The Bloody Way," a reputation that lasted well into the nineteenth century.[31] Anyone traveling alone on the so-called Jericho Road would have been considered reckless and foolish.

The inevitable happened. This Jewish man was brutally attacked, robbed, and left for dead. Two individuals passed by who could have helped but didn't—a priest and a Levite.

Priests were traditionally only the patrilineal descendants of Aaron who for generations offered daily sacrifices and other rites in the portable tabernacle and then the Temple of Jerusalem. Over the years, their numbers far exceeded the needs of the Temple, and thus qualified priests were divided into groups so that each had the distinct opportunity to serve only one week during the year.

Because Aaron and his priestly descendants were members of the tribe of Israel's son Levi, they were sometimes referred to as Levites. However, at the time of Jesus, Levite priests were even more numerous than descendants of Aaron. Coming from a specific family within the tribe of Levi, their duties in the Temple were restricted to menial tasks and responsibilities. A Levite's principal temple roles were singing Psalms during services, doing construction and maintenance on the Temple Mount, or acting as guards.

Samaritans, although technically part of the house of Israel, were, for several reasons, outsiders and considered enemies by Jews. Simply put, the hostility between the Samaritans and the Jews centered on religious purity. The Samaritans claimed that their beliefs constituted the true faith of ancient Israel prior to the Assyrian exile, preserved by those who remained in the land of Israel—as opposed to the tribe of Judah, which had been led into a second captivity. After most Jews returned from Babylon upon their release by Cyrus, they despised the Samaritans. Jews saw Samaria as a sinful kingdom full of idolatrous, heretical descendants of Israel. Samaritans had built their own temple on Mount Gerizim and claimed it as the original sanctuary. They were governed by their own Pentateuch. They claimed Judah had falsified a text produced by Ezra during the Babylonian exile. Moreover, Jews considered the Samaritans to be mongrels because they had intermarried with outside tribes and nations.

---

31. William Barclay, *The New Daily Study Bible: The Gospel of Luke,* 138.

The road through Samaria from Galilee to Jerusalem was by far the shortest route (ninety miles), but pious Jews often avoided it, especially if they were on their way to the Temple, for fear of becoming ritually unclean. Instead, they would take a route along the eastern shoreline of the Sea of Galilee and the Jordan, down through Peraea (a journey of approximately one hundred twenty miles), thus adding about a day and a half to their pilgrimage.

An Orthodox Jew traveling through Samaria would shake the dust from his feet upon leaving the territory as a sign that he wanted nothing to do with such people. The desire to avoid Samaria altogether was symptomatic of the mutual distrust, fear, and jealousy that led to feuds and often outright military intervention. Josephus reported on numerous violent confrontations between these enemies throughout the first half of the first century.

The priest in Jesus's parable was the first to happen upon his fellow Jew, who had been stripped of his clothes, beaten, and left for dead. He crossed all the way over to the other side of the road to avoid touching the bleeding, unclean stranger. Ironically, his decision not to touch the man was based on considerations of religious piety. He was most likely on his way to the Temple to perform his once-yearly service. If he touched this beleaguered man, who was bleeding or maybe even dead, he would have made himself ritually unclean and therefore disqualified from temple service. To requalify would have taken the priest at least a week of Mitzva cleansing and offering of sacrifices to become sufficiently pure to once again minister on the Mount in Jerusalem (Num. 19:11–13). By that time, his opportunity for his scheduled temple service would have passed. He would have to wait an entire year before it was his turn to participate again.

A Levite was the second man to pass by. Unlike the priest, he at least "walked over and looked at him lying there, but he also passed by on the other side" (Luke 10:32 NLT). Although he approached the fallen man, it is unlikely that he bent over his fellow injured Jew for fear of being attacked by robbers who might be hiding behind rocks waiting for an opportunity to surprise another unwary traveler. It was not uncommon for bandits to have a companion counterfeit an injury as a decoy.

The third person who passed by was a wealthy, despised Samaritan. He probably recognized the wounded man as a Jew. After all, the story takes place in Judea. For this reason alone, he had good reason to ignore him. Why take pity on the enemy? Yet he felt compassion for the beleaguered man and went over to him. He knelt down, touched the man, soothed his wounds with oil and wine as a disinfectant, and bandaged them. Then,

Jesus said, he put the wounded Jew on his own donkey and took him to an inn to be cared for. The next day he gave the innkeeper money, instructing him to "[t]ake care of this man. If his bill runs higher than that . . . I'll pay you the next time I am here" (Luke 10:35 NLT).

Until this moment, the scribes and Pharisees who had listened to the conversation between Jesus and the law-abiding lawyer undoubtedly sided with the priest and the Levite. They were nonplussed by the kindness the Samaritan showed his enemy. After all, temple service was a high privilege and should take precedence over a man left for dead by robbers. The scribes and Pharisees may have reasoned that the man who had been attacked must have been traveling alone and therefore stupidly vulnerable, or else this terrible event would never have happened to him. People with any sense traveled in groups on such a well-known and dangerous stretch of road. How stupid of him to bring this calamity upon himself by not taking necessary precautions. It was his own fault.

But Jesus was not content to leave it there. He wanted to make it absolutely clear who the real hero of the story was and why. So he pinned his interrogator down and asked him a specific question—a question that shifted the focus of the scribes and Pharisees from the smart thing the priests did to preserve their worthiness to serve in the Temple to the real hero of the story, the Samaritan. "Now which one of these three would you say was a neighbor to the man who was attacked by bandits?" (Luke 10:36 NLT). Because the question was limited to "the man who was attacked by bandits," there was only one possible right answer—the Samaritan ("the one who showed ... mercy"), because he loved his enemy and esteemed him as his neighbor (Luke 10:37 NLT).

Defining the Enemy: "Them" versus "Us"

Jesus's teachings on enemies takes into account the realization that we and those we oppose as "evil" cannot easily be divided into separate camps. Traditional lines defining "friend" and "foe" are not easy to draw. As N. T. Wright put it, the enemy at work is a "cunning enemy, much too clever to allow itself to be identified simply with one person, one group, or one nation."[32]

Speaking of the Kingdom of God, Jesus explained that good and bad evolve together side by side. In the parable of the wheat and the tares, Jesus

32. Wright, *Simply Jesus,* 123.

compared himself to a farmer planting "good seed" (Matt. 13:37 NLT). The Kingdom of God was like a farmer's land. Good seed was planted, but weeds took root alongside the wheat. Jesus said the weeds were those in the Kingdom of God that were under the influence of the "evil one" (Matt. 13:38 NLT). The wheat, of course, was his devoted disciples. The point of the parable was that the "good" and the "bad" grew together and were not entirely distinguishable until Jesus returned at his Second Coming.

The analogy was particularly insightful because tares, as they are referred to in the King James translation, were a type of plant that was barely distinguishable from wheat. Sometimes referred to as darnel, tares were a ryegrass that looked much like wheat in its early stages of growth.[33] It could be so damaging to a crop that Roman law prohibited sowing darnel among the wheat of even one's enemy.[34] Distinguishing between good and bad people (wheat and tares) was not always easy.

N. T. Wright sums up the situation: "The line between good and evil is clear at the level of God, on the one hand, and [Satan], on the other. It is much, much less clear as it passes through human beings, individually and collectively."[35] It becomes

> fatally easy to misunderstand, to draw lines wrong, to see "our present system" as automatically good, so that anyone who disturbs it—as Jesus was disturbing the system of the scribes and Pharisees—must be "satanic," must be from the dark side. That road leads to the "war of the sons of light against the sons of darkness," enabling "us" to see ourselves as "children of light," casting a surreal overdramatized shadow over "them," the "children of darkness." Jesus will have none of it.[36]

He required his followers to reserve judgment.

Jesus, in fact, was redrawing the lines of "good" and "evil" and who the real enemies were. His vociferous and sharp criticisms of the scribes and Pharisees upset the ruling establishment and turned what most people saw as "good" into "evil." He called the scribes and Pharisees "hypocrites" who "crush people with unbearable religious demands." He referred to them as "blind guides" who "cross land and sea to make one convert, and then you turn that person into twice the child of hell you yourselves are!" (Matt. 23:15–16 NLT). Conversely, he exonerated those who were traditionally

---

33. Craig S. Keener, *The Gospel of Matthew: A Socio-Rhetorical Commentary*, 386–87.

34. Ramesh Khatry, *The Authenticity of the Parable of the Wheat and the Tares and Its Interpretation*, 35.

35. Wright, *Simply Jesus*, 123.

36. Ibid., 125.

seen as unworthy—prostitutes, tax collectors, shepherds, lepers, the halt, and the blind. Traditional "enemies" were suddenly brought within reach of God's blessings. Friends who thought they were automatically on the right side had to be reconsidered. Jesus's view of evil and enemies was nuanced, and his followers could not simply say "our people" versus "those people."

Wright eloquently observes that from Jesus's perspective,

> The line between good and evil does not lie between "us" and "them," between the West and the rest, between Left and Right, between rich and poor. That fateful line runs down the middle of each of us, every human society, every individual. This is not to say that all humans, and all societies, are equally good or bad; far from it. Merely that we are all infected and that all easy attempts to see the problem in terms of "us" and "them" are fatally flawed.[37]

Wright argues in his book *Following Jesus* that by the time Jesus reached the apex of his ministry, the scribes, Pharisees, and Sadducees were of course looking for a way to dispose of him. Jesus had three choices. One option was to lead a revolt. The other was to retreat. He could have taken his disciples and followers up over the Mount of Olives, through Bethany, down to the Jordan into the wilderness, and away from trouble never to be heard of again—perfectly safe. Finally, he could stay in Gethsemane, wait for Judas, and then stand silent before his accusers to be martyred.

When Jesus chose the nonviolent and non-confrontational alternative, he pursued a path of holiness that most of us miss. He understood a secret that the "Adolph Hitlers of this world, never ever glimpse in their dreams: the secret that there is a different sort of power, a different sort of Messiah, a different sort of King. The Son of Man came, he said, to give his life a ransom for many."[38] With this third option, he took the "projected evil of the world" and drew it on to himself. "He would draw on to himself the pain of Israel," and "instead of projecting evil out on to the world, instead of keeping the pain in circulation by passing it on, he would bear its full weight in himself."

His way of being holy would show us a nonviolent way forward.

---

37. N.T. Wright, *Surprised by Scripture: Engaging in Contemporary Issues*, 115–16.
38. N. T. Wright, *Following Jesus: Biblical Reflections on Discipleship*, 46.

chapter 12

jesus and His inner circle

Each chapter in this section has been designed to look at Jesus's relationships with various demographic groups in first-century Palestine. The thinking has been, so far, that we can understand his character by tracking how he connected with specific segments of the population: women, outcasts, the poor, and the wealthy. At this point we want to turn our attention to one last, rather small cohort of Jesus's most ardent followers—his inner circles of disciples. Although each individual man or woman remained part of at least one of the previously described subsets, as they each became converted they were voluntarily reconfigured into yet another group; they became his closest allies and then his apostles who were endowed with power to testify of his glory.

The primary purpose of looking at this particular smaller component of the larger society is that this appraisal provides important lessons for us who are also committed to following him. That group, those men and women who loved him, often tried his patience and tested his devotion. Paradoxically, those closest to him seemed to have misunderstood his "work and [his] glory" (Moses 1:39). They misconceived what kind of a messiah he would be. As a consequence, with the possible exception of the women who were at first confused by his absence in the tomb, the disciples temporarily abandoned him after his death in the belief that his crucifixion proved he was not the anointed one they had anticipated. Nevertheless, it remains critically important to see that Jesus did not abandon them in return, either before or after his resurrection.

It may be that some will argue that drawing these lines to separate out slightly artificial groups can potentially limit our ability to look at the whole of his life, rather like being unable to see the forest because we're focused on the individual trees. We think, however, that the sub-title of this collection of essays—*Lessons from the Jesus of Nazareth*—makes the case for some sort of categorical organization for examining any number of angles and views of his life. That being said, in this last chapter in Section One, we will look at how Jesus interacted with members of the demographic group who were the most dedicated followers of his movement, those who walked the landscape of Palestine with him, observing his miracles, his moments of solitude, his anger, and his grief. Most importantly, we will explore how these disciples could not or would not hear his teachings regarding his death and resurrection three days later or what those events meant for his Kingdom. In this chapter we looked at the lessons to be learned from not only the apostles's incomprehension but also his reaction to their disbelief and subsequent disappointment. The lessons we learned are actually relatively simple ones, but ones we tend to need to learn over and over.

We have come to understand several things, at least in principle. First, to admit that the disciples' cultural context blurred the lens through which they viewed Jesus's messianic movement is to admit to the same trap in our own time and place. Just as their lenses obscured the full import and limited their comprehension of their teacher and messiah and his message, we are subject to the same clouded views. Their views—and ours—seemed to be masked by lack of knowledge or time, or the spiritual turbulence of their most private convictions. Second, despite their collective and individual inability to grasp his predictions, their haunting doubts, and their subsequent desertion of him, the resurrected Jesus returned to love and reclaim each one, including ourselves. He made them the leaders of the Jesus movement, the chief carriers of his message. He will do the same for us.

One Messiah among Many

Richard Horsley, professor of the Study of Religion at the University of Massachusetts, explains the general Jewish expectations regarding a messiah around the beginning of the Common Era.[1] He writes that while the promised messiah became an idea of particular importance to Christians, Jewish writings of the first century, on the other hand, do not commonly use "messiah" as the title for "God's [divine] representative or intermediary at the beginning of a new age of peace for Israel and the nations."[2] Belief that such a "radical and definitive change would be brought about by God [through] angelic agents of divine deliverance" was generally "not stressed" by Jews of Jesus's day.[3]

The weight of that statement must not be minimized in a conversation about Jesus as the Messiah or Christ, as Matthew identified him in

1. David Noel Freedman, ed., *The Anchor Bible Dictionary*, s. v. "messiah."
2. Ibid.
3. Ibid., s. v. "messianic movements in Judaism."

the first verse of his Gospel. Rather than looking for a divine being who would somehow intervene to bring about a redemption for mankind's sins as well as a general resurrection of the dead, Jews believed that relief would come from a lowercase "anointed one" in the person of a mortal king, referring to the rites of ordination common to priests, prophets, and princes in the Old Testament. When Samuel "took a flask of olive oil and poured it over Saul's head" (1 Sam. 10:1 NIV), for example, the anointing signified God's approbation as well as his delegation of authority, through his servant Samuel, onto a very earthbound head rather than on a divine one.[4]

In point of fact, Josephus wrote about a number of Jews who claimed special powers as God-ordained saviors; he called them "ambiguous oracles."[5] Each of the men he described claimed messianic status; they each made declarations to the effect that by force of arms they would come to the aid of their people. Several were men who Josephus saw as simply gangsters and thieves who seduced the restive poor into largely suicidal warfare. He spoke about charismatic zealots and still others who led rebellions and uprisings as "prophetic figures resembling Moses."[6] We mention several here.

Simon of Peraea (ca. 4 BC) was an especially notable messianic candidate. He had formerly been Herod the Great's slave. Under his leadership, his revolutionaries burned down Herod's royal palace in Jericho, along with other palaces or buildings in several locations throughout Palestine. The Romans decapitated him.

Israel Knohl, the Yehezkel Kaufmann chair of Biblical Studies at the Hebrew University of Jerusalem, has discovered a stone tablet measuring about three vertical feet that he believes tells of a man who was this Simon of Peraea. The inscription reads that the angel Gabriel prophesied that Simon would die and be resurrected in three days.[7] He was not.

---

4. The priests in Exodus and Leviticus were anointed (Ex. 29:29; Lev. 4:3, 5, 16). Leviticus says that consecrated oil was poured on Aaron's head to anoint and "to sanctify" him (Lev. 8:12 NLT). When Samuel anointed Saul as king with the same ritual, he said, "I am doing this because the Lord has appointed you to be the ruler over Israel, his special possession" (1 Sam. 10:1 NLT).

5. Anchor Bible Dictionary, s. v. "messianic movements in Judaism." Jonathan Klawans, *Josephus and the Theologies of Ancient Judaism*, 162.

6. Ibid.

7. Israel Knohl believes that this find calls for a complete reassessment of what it meant to be a messiah. In 2009, the National Geographic Channel addressed the question in a program called *The First Jesus?* Knohl views the blood of a slain

Josephus's list of messiahs included a certain Menahem ben Judah, the grandson of Hezekiah, the late eighth-century BC king of Judah. Ben Judah was one of the leaders of a splinter group of the Zealots, a band of assassins called the Sicarii from the Greek *sikarioi*, or "dagger men," who were considered terrorists. Ben Judah led an insurrection that overpowered the troops of Agrippa II, the seventh and last king of Herod the Great's dynasty. He attacked the palace overlooking the Dead Sea at Masada. Armed with weapons liberated from the palace, he and his followers then went to Jerusalem, where they captured the Roman Antonia Fortress overlooking the Temple Mount. Then Ben Judah proclaimed himself king. A rival zealot named Eleazar ben Simon eventually disposed of him.[8]

Finally, even though he came after Jesus, Simon bar Kokhba—the most notorious and *successful* messiah—must be included in the list. He organized yet another revolt against Rome, and during a three-year period he established a Jewish state of Israel. In the process of the revolt, bar Kokhba annihilated an entire Roman legion of 5,000 soldiers and its auxiliaries. His Jewish state was laid waste in AD 135, after the Romans captured and killed him along with thousands of his followers. According to Cassius Dio, a Roman consul and historian of the period, 580,000 Jews were killed, 50 fortified towns defeated, and 985 villages razed.[9]

Josephus himself felt that it was Vespasian, a man from a Roman equestrian family who rose to the senatorial ranks and then became the self-proclaimed "anointed" emperor of the Jews, who would ultimately bring a Roman-style peace through war to Palestine and Covenant Israel.[10] From Josephus' viewpoint, in the face of Roman military might, all of the self-proclaimed messianic rebels failed. In AD 70, the final insulting death blow for Jerusalem and the Temple came by way of the Flavian general Titus, the son of Vespasian and later emperor. Titus laid siege to the city, and in the end ransacked even the Holy of Holies. An honorific

---

messiah (Simon) as an essential part of the redemptive process that paves the way for a final Messianic Age.

8. See discussions of messianic movements in Jonathon Klawans, *Josephus and the Theologies of Ancient Judaism*, 92–136.

9. Ibid.

10. Ibid. Ironically, the destruction of the Temple and Jerusalem greatly weakened the influence of Judaism over the early Christian movement and therefore paved the way for Christianity to appeal to other diverse populations. Peter's Jewish slant on Christianity was diminished, and Paul's more inclusive and universal vision of what Christianity would become was accelerated.

arch constructed by Titus's brother Domitian still stands in Rome near the Senate. It celebrates the military conquests of Titus and Judah's humiliation at the hands of his army. One of the high relief panels on the inside of the arch below the intrados or inner curves of the arch itself features his troops parading the golden booty from the destroyed Temple. Soldiers at the center of the procession heft the pallet with the sacred menorah taken from the sanctuary on their shoulders.[11]

Josephus famously mentioned Jesus of Nazareth in his *Testimonium Flavianum* (known more commonly as *Antiquities*) almost incidentally. Although somewhat controversial because, as several critics have suggested, the text has been edited by Christian believers, the Louis Feldman translation has Josephus writing that Jesus "was the Messiah. . . . He appeared to them spending a third day restored to life, for the prophets of God had foretold these things and a thousand other marvels about him."[12] But we must take the scholars' use of this title of *Messiah* for Jesus in the context of Josephus's time period. For Jews in the ancient world, calling Jesus a messiah did not allude to a *future* divine savior or redeemer who would suffer for the sins of the world, as Matthew came to believe and testify. Rather, the title denoted in the Hebrew Bible was interpreted as having more immediate political results.

It is important to remind ourselves that the idea of an anointed one was linked to a ritually ordained king, like David or Cyrus the Great, whose forces would eventually rout the Romans and deliver the Jews from oppression so as to usher in a restored Kingdom of Israel—all in the very near future. He would bring the *Olam Haba,* the "world to come" or Messianic Age, of peace and prosperity. Political and social justice and change were the watchwords. The anointed one would be a political and religious leader who "would spearhead God's deliverance of his people" from Roman domination and humiliation.[13]

The pervasive faith in the eventual advent of a political messianic deliverer probably predisposed Jesus's inner circle of disciples to misunderstand the grand finale of his mission and the kind of messiah he would turn out to be. It seems entirely plausible that in the context of multiple messianic "oracles"—to use Josephus's term—those around Jesus focused on what

---

11. Mortimer Wheeler, *Roman Art and Architecture,* 156.

12. *Flavius Josephus: Translation and Commentary,* 18.3.3. On the controversy of Josephus's characterization of Jesus, see also John Meier, *A Marginal Jew: Rethinking the Historical Jesus,* 57–69.

13. David F. Wright, et al., *New Dictionary of Theology,* s.v. "messiah."

they wanted to hear and downplayed or ignored those parts of his message that controverted the political and cultural expectations of the day. From their perspective, Jesus appeared to be the right person for the job. He came announcing that the long-awaited Kingdom of God was about to be established on earth. He prayed that God Himself would help bring it about: "Thy kingdom come. Thy will be done in earth, as it is in heaven," he said (Matt. 6:10 KJV). More than anything else, his well-known charismatic gifts, miracles, and healings would certainly have seemed to demonstrate God's approval as well as the spiritual muscle to successfully throw off the Roman yoke. Certainly a person of his prowess and ability could fulfill Israel's cosmic vision of an age of peace and Jewish dominance.

In making these assumptions about Jesus, however, his followers—especially those closest to him—failed to understand the full import of his message, or they at least ignored it. His vision of what kind of a kingdom he would establish and his role as the promised messiah was radically different from the one Josephus described.

"We Have Found the Messiah!"

At first, it seemed that the fondest hopes for the advent of the anointed one who had been promised were finally realized at the baptism of Jesus; John the Baptist had testified that he was "the Lamb of God." The Holy Ghost was present as a dove, and God's voice was heard to introduce his son who he loved (Matt. 3:16–17; John 1:32–34). Shortly thereafter, the men who were with the Baptist at Bethabara beyond the Jordan and who had witnessed the extraordinary spiritual manifestations there, followed Jesus to the Sea of Galilee. John's Gospel records with a precision that speaks to the account's likely authenticity that "about four in the afternoon," Andrew found his brother Simon. He avowed, "We have found the Messias" (John 1:41 KJV). The NIV includes, for the benefit of readers who understood Greek, that John added, "that is, the Christ" (John 1:40–42).

To modern readers it may escape particular notice, but those present in Galilee would not have missed the full impact of Andrew's declaration. The J. B. Phillips Translation and at least a dozen other English translations include an exclamation point after his announcement to his brother—soon to be renamed Peter—as if to emphasize the enthusiasm at their hopes being realized: "We have found the Messiah!" Andrew declared (John 1:41 Phi).

Notwithstanding Andrew's announcement, however, the evidence throughout the four Gospels demonstrates that Jesus perplexed even his most devoted disciples, and that they failed to comprehend the full meaning of his genuine messianic status.

Perhaps the most famous abjuration of Jesus's predicted immediate future comes midway in Matthew's Gospel. As they walked toward Caesarea Philippi, Peter took Jesus "by the arm and began to rebuke" him (Matt. 16:22 NEB). Jesus had "plainly" taught his apostles that he would "suffer at the hands of the leaders, he would be killed and he would be raised on the third day" (Matt. 16:21 NLT). "This will never happen to you!" Peter protested, again with the enthusiasm denoted by an exclamation mark (Matt. 16:22 NLT). Jesus reprimanded Peter: "Get away from me, Satan! You are a dangerous trap to me. You are seeing things merely from a human point of view, not from God's" (Matt. 16:23 NLT).

Most of us will read this passage as one of the most stinging rebukes Jesus ever delivered to those who were his most devoted allies. The tone of the reprimand seems grossly antithetical to other exchanges between Jesus and the Twelve, such as in the prayer he offered in their behalf in the Upper Room on the night of their last Passover Seder (John 17:1–26).

It is difficult to hear inflection and tone of voice in the written word. In this case, however, it is critical to understand the tone, given that in this chapter we are attempting an analysis of Jesus's relationships with individuals in his inner circle. William Barclay considers the problem of the tone in this exchange first by commenting on Peter's background. He writes that Peter had been indoctrinated his whole life "on the idea of a Messiah of power and glory and conquest."[14] Yet here was this man he had given up everything for saying they were to go to Jerusalem where he would suffer, be killed, and then raised from the dead after three days (Matt. 16:21). For Peter, "the idea of a suffering Messiah, the connection of a cross with the work of the Messiah, was incredible."[15] Thus we picture his passion as he caught hold of Jesus and "took him aside" to straighten him out (Matt. 16:22 NIV). Barclay writes that Jesus must have been "a man wounded to the heart, with poignant grief and a kind of shuddering horror."[16] He also compares the urgency of Peter's reaction to the Devil's temptation in the wilderness. Barclay says Peter declared that Jesus must not, could not, do such a thing as let himself suffer such a disgraceful death at the

---

14. William Barclay, *Daily Bible Study, The Gospel of Matthew*, 2:172.
15. Ibid.
16. Ibid.

hands of the Romans, who in turn were provoked by the ultra-devout and hypocritical scribes, Pharisees and Sadducees. Like Peter, the Devil offered alternative, even violent, paths to power. Barclay concludes, "That is why Peter was *Satan. Satan* literally means *the Adversary.*"[17]

In Barclay's final commentary on Jesus's rebuke, he uses a passage from the writings of early third-century theologian Origen of Alexandria, who suggested an interpretation considerably more forgiving of Jesus's response to Peter's rash retort. Origen wrote copiously about Early Christian and Hebrew Bible texts, interpreting passages such as this one in Matthew's Gospel. Barclay offers Origen's idea on the problem and follows it with his own:

> Origen suggested that Jesus was saying to Peter: "Peter, your place is *behind* me, not in *front* of me. It is your place *to follow* me in the way I choose, not to try *to lead* me in the way you would like me to go."
>
> If the phrase can be interpreted in that way, something at least of its sting is removed. . . . [Rather than banish him], it recalls him to his proper place, as a follower walking in the footsteps of Jesus.[18]

Peter was certainly not the only member of Jesus's inner circle who did not comprehend his mission. Luke wrote that as they walked toward their last Passover Festival, Jesus began once again preparing them for what was to come:

> Gathering the twelve disciples around him, Jesus told them, "As you know, we are going to Jerusalem. And when we get there, all the predictions of the ancient prophets concerning the Son of Man will come true. He will be handed over to the Romans to be mocked, treated shamefully, and spit upon. They will whip him and kill him, but on the third day he will rise again." *But they didn't understand a thing he said. Its significance was hidden from them, and they failed to grasp what he was talking about.* (Luke 19:31–34 NLT; emphasis added)

Note that they did not "grasp" either his coming death or his ultimate resurrection (Luke 19:33 NLT). Whereas the Pharisees believed in a resurrection of the body, it was not something the Jews associated with a messiah. Theirs was an eschatological viewpoint in that they expected some kind of physical renewal to happen at the *final judgment,* a point in time long after the arrival of a messiah. As the Gospel of John explains, Mary

---

17. Ibid., 173; emphasis in original.
18. Ibid., 174; emphasis in original.

Magdalene and the Twelve "still hadn't understood the Scriptures that said Jesus must rise from the dead" (John 20:9–10 NLT).

Perhaps the most poignant example of the disciples' incomprehension of Jesus's mission is found in the Gospel of John. In the following passage, Jesus explained his mission more completely to his disciples than on any other occasion. According to John, his deep explanation came in a room reserved for their celebration of the Passover supper. Later, Jesus would ask his father to spare him: "My father! If it is possible, let this cup of suffering be taken away from me. Yet I want your will, not mine" (Matt. 26:39 NLT). But in the intimate context of the Upper Room, Jesus gathered his disciples and once more warned them that there were "things I still have to say to you . . . but you're not yet strong enough to take them" (John 16:6 NTWT). He explained: "Not long from now, you won't see me anymore. Then again, not long after that, you will see me!" (John 16:16 NTWT). The disciples responded as they had on other occasions when Jesus brought the sensitive subject of his demise to their attention. "What's he talking about? . . . What's this business about 'not long from now, you won't see me'? And what's this about 'going to the father'?" they asked (John 16:17 NTWT). It was so inconceivable that they repeated the interrogation: "What is this 'not long'? What's it all about? We don't know what he means!" (John 16:18 NTWT).

Then Jesus spoke about their future sorrow and disappointment: "You will weep and wail but the world will celebrate. You will be overcome with sorrow, but your sorrow will turn to joy" (John 16:20 NTWT). "Sorrow now," he counseled. "But I shall see you again, and your hearts will celebrate, and nobody will take your joy away from you" (John 16:22 NTWT). And then this prediction: they would temporarily abandon the cause they once lovingly embraced: "Look here: the time is coming (in fact, it's now arrived!) when you will be scattered, each of you to his own place" (John 16:32 NTWT).

"We Had Hoped"

The disciples' lack of comprehension led to despair and inconsolable, perhaps even angry disappointment when Jesus actually died as he had promised. But the ensuing days brought manifestations of a very physical Jesus that would change their minds. The first appearances were to several women early on a Sunday morning. They had returned to the burial site only "to find the empty grave and the folded grave-clothes" (John

20:1–10). All but Mary Magdalene ran back to the city to tell Peter and John that the body of Jesus was not there. They left Mary weeping because she supposed the body had been removed by the gardener. Mary addressed the voice of someone behind her who asked, "Why weepest thou?" She pleaded, "If thou have borne him hence, tell me where thou hast taken him, and I will take him away" (John 20:15 KJV).

The next verses in the New Living Translation are restrained. They say that they spoke and that she clung to him until it was time to part, when he gently said, with more tenderness than the remonstrance of the King James Version, "Cling to me no longer." Thus comforted and reassured, she rushed to find Peter, John, and the others; then she told them what had happened (Mark 16:9–11 NLT; John 20:10–18 NLT).[19]

Jesus appeared to other women, who like Mary Magdalene had gone to the tomb, found it empty, and then returned to find the others. As they made their way back to the disciples' hiding place, Jesus came to them as well. They ran to him, held his feet, and spoke with him. Jesus gave them instructions on what they should tell his disciples, and hence they became his first apostolic witnesses (Matt. 28:9–10).

He appeared to the eleven disciples who were "startled and frightened," and their hearts were "filled with doubt" at his sudden appearance in the Upper Room (Luke 24:38 NLT). In fact, they thought they had seen a ghost (Luke 24:37 NLT). We may assume they had gathered for mutual strength and comfort.

To reassure them, Jesus invited them to experience his resurrected self through their senses. "Look at my hands. Look at my feet. You can see that it's really me. Touch me and make sure that I am not a ghost, because ghosts don't have bodies, as you see that I do." Yet "they stood there in disbelief, filled with joy and wonder." As further evidence that he had returned in a perfected material body, Jesus had them bring food, and "he ate it as they watched" (Luke 24:39, 41 NLT). John wrote that on this occasion Jesus "rebuked them for their stubborn unbelief because they refused to believe those who had seen him after he had been raised from the dead" (Mark 16:14 NLT). However, we should give them some quarter inasmuch as we can only imagine the massive reorientation of their worldview as he stepped into the room to say, "Handle me and see!" (Luke 24:39 KJV).

---

19. It is worth noting that in the Joseph Smith Translation, the Savior instructed Mary Magdalene, "Hold me not" rather than the King James Bible rendition "Touch me not" (compare JST, John 20:17 with KJV, John 20:17).

Surely chagrined because they had doubted and disbanded, they received assurance that Jesus loved them and trusted them. He invested them with authority to go into the world as witnesses to the fact that just as he had promised, he had returned.

Later he came a second time to his disciples behind locked doors. This time Thomas, ardent cynic and skeptic, was present. Thomas had been despondent at the ignominious loss of his master. Given the circumstances, his disbelief is understandable. Thomas could only be fully satisfied when his own physical senses confirmed that Jesus indeed stood before him with a transcendent physical body.

Yet, Jesus once again "held out his hands for [all] to see, and he showed them his side" (John 20:20 NLT). Thomas stepped forward to see the marks of his crucifixion, referred to as the *stigmata*. He put his finger on the nail prints; Jesus allowed him to guide his hand "into the wound" on his side (John 20:19–29 NLT).

John records another appearance to seven of the inner circle on the shore of the Sea of Galilee. On this night they had fished through the darkness without netting even a single fish. In the early light of dawn, they perceived a man standing on the shore by a small fire. He called to them, telling them to cast their nets on the other side of their boat. The subsequent yield was overwhelming. Suddenly they recognized their Lord. Peter jumped from the boat to speed to the shore. As they ate the breakfast Jesus had prepared, he spoke with them for an extended period. Then Jesus charged Peter three times that if he loved him as he loudly professed, he must return to his apostolic calling. He said, "Feed my sheep" and care for "my lambs." This enormously important appearance fortified the lonely and disconsolate men who were left behind to lead the others who had committed to follow Jesus. Once again, Jesus's appearance provided a kind of mission statement regarding priorities for the nascent church (John 21:1–14).

Jesus's visits to those he had left behind did not merely span minutes or even one or two days. He continued to appear to and visit with his apostles "during the forty days after his crucifixion, . . . from time to time, and . . . proved . . . in many ways that he was actually alive"(Acts 1:3 NLT). Jesus appeared to at least another two thousand men, women, and children in the New World. He taught them, set up his church there, blessed both the adults and their children, and on multiple occasions invited each one to step forward to touch him (3 Ne. 18:36–38; 28:12).

Luke's account of a conversation between two of the disciples—Cleopas and, tradition says, James—reveals the depth of their wretchedness. As these forlorn followers walked toward Emmaus, a village about seven miles from Jerusalem, Jesus joined them incognito (Luke 24:16 NLT).

Jesus saw "sadness written across their faces" (Luke 24:17 NLT). Still in disguise, he asked the nature of their conversation. Cleopas' astonished reply was that this traveler must have been the only person in Jerusalem who had not heard what had happened.

At this point in the exchange the two men revealed the true source of their disappointment. Jesus from Nazareth, they said, "was a prophet, powerful in word and deed before God and all the people. The chief priests and our rulers handed him over to be sentenced to death, and they crucified him; *but we had hoped that he was the one* who was going to redeem Israel" (Luke 24:19–21 NIV; emphasis added). By their own admission, they had concluded that a dead messiah was no messiah at all. They said, "Some of our men ran out to see [the empty tomb] and sure enough his body was gone," as several women had reported (Luke 24:22 NLT).

Jesus responded with another exclamation and then a rhetorical question (we like the New English Bible translation for the first part and the New Living for the question): "How dull you are!" Jesus said (Luke 24:25 NEB). Then, "You find it so hard to believe all that the prophets wrote in the Scriptures. Wasn't it clearly predicted by the prophets that the Messiah would have to suffer all these things before entering his time of glory?" (Luke 24:25–27 NLT). As they walked, Luke reports that Jesus expounded on the prophecies and promises of the Hebrew Bible regarding a messiah. The story is so familiar it hardly needs repeating, but we include it all the same because it reflects such an important model for all of us. His response shows us his compassionate patience toward all of us whose commitment and faith ebb and flow.

At the end of their walk, the two disciples invited the stranger to eat with them and stay the night. As they sat at table and broke bread with him, they recognized the Lord, who then vanished (Luke 24:31).

Just as others who had heard that Jesus's body was no longer in the tomb had not therefore concluded that he had been resurrected, neither had Cleopas and James understood the kind of messiah Jesus had become. Many thought the body might have been stolen. Mary Magdalene and the other women who had become the "apostles to the apostles" rushed to find the other disciples to tell them that Jesus was very much alive. Mary said "she had seen him [but] *they didn't believe her*" (Mark 16:10–11 NLT; emphasis added).

What are we to conclude from all of these appearances? First, as N. T. Wright expressed it, the apostles and Jesus's followers mistakenly believed that Jesus would "fight God's victorious battle against the wicked pagans[,] . . . rebuild or cleanse the Temple[,] and . . . bring God's justice to the world."[20] Second, again quoting Wright, "the ancient world—with the exception of the Jews—was adamant that dead people did not rise again; and the Jews did not believe that anyone *had* done so or that anyone *would* do so all by themselves in advance of the general resurrection" at the end of times. Therefore, when Jesus died and defied both assumptions, says Wright, "every single disciple knew what it meant: we backed the wrong horse. The game is over."[21] This "stubborn unbelief" and inability to see past the customary teachings of their day explains why the apostles had been so disappointed. In their lonely and abandoned states of mind, despite a witness in Jerusalem, they went back to their individual professions, disillusioned and disconsolate. They simply gave up.

Yet, in the face of this seemingly impenetrable wall of cultural, psychological, and theological resistance to the kind of messiah Jesus became, something changed the attitude of the inner circle and first-generation Christians in very personal and reassuring ways. It came by way of a singular event that literally meant everything had been re-ordered. Why didn't the fledgling group of believers fade into obscurity after Jesus died as just another failed messiah movement? What could have possibly caused a group of disgruntled disciples to go out into the world at the peril of their lives and become not only his disciples but also his apostles, those who would proclaim that Jesus was resurrected? "Wishful thinking or mere blind optimism?"[22]

N.T. Wright's reasoning about the question and response between Jesus and Peter as they walked toward Caesarea Philippi goes something like this: When Jesus asked Peter the crucial question about his identity and mission, Peter answered that he, Jesus, was the messiah and the son of God. On this side of the resurrection we can be forgiven for reading that passage, says Wright, as if Peter had revelatory surety about Jesus's impending death and more importantly resurrection. However, Wright argues, the disciples saw him as a messiah who would bring God's covenant Israel to conquer the immediate oppressor. They simply did not believe

20. N. T. Wright, *Surprised by Hope: Rethinking Heaven, the Resurrection, and the Mission of the Church*, 47.
21. Ibid., 34.
22. Ibid., 40.

that the promised messiah would die at the hands of the Romans who he was sent to conquer. So when Jesus made numerous post-resurrection appearances to his disappointed disciples of his inner circle in Palestine, each of the accounts did at least two things.

Each encounter provided compelling testimony of a very physical, perfected, and immortal Jesus, who, as Wright is fond of saying, went "through death and out the other side again" into a new eternal "mode of existence."[23] Even though the disciples had misunderstood his multiple declarations about leaving and returning, it happened just as he had promised them. He did "not abandon [them] as orphans" (John 14:18 NLV). Instead, he came back to them in a body impervious to death and with power to save them and the entire human race from the oppression of death and cosmic obliteration. More important to their immediate despair, however, these post-resurrection appearances brought a kind of individualized peace to each of the miserable, disappointed disciples so that each could in turn provide not only the faith necessary to establish the Kingdom of God on earth, but also the tactile, sensory testimony of his reality as a resurrected being.

---

23. Ibid., 72.

section two
jesus and institutions

chapter 13

jesus and the kingdoms of this world

In the preceding pages we have observed how Jesus responded to individual souls in first-century Palestine. As we would expect of the Jesus who is the genuine Messiah, it is a portrait of a man with unwavering compassion who fed the hungry, healed the sick, forgave the sinner, searched after the lost, consoled the suffering, relieved the fearful, and loved the enemy. It is a Jesus who included within his inner circle slaves as well as the powerful, the wealthy as well as the poor, women as well as men, and always, always the outcasts.

The focus now shifts from his relationships with individuals to his connections to institutions, namely the Roman government and the Jewish religious establishment. The contrasts are remarkable. For the singular man or woman, Jesus was ever commanding, yet accessible and empathic. Yet when Jesus dealt with those who controlled the religious and political levers of power, those who represented the institutions of his day, he was often aggressively short. He was invariably and perilously critical. And he was judgmental. We see a side of his personality that was full of thundering condemnations. It was a Jesus who passionately challenged abusive and corrupt power structures that systematically spiritually disenfranchised and materially impoverished whole groups of people. He spoke from an entirely altered paradigm, summoning to earth a society he called the Kingdom of God.

The Temptations in the Wilderness

This chapter is intended to function as a hinge connecting two aspects of Jesus's ministry. It is therefore a kind of pivot point holding steady our first reflections on those narratives that illustrate his compassion for the one, while we open others that demonstrate the Jesus who found the institutions of his day insufferable. While it will always be critical to remember how he ministered to individuals, if we want to establish the more three-dimensional historical Jesus, it seems appropriate to shift our focus to the

Gospels' accounts of Jesus confronting both the political and religious systems of power. It seemed to us that the hinge we were looking for was the temptations experience that came directly following his baptism. Thus, the title of this chapter comes from the accounts of Jesus's forty-day trial in the Judean wilderness.

All three of the synoptic Gospels speak of the self-imposed ordeal. Mark's version is contained in two cryptic verses. He tells us that "immediately" after Jesus's baptism, he went into the desert for forty days, where the devil tempted him, and because he was among wild animals, angels "ministered" to him (Mark 1:12–13 NLT). Matthew and Luke, on the other hand, make use of a time-honored literary structure to tell us of the tests put to Jesus as he prepared to commence his messianic responsibilities.

Some debate exists over the literal authenticity of the Temptations story because of its striking, fantastic events and formulaic literary structure. After all, none other than the Devil himself transported Jesus in a flash! (exclamation mark included) from the wilderness to the pinnacle of the Temple in Jerusalem and then to the top of a mountain. And in addition, there are three neatly devised temptations written in a kind of hierarchy of importance. Certainly at its most essential level, this trials narrative is a literary device Matthew and Luke employed to powerfully describe an experience of prodigious importance. Therefore, Mark's account is the most basic one, and because of its brevity and lack of formulaic, almost mythical structure, it is the one we may easily accept as a simple report of this experience. Nonetheless, like the other accounts, it also expresses Jesus's perfect discipline in response to evil enticements, such that Matthew and Mark tell us he was able to keep company with angels.

Matthew and Luke may clothe the testing in the elegance of traditional poetic forms, but the themes in all three accounts of Jesus's forty days in the wilderness remain the same. Whether cryptic or elaborate, they are fundamentally about elemental temptations that confront all mortals. And so we list them all but then focus on Matthew's last one:

1. The allure of selfish physical indulgence.
2. The demand for miracles as prerequisites for belief in God's fidelity.
3. The seduction of worldly power and earthly glory.

By the end of the wilderness trials, Jesus would enter the ministry and multiply loaves of bread not to satisfy his own hunger but to feed the hungry pilgrims. In the desert he did not draw attention to himself by demanding that God would send angels to save him from falling. In the world he used miracles to heal the sick and raise the dead, worrying that the added attention might distract or prevent him from preaching his message (Mark 1:43–45). Finally, the third trial was the crucial one for us at this juncture. "All the kingdoms of the world and their glory" were offered if only he would acquiesce to their inherently evil structure and to the Devil, the master of the kingdoms; yet we know that he did nothing of the sort (Matt. 4:8 NLT).

Immediately following the time in the wilderness, he went to the Galilee. There Matthew wrote that he began to preach about the Kingdom of God. "Repent of your sins and turn to God, for the Kingdom of Heaven is near," he said (Matt. 4:17 NLT). Then he taught the corpus of laws that governed the Kingdom: loving one's enemies, shunning not only violence but also anger, renouncing the old "law that says the punishment must match the injury," and practicing pure, unseen acts of charity (Matt. 5:21–26; 38–48; 6:1–4 NLT). He prayed that God's Kingdom in Heaven would be brought about on earth by his disciples through *active* but peaceable means rather than the *passive* aggression of the former slaves of the Exodus or the hypocrisy of the corrupted religious and political kingdoms of his day. In the end, Jesus's trials narrative offers us an opportunity to consider the stakes, as it were, as he emerged from the desert committed and ready to engage with the kingdoms he had declined to lead.

The Worldviews of First-Century Palestine

To more fully situate Jesus *vis a vis* the institutions of his own day, we should next review a few of the essential philosophical and religious contexts for those institutions, what theorists and epistemologists sometimes refer to as the *Weltanschauung* of the era and of individuals living in it. The term moved into English laterally and literally from two German words *Welt* (world) and *Anschauung* (view or outlook). The eighteenth-century German philosopher Immanuel Kant probably wrote about it first. Kant's near-contemporary Georg Friedrich Hegel, another German philosopher, popularized it. Epic trials narratives and mythologies—including any number of examples in Old Testament and Greco-Roman epic poetry texts—are linguistic manifestations of a civilization's *Weltanschauung*. We offer three definitions. The first and most basic is from Merriam-Webster. When English "first adopted it from German in the mid-19th century,

Weltanschauung referred to a philosophical view or apprehension of the universe. . . . [It can] describe a more general ideology or philosophy of life."[1]

The second definition comes from Jonathan Haidt's *The Righteous Mind: Why Good People Are Divided by Politics and Religion*, an insightful 528-page analysis of the reason nations become so bitterly divided.[2] Haidt's thesis is, simply put, that the worldviews of each side cannot be reconciled to the other. As the book's title suggests, the divide is very nearly an irreparable one because each nation takes their view of the world as the "righteous" one. He then offers details for what he sees as such a total breach of comity, arguing that the worldviews of nations and political parties are based on assumptions and definitions of morality in government and everyday relationships.[3] Therefore, the prism through which each side interprets the motives of the other is a kind of gut holier-than-thou intuition—what he defines as a worldview.[4] Every side believes in the superiority of its morality and of its systems, despite the system's inconsistencies and hypocrisies. Hence, the worldviews create both ideological and political segregation.

Haidt's arguments about contemporary worldviews are especially compelling when he writes that demographics—living in and belonging to what he calls "lifestyle enclaves" governed by equally segregated religious and socio-economic systems[5]—are the problem. It is equally compelling to view Roman and Jewish societies through Haidt's lens, with their civil and religious canons, dispensed in temples and tribunals. We then pair that first definition of *Weltanschauung* from Merriam-Webster with Haidt's to observe that when the "general ideology or philosophy" of accommodation and assimilation of Rome met the highly exclusive "ideology or philosophy" of the Jewish religious establishment everything was per force segregated into camps, each seeking to dominate and exploit the other.[6] By placing Jesus in the midst of it all as a messiah with a powerfully different sort of worldview, we get a picture of the conditions that blighted the kingdoms of the Ancient World that Jesus came to upend with his Father's Kingdom (Luke 11:2).

After his trials in the wilderness, Jesus came to the ministry rejecting the worldview that his Kingdom ought to utilize commonly accepted

---

1. *Merriam-Webster.com*, s.v. "weltanschauung" (accessed October 27, 2017).

2. Jonathan Haidt, *The Righteous Mind: Why Good People Are Divided by Politics and Religion*, 73. Ebook.

3. Ibid., loc. 130.

4. Ibid., loc. 191.

5. Ibid., loc. 5210.

6. Ibid., loc. 5454.

psychological and political power structures to achieve its ends. When the Devil swore that Jesus could have inestimable glory, that promise was based on the use of tyranny and torture. On the other hand, Jesus's world-view rested on the idea that the Kingdom of God was non-compulsory. This was clearly set out in the opening verses of the Sermon on the Mount known as the Beatitudes (or Blesseds), where Jesus proclaimed that it would be the merciful and pure-in-heart peacemakers who would be called "children of God" in the Kingdom of Heaven (Matt. 5:7–10 NLT).[7] At the very opposite end, the kingdoms of the world were founded on coercion, intimidation, extortions, the use of force, and wholesale violence.

A second principle that divides the Kingdom of God from the kingdoms of the world is based on the second great commandment, to love one's neighbor; by extension, it required an entire society to be based on principles of equality. Jesus and his apostles taught first generation Christians that they should have "all things in common." Therefore, they "sold their possessions and goods, and parted them to all men, as every man had need" (Acts 2:44–45 KJV). Jesus taught that economic justice would bring with it social and spiritual parity, leading to what God envisioned for his children—what Paul later referred to as the assurance that all are destined to become "joint-heirs with Christ . . . glorified together" (Rom. 8:17 KJV).

In Luke 14:15–23, Jesus compared the Kingdom of God to a feast, one very different from the typical banquets sponsored by the privileged classes of society of his day. Rather than inviting only the wealthy and prominent, everyone who accepted Jesus's invitation to the Kingdom would be seated regardless of their status—people off the street next to the prominent, female next to male, socially high next to socially low, and ritually pure next to ritually impure. His seating arrangements illustrated (in a very understandable way) his worldview. John Dominic Crossan calls this banquet an example of "table commensality." Eating together in this way eliminated society's "vertical discriminations and lateral separations."[8] By inviting everyone, Jesus illustrated the equal privilege that was at the heart of the Kingdom of God. None were to be excluded; all were to be seated at the table equally. This eating and drinking arrangement, which

---

7. In Mormon theology the non-compulsory nature of God's Kingdom is described in Doctrine and Covenants 121:41–46: "No power or influence can or ought to be maintained . . . only by persuasion, by long-suffering, by gentleness and meekness and by love unfeigned . . . and thy dominion shall be an everlasting dominion, and *without compulsory means* it shall flow unto thee forever and ever" (emphasis added).

8. John Dominic Crossan, *Jesus a Revolutionary Biography*, 67–70.

created brother and sister relationships amongst the community of Jesus's disciples, is figuratively repeated in the celebration of the Lord's Supper in Christian churches throughout the world.

Crossan also described the Kingdom of God in terms of a well-run household, as a place where the love and good deeds of all its members fulfill the unique needs and desires of the entire group. In such an environment, relationships are not coercive but sympathetic. Does everyone in the household have enough food, clothing, and shelter? Does a sick child get special care? Is a pregnant woman or nursing mother given special concern? Does everyone have a fair share of everything? Does everyone have enough? Are all the members of the household loved and supported? If such questions could not be answered in the affirmative then Jesus would not have approved. A household where some members are exploited or some have far less than they need, while others have far more than they need, is a household that horrified the conscience of Jesus, destroyed the integrity of the household, and dishonored the householder.[9] According to Petr Pokorny, a German professor of theology, "The provocative element of Jesus's [worldview] was mainly his expectation of the Kingdom of God as a new social structure fulfilling the justice of God."[10]

A third definition of *Weltanschauung* or worldview is one from Michael Lind, a well-known political scientist, who writes that a "worldview is a more or less coherent understanding of the nature of reality, which permits its holders to interpret new information in light of their preconceptions."[11] Lind's definition is one that explains the meaning of *Weltanschauung* in behavioral terms. Assuming we can, for the purpose of clarity, generalize about whole populations, the key phrases in his definition, not only for Jesus but also for Jews and Romans of his day, can be written here in the form of a question: What were Jewish and Roman "preconceptions" about their worlds—their *Weltanschauung*—through which they "interpreted" the teachings of Jesus? And, in the alternative, what was Jesus's worldview through which he "interpreted" Rome and the Jewish religious establishment? In the chapters that follow we will explore several answers to those questions and attempt to explain why the kingdoms of the world were irreconcilable and eventually on a collision course with the Kingdom of God.

---

9. John Dominic Crossan, *The Greatest Prayer: Rediscovering the Revolutionary Message of the Lord's Prayer,* 14, 45, 50, 78.

10. Petr Pokorny, "Jesus' Death on the Cross: Literary, Theological, and Historical Comments," 906–7.

11. Michael Lind, "The Five Worldviews that Define American Politics."

chapter 14

jesus and systemic injustice

John the Baptist began preaching in the wilderness that a new Kingdom was coming, shouting, "Repent of your sins and turn to God, for the Kingdom of Heaven is near" (Matt. 3:2 NLT). Using the language of Isaiah, John proclaimed that he was the one "clear[ing] the road for him" who would be a new sovereign on the earth (John 1:23; Isa. 40:3; Matt. 3:2–3 NLT).

The crowds who heard John would have known exactly what text he was referencing and to what end. They would have known he meant he was acting as a forerunner for someone they believed Isaiah had promised would be of salvific importance, one who would come with authority to supplant the kingdoms of the world and redeem oppressed Israel. Indeed, those who heard John were also well aware of the customs regarding a king's arrival; they knew about a harbinger who would make a way through whatever might lie in the new monarch's intended line of march.

John became known locally for preaching that Israel should anticipate such a new king, a messiah or "anointed one." It was for that reason that the crowds came from Jerusalem to Bethabara's *micvehs*, the ritual baths at the edge of the Jordan River—the place John used for covenant, cleansing immersions. Their numbers included the wealthy, tax collectors, Roman soldiers, and a number of Pharisees and Sadducees who came to determine John's motivations and authority (Luke 3:14–15; Matt. 3:7; John 1:24).

Focus for a moment on the exchange between John and the Pharisees and Sadducees from Jerusalem. In Matthew's account, John specifically singled them out, calling them a "family of snakes" attempting to escape God's "coming wrath" (Matt. 3:7 NLV). The Anchor Bible explains that the epithet was distinctly uncomplimentary: a "viper's offspring was a common expression at the time, indicating those filled with malice" and even children "not from a legitimate union."[1] In the context of preparing the way for the new king via a baptismal ritual for those willing to become

---

1. W. F. Albright and C. S. Mann, *The Anchor Bible Series, Matthew* 26–27.

part of the new Kingdom, John did not stint on his stunning condemnation of these particular observers; in effect John quite literally called them "snake bastards."[2]

We may assume that such a crude insult had its desired effect coming from someone like John. Most commentaries use internal evidence in the Gospels to describe him as a Nazarite or an Essene,[3] two extreme ascetic sects living exclusively in the Judean desert. The Pharisees and Sadducees generally and specifically considered themselves of higher classes than both groups. They disdained the desert-dwelling sects' views on doctrinal orthodoxy, and they enjoyed status and power in Jerusalem's religious hierarchy. And yet it is worth pointing out that Matthew mentioned the Pharisees nearly six times more frequently than the Sadducees. Each time he portrays both as rigid, status-conscious, and often corrupt, possessing neither kindness nor conscience.

Besides knowing John's lower status and class, we also discern something of his more rough appearance from clues in the text. For example, the apparel and grooming of men from Jerusalem must have contrasted sharply with John's "clothes woven of coarse camel's hair," with a "leather belt around his waist." His hair was probably wild, dirty, and uncut, and he must have been bone thin inasmuch as his diet consisted of desert "locusts and wild honey" (Matt. 3:4 NLT).

The Pharisees and Sadducees were outraged, disturbed, and affronted by a man of such a low status condemning them. He added more insults, saying they should not assume they were saved simply because they were "descendants of Abraham" and of the house of Israel—God could create children of Abraham from the very stones (Matt. 3:9–10 NLT).

And then Jesus, coming from Galilee, entered into the midst of this seminal event. Upon the death of Herod the Great, Imperial Rome had separated the remote province from the rest of Palestine, and Jesus had come from this region's entirely insignificant village of Nazareth. John

---

2. Ibid.

3. Bible scholars refer to Luke 1:5, 15; 5:33 to identify John as a descendant of Aaron through his mother and of the "priestly order of Abijah" through his father. Furthermore, they speculate that he was also a Nazarene, largely based on Luke's account that John would "never touch wine or other strong drinks" as well as the description of his clothes and diet, conditions of membership in a sect known as the Nazarites. In addition to abstention from wine, their vows, which could apply to a lifetime commitment or a shorter duration, included never cutting their hair, never touching dead bodies, and participating in a ritual *micveh*.

had been declaring in full voice to the assembled crowds that the king was coming—someone who would be greater than any of those there at the baptismal site, those sophisticated urban Judean crowds who lived at the center of Israel's orthodoxy.

The Gospel of Mark says John felt he was "not even worthy to stoop down like a slave and untie the straps of [Jesus's] sandals" (Mark 1:7 NLT). The implication of John's comment is clear. In the ancient world, slaves were what Aristotle called "living tools" who were "universally despised" and without "honor."[4] Day laborers (who belonged to no one and thus had no means of support whatsoever) and untouchables (the diseased unclean; see Chapter 7) were seen as the lowest of the low in the demographic hierarchy of the Middle East in the first century. They were rarely provided genuine status or meaningful access to the levers of power. Yet John said he wanted only to accept as his duty to "untie the straps" on Jesus's unquestionably dusty, dirty, worn sandals in order to be near this new king!

The details of Jesus's visit to John are important for several reasons. The first is that the particulars of this gathering provide important information about the major players in the drama to follow—their class, status, and power in the political and religious systems of first-century Palestine. It is here, for example, that we meet the Pharisees and Sadducees for the first time. They would become the arch-antagonists of the Jesus messianic movement. Together with the scribes (those charged with copying and interpreting scriptural texts), the Pharisees and Sadducees would be reviled and rebuked by Jesus as well as by John and others throughout the Gospels. We often consolidate them into one entity—the "PhariseesandSadducees"—with little allowance for nuance, as if they were a monolithic stereotype for the religious enemy. John's Gospel was especially guilty of combining "all Jesus's opponents except the chief priests, into one category, the Pharisees."[5]

However, these Jews of the elite upper classes arguably *were* more formidable and worrisome than the occupying Roman legions. The soldiers garrisoned in Caesarea Maritima were the empire's peacekeepers who kept their accommodating distance from the goings-on in the tiny province unless there was a disturbance in the order of things. But here, as we meet those infamous antagonists in the opening scenes of all four Gospels, John's and Jesus's interactions with the Pharisees, Sadducees, and scribes give us a snapshot of the who's who of the Jesus narrative.

---

4. S. Scott Bartchy, "Slaves and Slavery in the Roman World," 170.
5. Anthony J. Saldarini, *Pharisees, Scribes, and Sadducees in Palestinian Society,* 196.

The second reason to examine the details of the baptism story is to be introduced to the Roman-Jewish power structure. Despite the two relatively new Roman cities of Sepphoris and Tiberias, Galilee (together with the region on the eastern banks of the Jordan called Perea) was considered unsophisticated and rural. It was officially part of a tetrarchy ruled by Herod's weak and corrupt son, Herod Antipas, one of three Roman client kings. John, in provocative and seditious language at the baptismal site, "publicly criticized [Antipas] . . . for marrying Herodias, his brother's wife, and for many other wrongs he had done" (Luke 3:19 NLT).

Luke chronicled the rest of the rather dismal Roman hierarchy with a list: "Tiberius [was] the Roman emperor. Pontius Pilate was governor over Judea [including Samaria]. Herod Antipas was ruler over Galilee; his brother Philip was ruler over Iturea and Trachonitis [regions even further north of Galilee]; Lysanias was ruler over Abilene [in parts of what is now Syria]. Annas and Caiaphas were the high priests" in Jerusalem (Luke 3:1–2 NLT).

Thus Luke laid out the interconnection of the hierarchy of political power that flowed downward to the "kings on strings" who were tethered to Rome and then to the high priests. Taxes for Rome were collected through both the religious and the political establishments. The client kings' financial obligations to Rome bought protection in return. Small local kings, no matter how corrupt, could generally count on Roman legions for protection against other states outside the empire. Likewise, the high priests in Jerusalem could count on similar protection, provided their financial dues were paid and they successfully tamped down agitators like John and Jesus.

At the moment of Jesus's baptism, Israel was in the hands of Annas and Caiaphas, who were descendants of Zadok, the high priest during David's reign. Their lineage conferred on them uncontested power over the religious life of all Israel. In addition, they controlled the coffers of the Temple and the ranks of ordinary priests who were the Temple functionaries. Their class, status, wealth, and power were unparalleled. John's claims of a new Kingdom and of a new king were yet another challenge to the social structures and political systems of the day.

Finally, by briefly examining the sociopolitical makeup of the characters at Jesus's baptism we can extrapolate an understanding of a larger view of what the devil in his encounter with Jesus in the wilderness called the "kingdoms of the world."

Like So Much Dead Wood

The scene at the baptismal site at Bethabara brought together each of the constituencies that populated a world based on what Marcus Borg calls "the domination systems in the Jewish homeland" of first-century Palestine.[6] In a 1999 sermon, Borg said that these social and political structures were "marked by an economics of exploitation, a politics of oppression, . . . legitimated most frequently with a religious ideology, legitimated in the name of God."[7] Borg identified "systemic injustice" as one of the seminal themes of Jesus's approximately three-year ministry and said it was the "single greatest source of unnecessary human suffering, of unnecessary social misery . . . caused by cultural systems, by the structure of [a society]."[8]

Throughout his ministry, Jesus faced each of the classes and communities that attended his baptism. First and with perhaps the strongest claim to authority over other Jews, the Sadducees were the aristocratic members of a class whose power came from their priestly control of the Temple on one side of the religious divide and the accommodation of their Roman overlords who had backed Herod the Great and his reconstruction of the Temple on the other. While a minority of the Jewish power structure, their authority—via Rome and Judea—was in reverse proportion to their numbers.

Next and competing with the Sadducee's claims of priestly authority were the Pharisees, who also held considerable power and status. While some may have been priests, they disdained the Sadducee's control of the Temple and fealty to Rome. Lacking the hierarchical priestly authority, they appealed to a scribal authority gained through intense study of every "jot and tittle" of the Law. They sought to democratize the sanctifying ceremonies of the Temple by extending the daily ritual living requirements of the priests to the domestic lives of all Jews. In John's Gospel, these were mostly like the "priests and Temple assistants" sent to question John the Baptist's authority, asking, "If you aren't the Messiah or Elijah or the Prophet, what right do you have to baptize?" (John 1:24 NLT).

While the Gospels (particularly John's) tend to depict the Pharisees and others within the elite retainer class in the worst possible light, we must recognize that many—or perhaps most—of them were undoubtedly kind and honest men and women. Some became disciples of Jesus:

---

6. Marcus J. Borg, "Jesus and the Christian Life."

7. Ibid.

8. Ibid.

Nicodemus and Joseph of Arimathea come immediately to mind (Acts 5:34; John 3:1; Mark 15:43). And the most famous Pharisee was the Apostle Paul. Of course, he was hardly kind and was certainly not a disciple at first, but he was a Pharisee and the son of Pharisees (Acts 23:6), and he was taught by Gamaliel himself (Acts 22:3).

Together, the hegemony of the religious, military, and political elite perpetuated the oppression and degradation of God's children. Inasmuch as Jesus, the promised messiah, began his ministry at Bethabara beyond Jordan (John 1:28), it is fitting that one of John's retorts to the gathered crowds was a metaphor that did not cast Jesus as a docile cleric but rather as a weapon meant to cut the corruption out of the world's kingdoms. John announced that Jesus was an "axe" that would be "laid unto the root of the trees: therefore every tree which bringeth not forth good fruit is hewn down, and cast into the fire" (Matt. 3:10 KJV).

John's prophesying had already egregiously ruffled the feathers of his religious superiors. Not only was the religious establishment alarmed at his behavior and professed allegiances, but also at his attitude towards the governments of the client kings. Rome itself would soon be annoyed, challenged, and worried. Why the concern? What would Jesus's Kingdom change? The answer, in a word, is *everything*. In Jesus's Kingdom, everything connected to class structure, status, and power evidenced at the baptismal scene would change.

Systemic Injustice

Recall how Borg defined systemic injustice in Jesus's day—as well as in our own—as a social order that resulted in excessive inequality of wealth and station because of the way in which the prevailing establishment was structured. It was a configuration that devalued the contributions made by some of its members and allowed the ruling elite to prosper at the expense of the many. It inevitably included a disparity in wealth and social status and often resulted in the violation of basic and innate human privileges. In a religious context, systemic injustice became the overarching moral issue because it involved the methodical but taken-for-granted mistreatment of God's children.

Furthermore, systemic injustice was inevitable as long as the kingdoms of the world dominated. As we discussed in the previous chapter, those kingdoms—then and today—are based on coercion, greed, and social/spiritual inequality. Systemic injustice—then and today—is a structure that exalts the rich and debases the poor. As a consequence, elite classes are formed that benefit from most, if not all, of the wealth and power within the society. By its very nature, it is oppressive and exploitative and perhaps the single greatest cause of human suffering in the world.

To explain further how Jesus defined systemic injustice, Borg suggests that several questions can reasonably be asked that expose systemic injustice in any society:

- To what extent does a culture benefit at the expense of the many, or does the culture serve all equally?
- Does the society produce a large impoverished class or result in an equitable distribution of its resources?
- Does the society produce conflict or peace?
- Does the society nourish the future?[9]

The answers to these questions highlight the extreme disparity between the social classes at the time of Jesus. He lived in a highly brokered empire in which the religious and secular institutions dehumanized and made expendable whole classes of people. Historians estimate that the rulers and governors comprised about one percent of the population and owned about 50 percent of the land or wealth. The ruling priests, in turn, owned another 15 percent of the land and wealth. The retinue of bureaucrats and soldiers who served the elite came next. Although small in number, they were well-fed and cared for but did not control the levers of power, wealth, and status. Just below this group were a few merchants who evolved upward from the lower classes.

At this point there was a great divide—on the other side of it was the vast majority, close to 70 percent, who made up the peasant class. This group was always on the brink of economic ruin. They produced the bulk of the wealth, but the fruits of their labors went to the upper classes. At the lower end of the socioeconomic scale were the artisans, who made up about 5 percent of the population. Jesus's father, Joseph, was part of this group. While traditionally described as a carpenter, the underlying Greek word *tekton* could refer to any artisan, including those who made wooden yokes for beasts of burden and stone masons in the cosmopolitan city of Zippori, just 3.7 miles from the village of Nazareth where Jesus's family lived.

At the bottom of the heap were the expendables. These were day laborers looking for any kind of part-time work to feed themselves and their

---

9. Marcus J. Borg, *Reading the Bible Again for the First Time: Taking the Bible Seriously but Not Literally*, 139.

families. Many were destitute—families ravaged by disease, debt, drought, or death who had lost everything and been pushed off the land and into begging. These were the people Stephen Patterson describes as those who were "squeezed out deliberately as human junk from the system's own evil operations."[10] And finally, in addition to all the merchants, tektons, and day-laborers were a mass of people labeled as slaves (or "servants"). The ubiquitous practice of buying and selling or seizing by conquest other human beings allowed all the other evils of systemic injustice to thrive.[11] As a largely agrarian society, Palestine depended upon slaves as free laborers who were an integral part of the field workforce and of many households. The cities' slave populations were assigned domestic duties of every sort. However, their status was pre-determined and relegated any hopes whatsoever for genuine integration into the ranks of the privileged of society to magical thinking. In the New Testament the practice was absolutely taken for granted (Luke 12:46–48). In that way it was particularly heinous because it wore a mask of normalcy and necessity. Slavery "was as much a part of the fabric of society as any other human relationship."[12]

---

10. Stephen J. Patterson, *The God of Jesus: The Historical Jesus and the Search for Meaning*, 60–62.

11. The Romans inherited the institution of slavery from the Greeks and the Phoenicians, whose institutions were even more draconian. However, as Rome grew, entire conquered populations were enslaved to work on farms and in households.

12. One of the most craven practices was one that made slaves out of those who could not pay their debts. It was the most common way for a Jew to become a slave. Such situations generally arose in the context of a farmer borrowing money at exorbitant interest rates to finance his crops even though Jewish law banned the charging of interest. The Jewish religious elite took another portion of what a farmer produced in tithes and offerings. The Romans then took their share in taxes and tributes. Any inability to cope with financial pressures resulted in bankruptcy and in entire families being sold into slavery to service the unpaid debt. Despite the fact that under Jewish law slaves were supposed to be freed after six years of labor (Ex. 21:2–4; Deut. 15:12), there is evidence that this practice was widely ignored.

Slaves participated at every level although their status differed widely. In some instances slaves were considered part of the family and treated passably well. Those who were literate were tutors. Others performed secretarial duties. Sometimes they were more educated than their owners. Slaves who lived respectable lives were generally attached to rich and powerful urban households (Matt. 24:45–51; 25:14–30; Luke 12:42–48; 19:11–27). But most often slaves were organized into "agricultural chain gangs of the great estates," or in the abysmal conditions of mines.

From a twenty-first-century perspective, it may not be difficult to argue that although some slaves may have fared better in terms of food, clothing, and shelter than the expendable day laborers and unclean, they remained someone's property and hence their lot was the worst of the worst. However, in Jesus's world, filled with demoralizing injustice at every level, to rank the lot of an ostensibly free man with a stomach that was forever empty over that of a well-nourished slave with a promise of continued shelter is a ridiculous comparison.[13]

Judaism and Systemic Injustice

Jesus was born into an ancient society constrained by millennia of social, theological, and political practices perpetuated by the minority ruling elite and facilitated by a vast majority of souls who knew of no other way. Periodically prophets would rail against the system in the name of God. But the great, malodorous colossus of ancient Rome and its client states were sustained on a diet of forever-oppressed individuals, the very ones Jesus came to invite into a new, righteous Kingdom.

So, after his trial in the desert and at the formal beginning of his ministry, Jesus announced his objectives in the humble village of his youth. Consider how it must have stunned those who heard it: "The spirit of the Lord is upon me, for he has anointed me to bring Good News to the poor. He has sent me to proclaim that captives will be released, that the blind will see, that the oppressed will be set free" (Luke 4:18 NLT). Jesus concluded his inaugural sermon by proclaiming the "'acceptable year of

---

Some ended up as prostitutes. These unfortunate human beings were most often baby girls literally abandoned on street corners by their parents as an acceptable form of "family planning" in the Roman world. By some estimates there were over 12 million slaves, or 16 to 20 percent of the population, in the Roman Empire. See Craig A. Evans, ed., *The Routledge Encyclopedia of the Historical Jesus*, 577.

13. One of the most despicable parts of slavery not mentioned in the New Testament but which we cite here to illustrate the depravity of the systemic injustice of human ownership was the practice of purposeful selective breeding in the homes of their masters. Like beasts of burden or machines in the factories of the modern world, these human engines enabled those at the top to be handsomely benefited and to live the comfortable lives to which they had become accustomed. In the event of an infraction of even the smallest kind, it was perfectly permissible to inflict physical punishment and torture. Some towns even hired professionals to flog, crucify, and burn slaves alive. Other slaves were fed to animals in the arena as the Romans applauded.

the Lord,' an allusion to the year of Jubilee (Lev. 25:8–10), the end of the fifty-year cycle, when all land that had been confiscated as a result of debt or otherwise unjustly acquired was to be returned to its original owners."[14] Jesus undoubtedly made reference to this practice because it was being ignored. But this was only the beginning. Later on in his ministry he required much more of those he invited into the Kingdom of God: "Go and sell *all you have* and give the money to the poor," and then "come, follow me" (Matt. 19:21 NLT; emphasis added).

By the time a mature Jesus officially began his ministry, many of the specified traditions of the Pentateuch were being reinterpreted to fit the traditions of Hellenized Roman culture, mainly in urban contexts. Strict rules about the treatment of slaves (Lev. 25:39–55) and rules stating that fugitive slaves could not be returned to their owner but must be accepted into the household where they sought refuge (Deut. 23:1–5) were being ignored. Debts were no longer forgiven. Land was not universally shared. Wealth was commonly hoarded.

Just as other Old Testament prophets had done, but by way of a number of parables, Jesus talked about multiple manifestations of injustice. He told his disciples a story about a rich man who was splendidly clothed and who lived each day in luxury. At his door lay a diseased beggar named Lazarus who, as dogs licked his open sores, longed for scraps from the rich man's table. Both died. The rich man then found himself in hell and Lazarus in heaven, at Abraham's bosom. "The rich man shouted . . . 'have some pity! Send Lazarus over here to dip the tip of his finger in water and cool my tongue, because I am in anguish in these flames.'" In the account, Abraham ignores the rich man's cries for relief just as the rich man had ignored Lazarus's appeals for relief (Luke 16:24 NLT).

In another story, Jesus spoke of his feelings about the dehumanizing practices related to oppressive debt and forgiveness. He compared God in his heavenly kingdom to an earthly king who decided to bring his accounts up to date with his servants who had borrowed money from him. One debtor owed him the equivalent of millions of dollars. And because he could not pay, the king, following the debt customs of his day, ordered that he be sold into slavery, "along with his wife [and] his children." Everything the debtor had was to be liquidated to pay the debt. The servant "fell down before his master and begged him, 'Please be patient with

---

14. Obery Mack Hendricks Jr., *The Politics of Jesus: Rediscovering the True Revolutionary Nature of Jesus' Teachings and How They Have Been Corrupted*, 20.

me, and I will pay it all.'" The king took pity and forgave his debt (Matt. 18:25–26 NLT).

Jesus continued, saying the servant, now freed of his monetary obligation, decided it was time to collect his own debts, which were minor in comparison to what he had owed the king. He went to a fellow servant who owed him a few thousand dollars and was merciless. He "grabbed him by the throat and demanded instant payment," refusing to forgive the debt. When the king found out, he called the servant "evil," saying, "I forgave you that tremendous debt because you pleaded with me. Shouldn't you have mercy on your fellow servant, just as I had mercy on you?" The king sent the man to prison to be tortured until he had paid his entire debt to the king (Matt. 18:28–34 NLT).

Jesus's explanation of the parables was applicable to his day, but it is perhaps more important to those who profess to follow him in any age: He said the intent of his parables was to teach that those who participated in the mean-spirited practices of Judaeo-Roman society were to be condemned. "That's what my heavenly Father will do to you if you refuse to forgive your brothers and sisters from your heart" (Matt. 18:35 NLT).

The harsh punishment the king of the parable (God) meted out to the unforgiving debtor must give us all an occasion to reflect on forgiveness. Clearly, Jesus did not focus on personal virtues alone but also society's justice. It was not simply a matter of saying to the rich and powerful of his day and ours, "Be good" and donate more to your favorite charity. As Borg has often pointed out in his writings on systemic injustice, the elite can be good, devout, responsible, courageous, kind, gentle, charming, intelligent, committed to family, loyal to friends, and so forth. Moreover, those who benefit from the system do not always intend systemic evil. The privileged do give to charity. Nevertheless, Jesus wanted much more. Such charitable efforts were mere balms for the underlying and diseased wound. His aim was to radically alter the world's customs and structures that brought about the situation in the first place. The problem was an agreed-upon way of doing things that brought the poor and vulnerable to ruin.[15] Therefore, political and economic configurations did and still do matter because they can fundamentally and adversely affect the lives of individuals.

The early Christians attempted but did not fully live up to Jesus's hope for a Kingdom of God where all would be economically and socially one.

---

15. Marcus Borg and John Dominic Crossan have written extensively on the subject of systemic injustice. See for example Marcus J. Borg, *The God We Never Knew: Beyond Dogmatic Religion to a More Authentic Contemporary Faith.*

On the economic front, Peter and the Apostles established an order in which "they shared everything they had" (Acts 4:32 NLT). But there was an innate resistance to this reordering of society. The impetus to be "one in heart and mind" (Acts 4:32 NLT) also proved to be difficult, but was not entirely unsuccessful. Particularly on the issue of slavery, the idea that there should "no longer [be] . . . slave or free" was never fully realized (Gal. 3:28 NLT). Slavery was such an integral part of the ancient world that the whole society was built on it, and the fledgling early Christian church was never in a position to challenge it. If Christianity had taken slavery head on, it would have failed. However, Christian teachings made way for horizontal relationships where converts could call one another brother and sister. By the third century, early church designs translated the idea of equal status before God by making the entire worship space (the nave) on one level where all stood side by side.

Jesus believed that the Kingdom of God, founded upon communitarian principles, was locked in a battle with the kingdoms of the world, founded as they were upon individualism as a justification for materialism, avarice, and personal aggrandizement. Suffice it to say that when Jesus squared off with the institutions of his day—whether it was the Romans, the temple leaders, or the religious elites—he severely condemned them and ultimately sought to replace those institutions with his Father's Kingdom. He did not sponsor outright resistance to Roman authority or indeed to the entire social structure, but his teachings completely undermined the moral authority of both. From the beginning of his ministry at the baptismal site beyond the Jordan until its end on the cross at the hill of Calvary, he spoke about the corrupt political and religious institutions of his day. With the same verbal intensity he used to describe the leaders who came to challenge John at his baptism, he spoke on the Temple Mount at his last Passover Festival: They "crush people with unbearable religious demands and never lift a finger to ease the burden." They were "hypocrites . . . blind guides . . . fools . . . snakes . . . and sons of vipers" (Matt. 23:4, 15–17, 33 NLT). When he spoke about the institutions of his day, the intensity of his indignation rose to the level of white-hot anger.

chapter 15

Jesus and the Roman Empire

In August 2012, Robert Hughes, the irascible art critic for *Time* magazine, published *Rome: A Cultural, Visual, and Personal History*.[1] Less than a year later, the subhead for the magazine's obituary of Hughes referred to that history and said that he wrote with "thundering eloquence" in his last book, his homage to the Eternal City and the Roman Empire.[2]

So, we begin a chapter on Jesus and the Romans with selections from Hughes's powerful description of Gaius Julius Caesar Octavianus (63 BC–AD 14), the son of a wealthy equestrian, plebian family—known to the world then and now as Augustus (roughly translated as "worthy of veneration"), the title the Roman Senate bestowed on him. For just over forty years, Augustus was the absolute and undisputed sovereign of the empire, which included tiny Palestine at the time Jesus was born. His stepson Tiberius Claudius Nero, ruler of the empire during the 3-year ministry of Jesus, succeeded him in AD 14. History records that Tiberius was revered as a brilliant general but despised as a largely absentee emperor until his death in AD 37. Logic would suggest that because Tiberius's reign corresponds to the years of Jesus's ministry, the most apt analysis of Rome and its government would involve Tiberius. But it is the enduring iconic presence of Augustus—in fact, the entire age of the so-called Augustan Peace—that better suits our investigation of how the kingdoms of the world diametrically opposed the one Jesus proposed.

At the age of thirty-two, in 31 BC, Augustus finally vanquished all other political contenders after more than a decade of political upheaval following the murder of Julius Caesar. Born Gaius Octavius Thurinus, he had been noticed for his military prowess by age eighteen and became the adopted son of his great uncle Julius Caesar—thus becoming officially known as Gaius Julius Caesar Octavianus. He next took on the title of Gaius Julius Caesar Divi Filius (Son of the Divine) as a reference to his deified adoptive father. At one point he replaced Gaius Julius with

---

1. Robert Hughes, *Rome: a Cultural, Visual, and Personal History.*
2. Michiko Kakutani, "An Idea as Much as a City."

Imperator (the designation used by his troops after a military success), officially becoming Imperator Caesar Divi Filius.

Later, the Senate voted to give him yet two more honorifics: The first was *Princeps,* from the Latin phrase *primum caput,* or "the first head." It had customarily been meant for the most aged and illustrious member of the Senate. But giving him the title meant he was the regnal leader with custody of the largest empire the world had ever known. The second was Augustus, his most popular name. This title both had religious overtones and implied authority over literally everything and everyone. While he had come to power through sheer brute and merciless military force, this title was to serve as the Senate's recognition and recommendation of a new, more altruistic and benevolent persona for Octavius, regardless of whether or not he deserved such a designation. He would receive additional titles fairly regularly. In 13 BC, Augustus was made Pontifex Maximus, or head of the college of priests of the temple cult of Jupiter. With each title, his public image was further refined and his powers were increasingly consolidated. By the age of fifty, he was known as Imperator Princeps Caesar Divi Filius Augustus and Pontifex Maximus—or simply, Augustus.

The Image and Peace of Augustus

Robert Hughes reported that there are more than two hundred surviving busts or full-length statues of Augustus in various idealized poses. Their function was similar to billboards along the vast matrix of the empire's roads or like sponsors' logos plastered at virtually every Roman city's sports arena, theater, racetrack, bath, and even temple. Some statues show him wearing his priestly vestments. Others show him as a flawless younger man wearing a civic crown of laurel branches. Still others have him wearing a Gorgoneion amulet or protective charm. Sometimes he is colossally sized, seated on a throne holding a *fasces* as a symbol of his consular authority. His profile also appeared on coins, reminding citizens through each financial transaction that they were indebted to him for their livelihood.

Hughes cites a leading archaeologist who estimates that existing images represent "25,000 to 50,000 portraits in stone all told." Sometimes blunt but always-idealized instruments of propaganda, they were made to be distributed throughout the empire.[3] Perhaps none of the images is more famous than the *Augustus of Prima Porta.* This life-sized Augustus

---

3. Hughes, *Rome,* 58.

stands in full ceremonial armor, complete with a flowing cape attached at the neck, with the hemmed end draped over the left arm. His weight is on his right leg, his left hip slightly elevated above a bent left leg to give the appearance of restrained motion at rest. His right arm is extended toward an unseen audience. His head is slightly turned to address that audience. Hughes described the work:

> The statue is perhaps not, in itself, a great work of art; but it is competent, effective, and memorable, . . . showing the hero . . . in the act of giving a speech either to the state as a whole or, more probably, to his army, on the eve of battle. As an image of calm, self-sufficient power projecting itself upon the world, it has few equals in the domain of sculpture.[4]

Augustus wears a woolen tunic beneath the breastplate of his *cuirass* that has been carved in low relief. Like a scene from a frieze on a building, the center of the breastplate shows a baggy, unkempt barbarian in the act of handing over a military standard to the Roman general before him—presumably Augustus. The narrative of the breastplate suggests that Augustus has once again fulfilled his destiny. He has triumphed over his sworn enemies. The two figures are surrounded by various figures representing gods from the Roman pantheon and other figures interpreted as the personifications of Spain, Gaul, and perhaps Germany.

The message of the armor could be several things. Foremost among these possible messages is the gods' approbation of Augustus and his battlefield version of peace. The little "love god Eros next to Augustus' right leg is there to remind us that his family, the Julians, claimed to have descended from the goddess Venus, so its presence reinforces the belief that Augustus was a living god."[5] His face is recognizable as an idealized image of a younger Augustus. The body beneath the armor is perfectly godlike.

The original bronze sculpture was "cloned, copied and disseminated" throughout the empire as the ultimate and "indispensable" instrument of propaganda. Taken as a whole, the message distributed throughout the empire via the images was clear: Augustus, son of a god, descendent of a goddess, merciless and yet merciful commander of armies and navies, builder of roads and cities, had brought peace, unity, and prosperity to the empire by virtue of his military cunning and the approbation of the gods.[6]

---

4. Ibid., 57.
5. Ibid., 58.
6. Ibid.

But, says Hughes, we are required to pause after such a litany of successes. The picture we have of ancient Rome during the era of Augustan Pax Romana is obviously one we see only through the art of the privileged patrician classes. The sculptures long ago lost the bright colors that once covered their surfaces. Now we see "[w]hite cylinders of stone gleaming in the sun, . . . white ramps, white colonnades, flights of white steps, . . . white foam from splashing fountains . . . [and] white people wearing white togas. . . . Lots of dignified Romans."[7]

This image of Rome and its various colonies and provinces is, of course, wholly inadequate, not to mention inaccurate. Hughes says the real city of Rome was more like "Calcutta-on-the-Mediterranean—crowded, chaotic and filthy."[8] The whole empire was not much different. It was populated by an alarmingly small percentage of privileged upper classes. At their worst, they were atrociously cruel to their slaves. Their cruelty came not so much from a conscious espousal of wickedness but because of a millennia of obliviousness born of built-in systemic injustices. They were likewise sometimes promiscuous in their private lives for the same reasons.

The patricians consumed the world's goods, grains, and treasures in reverse proportion to their small population. They maintained power in the empire by suppression, even obliteration, of dissent and by the toady pseudo-fealty of their client kings like the Herodian dynasty in Palestine. And perhaps worst of all, they lived and died in a world devoid of awareness that life and society's structures could be any different.

Augustus brought about only relative stability and peace. The Senate and equestrian upper classes acquired great wealth—and enormous numbers of slaves—from the spoils of conquered peoples, oppressive taxation, and increased profits from trade that grew as the empire expanded. Slavery was ubiquitous. Even slaves had slaves. Resistance, resentment, and rebellion were always at a slow boil beneath the facade of an empire at peace.

Augustus instituted a number of social programs as a means of appeasing possible unrest from the masses. In the city of Rome, there was a monthly distribution of free grain for each family. There were numerous free public baths. The race course and other entertainments were often free to the populace, although lower classes and women were always relegated to the "cheap seats" furthest from the action. Those who served in the Roman military (about 25 legions or about 300,000 soldiers) were well taken care of. Its members received monthly stipends and discharge pay-

---

7. Ibid., 59.
8. Ibid.

ments. They were granted full citizenship and land grants. High-ranking military officers received land at retirement, usually at key geographical points such as Caesarea Maritima, located throughout the empire to be its eyes and ears and to deter discontent. According to N. T. Wright, Augustus's legions, together with his client kings, took necessary steps to ensure, "in their bloody and brutal way, that the locals stayed 'peaceful' and knew who was in charge."[9]

Furthermore, what has come to be recorded as an era of universal peace, in part because of the consolidated power of Augustus, was also a product of his efficient propaganda machine. Wright says Augustus's "projected vision of tranquil peace was perched on top of a world of horror and violence. Wrath and arms continued to dominate classical culture."[10]

Nicholas Perrin, professor of biblical studies at Wheaton College in Illinois, agrees:

[Augustus was] the human incarnation of . . . virtues that up to that point had been personified only within the pantheon of Roman gods. Such was the expansion of the emperor's public persona, a correlate of his expanded political power, that it began to make the gods redundant. All of this meant that any challenge to the religious supremacy of the emperor could be perceived as an act of political subversion.[11]

This included Jesus and his disciples who were born into a world in which Rome was firmly in political control of its people, and political control had "religious entailments. *Christians were religious and political deviants.*"[12]

The Names and Peace of Jesus

Unlike Augustus, there are no known contemporaneous depictions of Jesus's physical appearance. The common image of Jesus as tall, fair-skinned, blue-eyed, with blondish hair and beard, and wearing immaculate white robes is a modern construction. What little we can say about the appearance of Jesus is that according to Matthew's Gospel, he was ordinary enough as to be virtually indistinguishable from others on the night he was arrested in Gethsemane. When the temple soldiers, Jewish leaders,

9. N. T. Wright, *The Day the Revolution Began: Reconsidering the Meaning of Jesus's Crucifixion*, loc. 1110 of 7473, Kindle.
10. Ibid.
11. Nicholas Perrin, "The Imperial Cult," 127.
12. Ibid.; emphasis in original.

and Judas Iscariot arrived at the garden to arrest him, their only sure way of getting the right insurgent blasphemer was to have Judas kiss him.

The very few images of Jesus we do have are often of dubious provenance. For example, in 1898, an Italian lawyer and amateur photographer noticed that the negative he had made of the famous relic known as the Shroud of Turin (purported to be the wrapping cloth used in the tomb at Jesus's burial) appeared to be the image of a thin-faced bearded man with long hair. [13] The shroud offers us only a ghostly and very much disputed and confusing look at Jesus's image. The authenticity of the shroud has been widely debunked, leaving us no closer to his appearance. There is neither skeleton nor decayed remains that can offer a means to measure his height or collect DNA evidence.

In 2014, Richard Neave, a medical artist retired from the University of Manchester in England, used physical anthropology, forensic anthropology, and "computerized tomography" to create a generalized image of a man from the first-century Ancient Near East. Neave's image is a scientifically based extrapolation suggesting that because Jesus was part of that culture, he most likely had dark eyes, hair, and complexion. As an average Semite of the time, the team posits that he would have stood just over five feet tall and probably weighed around 110 pounds. In keeping with Jewish tradition, Jesus was likely bearded. Because Paul points out in a letter to the Corinthians that if a man has long hair, "it is a disgrace" (1 Cor. 11:14 NLT), Neave's team depicted Jesus with short curly black hair, a portrait that would startle most contemporary Christians. [14]

One of the earliest images of Jesus comes on a sarcophagus belonging to a man named Junius Bassus who died in the mid-fourth century in Constantinople. Bassus's sarcophagus offers a look at how early Christians only imagined Jesus, defining him by his simple, unadorned philosopher's robes and sandals. This Jesus is beardless and young. He sits on a throne with a scroll (probably meant to represent the canon recently organized by Constantine at the Council of Nicaea) in one hand and a key (apparently

---

13. Carbon dating of a minute piece of the corner of the shroud places the fabric's date at somewhere in the fourteenth century. Consequently, its authenticity is much in dispute. As recently as 2016, Pope Francis commented on the shroud but without vouchsafing its origins. See John L. Allen Jr., "Pope Francis and the Shroud of Turin."

14. See, for example, Morgan Whitaker, "Forensic Science Reveals How Jesus Really Looked."

offered to Peter as a symbol of authority) in the other. Other metaphoric depictions come no earlier than the third century.

The titles for Jesus are variously recorded in the Gospels. Like the titles acquired and bestowed on Augustus, they reveal a great deal about him and how his disciples saw him. He was known as the Lord, the Son of Man, the Son of God, the Son of David, and variations of the titles the Christ, the Messiah, and the Anointed One. He was called Rabbi, Teacher, Logos, and the Lamb of God. More importantly and paradoxically, he emphasized how he viewed his own role by calling himself a servant while also affirming to Pilate that he was King of the Jews.

In John's Gospel we not only see these titles but also metaphorical descriptions Jesus offered of himself. These are what New Testament scholars have often called the seven great "I Am" declarations, and they are unusually revealing of Jesus's character and the nature of the Kingdom of God. "I am the bread of life," he said, "the light of the world," "the gate" to the sheep's fold, "the good shepherd," "the way, the truth and the life," "the vine," and most importantly, "the resurrection and the life" (John 6:35; 8:12; 10:9, 11; 14:5, 6, 11; 11:25, 26 NLT). Notice how these contrast with Augustus's titles, which were connected to an earthly kingdom that he kept at peace by violence and perpetual military conquest. By way of contrast to Augustus's, the titles given to or claimed by Jesus are metaphors for the leader of a kingdom that gives peace to each citizen, that provides a nurturing shepherd who keeps his flock safe, that offers enlightenment and truth to all regardless of station, and that promises a continuation of lives. The differences are stunningly obvious.

Palestine, Jesus, and the Romans

During the first century BC, Rome controlled every level of power in Palestine. Julius Caesar and the Senate had installed Herod, a Jew in name only, as the king. Throughout Herod's reign, his relationship with the populace was a hostile one, despite the fact that he had begun the massive project of rebuilding the Temple on the grandest scale imaginable.

Herod heavily taxed the people of Judea, Samaria, and Galilee. He taxed them to support his temple campaign and to build a lavish new port city on the Mediterranean he named after Caesar and a new palace high above the Dead Sea. Adult males paid a number of other taxes and tributes to Rome. They paid others to Herod. And they paid still others to the families of the high priests controlling the temple coffers. Men paid an annual tithe, or temple tax, of half a shekel in the spring of every year for temple maintenance, the purchase of sacrificial offerings, and support of the temple priests. Men and women both paid a one-denarius poll tax (the equivalent of about one day's wage). They paid it not for the right to vote as we might expect today but as tribute money going directly to Rome. They paid taxes on land and on slaves when they were bought or sold or even emancipated. They even paid a 1 percent income tax on the head of the household's annual increase. All of this escalated economic pressures on the masses and threatened their livelihoods. Families were impoverished. Those who could not satisfy debtors were sold, sometimes with their family members, into slavery. The disintegration of the family and of village life was common.

Herod's sons were no less corrupt than their father. Herod Antipas, king of Galilee during the ministry of Jesus, was as depraved as any of the worst patricians in Rome, where he had been sent to be educated. Herod's son Archelaus was so ineffectual in tamping down rebellions in Judea that Pontius Pilate, a fairly insignificant member of the equestrian or military class, was sent to govern Jerusalem and its surrounding country as well as Samaria.

In this environment of the grossest kinds of cruelty and political corruption, it is no wonder that a segment of Jewish society, with some regularity, sought to forcibly overthrow the Roman authority in Palestine and once again establish an independent Jewish nation. Messiahs rose and then disappeared without bringing back the idealized past glory and integrity of Israel. Perhaps the most well-known, even glorified as heroic, rebels were the Zealots who were organized to oppose their Roman overlords after the fall of Jerusalem to Titus and his legions.

Given the litany of abuses and burdens faced by men and women of the empire, we might ask: How did Jesus feel about Roman abuses, and in what ways did Jesus oppose Rome's power and the ostensible peace? The latter half of this question requires a somewhat nuanced answer. In the Gospels, Jesus directly confronted or commented on Rome and imperial domination on roughly eleven occasions. We will discuss three to answer the previously-posed question.

The first clash we cite between Jesus and Rome involved the issue of imperial taxation and tribute. It illustrates a Jesus whose attitude toward the empire with all its depraved violence was not quarrelsome. He was cunningly non-confrontational. All three synoptic Gospels (Matthew, Mark, and Luke) record that the exchange came late in his ministry. Jesus had come for the last time to Jerusalem to celebrate the Passover. There, the Pharisees and a group Matthew calls the Herodians (a political party supporting the

Herodian dynasty as a last hope for Judean independence) questioned Jesus about taxes.[15] In a clumsy effort to gather evidence against Jesus, their question came cloaked in obsequious flattery: "Teacher, we know how honest you are," they said. "Now tell us what you think about this: Is it right to pay taxes to Caesar or not?" (Matt. 22:15–17 NLT).

Jesus's reply needs minor contextual information to best understand it. First of all, the question was not an ethical one. As subjects rather than citizens of Rome, Jesus as well as the disciples and most Jews did not have the option to not pay a poll or head tax. Second, at the outset of the reign of every new Caesar, coins were minted and imprinted with his image, whether the emperor was young or old. In this case the coin was a denarius, which was the required tax rate. It was stamped with the image of Tiberius, whose valuable metal it was.

The dilemma for Jesus was that if he had answered that he would not pay the tribute money, he would have been reported to the authorities by the Herodians and most likely arrested. If he had answered yes to paying the tax, readers of the Gospel when it was written in the late first century would have understood that the poll tax supported a pagan temple dedicated to Jupiter, Mars, or even Tiberius himself. For the Pharisees, then, paying the tribute was a blasphemous act.

So Jesus asked to see a coin. And his answer to their query was a rhetorical statement simply about ownership. He answered that he and everyone else in the empire should "give to Caesar what belongs to Caesar [the coin], and give to God what belongs to God" (Matt. 22:21 NLT). Marcus Borg and John Dominic Crossan add additional insight about this coin. They write that another key to understanding the incident of the disputed coin is that Jews were allowed to have their own copper coins that lacked Caesar and symbolic imagery to avoid idol worship. Jesus would have known that the Rome-aligned Herodians would have preferred the Caesar-stamped rather than copper coins. So when one of their pack pulled Caesar's coin out of his pocket, he revealed his true allegiance, and that of his group. So in a way, Jesus sidestepped their trap and turned the challenge against them by showing that they cared more for Caesar than God.[16]

---

15. Matthew records another conflict with the Pharisees over a tithe owed to the temple priesthood (Matt. 17:24–27). The encounter we speak of here, however, was on the occasion of a confrontation between Jesus and the Pharisees over a poll tax to be paid to Rome.

16. Marcus J. Borg and John Dominic Crossan *The Last Week: What the Gospels Really Teach About Jesus's Final Days in Jerusalem*, 63–65.

Either commentary includes Jesus's measured response; it was a powerful message about one's place in a worldly kingdom, especially given that he had previously announced that he had come to inaugurate an alternative Kingdom of God. The exchange left the Pharisees, and the Herodians, fuming and speechless.

Our second example of Jesus's attitudes about Rome's power is an occasion when Jesus told his followers not to retaliate or use force against one's enemy. "You have heard," he said, "that the punishment must match the injury," a reference to a commonly held view in the ancient world we would recognize as "an eye for an eye" system of justice. Imperial and unjust domination could be returned with equal amounts of force. To the contrary, Jesus explained. "Do not resist an evil person!" (Matt. 5:39 NLT.) Here William Barclay explains the context for what followed. He writes that the text referred to the fact that "[a]t any moment, a man might feel the touch of the flat of a Roman spear on his shoulder, and know that he was [unjustly] compelled to serve the Romans, probably in the most menial way." Hence, Jesus said that if a Roman soldier demands that "you carry . . . gear for a mile, carry it two miles" (Matt. 5:41 NLT).[17] Clearly, Jesus would not have had his followers forcibly resist Roman authority. Rather, as discussed in Chapter 11 of this volume, Jesus encouraged various forms of nonviolent resistance to such oppressive acts.

Our last example of Jesus's opposition to Rome came as he stood before the prefect Pontius Pilate to be judged. The night before, Jesus had been accused of blasphemy by the high priest Caiaphas and his high council. Jesus had maintained that he was the kind of messiah whom they would see "seated in the place of power at God's right hand and coming on clouds of heaven"—a claim that under Jewish law merited capital punishment (Matt. 26:64 NLT). The Jewish leadership, however, was not allowed to mete out such a sentence. Only Roman officials could put someone to death. Caiaphas knew the Romans would take little notice of a Jewish blasphemer. On the other hand, he knew that Pilate would take seriously an assertion that Jesus was the messiah, the "king of the Jews," a revolutionary who was perfectly capable of fomenting destruction of the peace of Rome and Roman authority.

When Jesus was brought before Pilate to be condemned, he did not resist. Pilate immediately addressed his most pressing concern. "Are you the king of the Jews?" Jesus's answer was enigmatic. "You have said it"

---

17. William Barclay, *The New Daily Study Bible: The Gospel of Matthew*, 1:168.

(Matt. 27:11 NLT). In the course of further accusations, "Jesus remained silent" (Matt. 27:12 NLT). The Gospel of John gives more detail. When Pilate asked Jesus why the leading Jews had brought him to trial, he admitted that he had a Kingdom but that it was *not of this world*. In the context of Jesus's teachings on nonviolence, his comment that his Kingdom was an unearthly one must have assured Pilate that he would not use force to accomplish his purposes. At this point, Pilate queried, "So you are a king?" Jesus answered, "*You* say I am a king" (John 18:37 NLT; emphasis added). Apparently, Pilate remained unconvinced that Jesus was a threat, an active insurrectionist. The safest course for Rome, however, was to take no chances and accede to what Jesus's enemies had demanded (John 18:38–40).

In all three encounters with the empire's armies and leaders, Jesus did not actively resist their authority. Furthermore, his behavior was entirely inconsistent with the tactics of the Zealots and other revolutionaries who condoned the use of arms to overthrow Rome. Throughout his ministry, Jesus had unfailingly taught his followers to "love your enemies, bless them that curse you, do good to them that hate you, and pray for them which despitefully use you" (Matt. 5:44 KJV). He even went so far as to teach them to "resist not evil." Then, by way of example, he said, "Whosoever shall smite thee on thy right cheek, turn to him the other also" (Matt. 5:39 KJV). Such an allocution was filled with cultural nuance. For example, a soldier or master could legally backhand someone they viewed as subservient. But open-palmed slaps were for persons on the same level. However, by asking his disciples to present a second cheek for any kind of slap, he indicated that no one—regardless of the social standing of the aggressor or the recipient—was permitted to choose violence in interactions with another human being.

In addition, by citing that common form of violent exchange he did not mean we should acquiesce to evil or fail to preach and teach that true disciples were to find peaceful ways to resist it. Discipleship meant that violence was never a first, second, or even third response to aggression.

The fact that Jesus was not willing to foment the overthrow of Rome by force did not mean that he in any way endorsed what Rome stood for. Indeed, his agenda was ultimately on a collision course with his Roman overlords because he came to inaugurate an alternative Kingdom. His Kingdom of God, had it been successful, was meant to supplant the empire and, for that matter, any other earthly dominions.

Roman Imperial Theology

Rome was a deeply religious society and attributed its success as a world power to its collective piety in appeasing its gods. From the most elite men and women of the ancient world to the most humble or insignificant, every soul was taught an obligation to offer prayers and libations to various deities at temples as well as at household shrines. In fact, the Roman calendar was built around religious observances. Throughout the empire, Romans had as many as 135 days a year dedicated to religious festivals.

The spiritual life of the empire was built on an implicit yet unambiguous belief that Roman expansionism was a matter of its divine destiny. Military triumph was therefore at its center of worship, with temple rituals dedicated to the vast pantheon of pagan gods as well as to living and dead emperors as a way of indemnifying that military success. Every Roman general displayed his piety by dedicating a portion of the spoils of his campaigns to the gods, most especially to Jupiter, lord and master of all the gods, the *dies pater* or "shining father." As the god of light and sky and the protector of the state and its laws, Jupiter was the embodiment of an omnipotent ruler. Throughout Italy he was worshiped in temples and at shrines on the summits of hills. His oldest and most auspicious temple was on Capitoline Hill in the center of the city. There, the succession of Caesars made their most ostentatious oblations.

As we mentioned at the outset of this chapter, the centerpiece of Rome's propaganda machine in the first century, even as far away as Palestine, was Augustus, the undisputed ruler of the empire for more than forty years. He was *The Lord*. He was even spoken of as the redeemer and savior of the world. The first-century lyric poet Horace wrote, "Our children [are] made fewer by their parents' sins." Then he asked, "To whom shall Jupiter assign the task of atoning for our guilt?" His answer: "Augustus."[18]

What these mortals-cum-gods had in mind for Rome was to spread its influence throughout the known world and bring about the destined and enduring state of political peace. The method for attaining this Pax Romana was straightforward. It began with religion and ended with violence—always violence. In assuming his role as *Divi Filius,* or son of God, Augustus was both a military leader and head of state as well as the high priest whose right it was to speak for the gods. All this gave Rome and its

---

18. Marcus J. Borg and John Dominic Crossan, *The First Paul: Reclaiming the Radical Visionary Behind the Church's Conservative Icon*, 68.

minions the assurance that Roman dominance as a world power had been predetermined by the gods—a Roman "manifest destiny," as it were.

Thus the emperor/god and his gods guaranteed that peace would be brought about by military victories and thereafter maintained by military might. Palestine under Roman rule, as well as every other client state or province of the empire, was a harsh and brutal environment for most men and women. H. H. Scullard, British historian and editor of the Oxford Classical Dictionary, writes that the objective of Augustus and the legacy of his kingdom were based on the exercise of "a predominant military power, and . . . the ultimate sanction of his authority was force, however much the fact was disguised" as a benevolent peace.[19]

The Theology of Jesus

Ironically, Jesus the messiah had an identical objective—peace—but he sought to achieve it in a different way. Whereas the glue of Pax Romana was intimidation and force, Jesus declared that his Kingdom would coalesce around only two commandments: to love God and to love others. Love meant that his Kingdom would be based on compassion,[20] a way of governing where everyone's needs would be respected.

In the Biblical tradition, a society based on love and compassion in the King James Bible is referred to as a "righteous" society. In a number of modern translations the word "righteous" is equated to the word "justice."[21] Hence, in Jeremiah the voice of God declares, "I am the Lord

---

19. H. H. Scullard, *From the Gracchi to Nero: A History of Rome from 133 BC to AD 68*, 211.

20. As Joseph Smith wrote, "Thy dominion shall be an everlasting dominion, and *without compulsory* means it shall flow unto thee forever and ever" (D&C 121:46; emphasis added).

21. In the King James Version, the word "justice" is used 28 times in the Old Testament and not once in the New Testament. In the New Living Translation the word "justice" is used 173 times in the Old Testament and 22 times in the New Testament. For example, in the King James Version Matthew 5:6 is rendered, "Blessed are they which do hunger and thirst after righteousness: for they shall be filled." In the New Living Translation the same verse reads, "God blesses those who hunger and thirst for justice, for they will be satisfied." In the context of people who are hungry, the word "justice" (meaning restorative justice) fits better and gets to the root of what Jesus is really speaking about. Edward Kessler, the Founder and Executive Director of the Center for Jewish Christian Relations in Cambridge, points out that in the Old Testament humankind is "just" by

who demonstrates unfailing love and who brings justice and righteousness to the earth" (Jer. 9:24 NLT). Jeremiah warned, "This is what the Lord says: Be fair-minded and just. Do what is right! Help those who have been robbed; rescue them from their oppressors. Quit your evil deeds! Do not mistreat foreigners, orphans, and widows. Stop murdering the innocent!" (Jer. 22:3 NLT). Clearly, God in the Old and New Testaments expects the sovereigns of kingdoms or nations of the world to follow the mode that Jesus would exemplify, or as N.T. Wright is fond of saying, to be "image bearers" of God by loving and caring for one's neighbor.[22]

The words "righteousness" and "justice" as used in the Bible do not resonate within our own culture in the same way. Today, when we speak about "righteousness" we think about an individual who is virtuous, honest, prayerful, and religiously observant. When we think about "justice" it is usually in connection with our punitive legal system. We take it to mean that those who do wrong are appropriately punished—*retributive justice*. In the Bible, however, to be "righteous" or "just" means to provide for and restore the physical and temporal needs of the oppressed, downtrodden, and suffering—*restorative justice.*[23] Such a society is the polar opposite of Roman systemic injustice that robbed the poor, overlooked the widow and the orphan, and enslaved foreigners.

Jesus and the prophets who came before raged against unfair, unrighteous, and unjust societies. The largesse of the community was to be available to everyone. Disparity between the rich and the poor was morally wrong. They forcefully spoke against the practices that ground the faces of the poor into the earth, that sold goods for more than they were worth, and that provided for the few to live in opulence while others lived in only dirt.[24] Philo of Alexandria, a first-century Jewish philosopher, expressed

---

imitating God and acting in accordance with God's laws. Imitating God means clothing the naked, visiting the sick, comforting those that mourn, and burying the dead. See Edward Kessler, "The Jewish Concept of Justice."

22. Wright, *Day the Revolution Began*, loc. 2470 of 7473. Kindle.

23. Sometimes, in order to help clarify the way "righteousness" and "justice" are used in the Bible (as opposed to modern usage), Biblical "righteousness" is referred to *restorative* instead of *retributive* and "justice" is referred to *distributive* instead of *punitive.*

24. Lev. 19:13; Mal. 3:5; Jer. 22:3; Isa. 3:5; Amos 6:1–8, 10–13; Isa. 3:14; Matt. 19:16–30; 19:21; Luke 3:14;10:7; James 5:4.

it this way in his *Special Laws*: "Equality is the mother of justice" and "justice is the offspring of equality."[25]

N. T. Wright described the Kingdom of God as a fair society and as the "climax of [Jesus's] work of inaugurating God's Kingdom on earth as in heaven." It was the

> . . . victory over the destructive powers let loose into the world not simply through human wrongdoing or the breaking of moral codes, but through the human failure to be image-bearers, to worship the Creator and reflect his wise stewardship into the world.[26]

Jesus taught that ultimately the kingdoms of the world would fail. They would be replaced with the Kingdom of God. Any Roman-like society based on violence, intimidation, and social and economic inequality would self-destruct. But Jesus's Kingdom, based on compassion, justice and righteousness would not need to rely upon coercion to be unified. By putting the wellbeing of everyone at the forefront, the Kingdom of God would be the kind of community that first generation Christians desired, where "the believers were united in heart and mind because all were equally valued and cared for. And they felt that what they owned was not their own, so they shared everything they had" (Acts 4:32 NLT). Consequently, "[t]here were no needy people among them" (Acts 4:34 NLT).

Perhaps a simpler way of expressing the difference between the empire of Augustus that we have briefly described and the Kingdom Jesus taught of in the Gospels has been distilled by Marcus Borg and Dominic Crossan. They created a kind of formula for peace:

For Rome, peace came in this order:
RELIGION—WAR—VICTORY—PEACE.[27]
For Christians, peace came in this order:
RELIGION—NONVIOLENCE—JUSTICE—PEACE.[28]

They add, "There will be peace on earth, said Roman imperial theology, when all is quiet and orderly. There will be peace on earth, said [Jesus], when all is fair and just."[29]

As Jesus anticipated the violence of Golgotha where the Romans would handily dispatch the "King of the Jews," he reassured his disciples:

---

25. Philo, in Joseph L. Baron, ed., *A Treasury of Jewish Quotations*, 106.
26. Wright, *Day the Revolution Began*, loc. 2471 of 7473. Kindle.
27. Borg and Crossan, *First Paul*, 89.
28. Ibid., 88.
29. Ibid.

"Peace I leave with you, my peace I give unto you." Undoubtedly, in the context of his impending departure, he was not speaking about the ultimate peace that he would one day bring to the world when the Kingdom of God came as promised. Rather, he was offering the disciples a spiritual tranquility in the face of excruciating personal hardships.

Leo Tolstoy expressed the peace Jesus spoke of. It could only come about, he wrote, when the warring peoples of the earth would come to realize that

> in order to annihilate evil we must not employ violence against it, but must destroy it from the root with love. Men said: 'We will not listen to him, he is a fool; he advises not to oppose evil with evil so that evil may overwhelm us.' I [Tolstoy] say that according to Christ's teaching, evil cannot be eradicated by evil; that all resistance of evil by violence only intensifies the evil, that according to Christ's teaching evil is eradicated with good. *Bless them that curse you, pray for them that abuse you, do good to them that hate you, love your enemies, and you will have no enemies!*[30]

---

30. Leo Tolstoy, *Lift Up Your Eyes: The Religious Writings of Leo Tolstoy,* 317–18.

chapter 16

Jesus and the Religious Establishment

All good dramas require a hero, and all true heroes must face an exceptional villain. In the drama played out in the four Gospels, identifying the hero is effortless. Likewise, we might expect that identifying the adversary would be equally easy. We might reflexively conclude that it was the first-century Roman overlords. After all, they accomplished the celebrated *Pax Romana* through brutal military power, and they maintained it by the threat and consistent use of the same. We also know they were, as N. T. Wright suggests, grossly "insensitive" and "arrogant" toward the people they conquered. And they were the "archetypal idolaters."[1]

By the standards of the day, Rome's governance in Palestine was built on a type of oxymoron. Rome's powerfully benign accommodation of indigenous customs, social organizations, and religious practices was initially admired. There was on the surface—and on the surface *only*—a general recognition of Rome's legitimacy through its strength. In fact, the author of 1 Maccabees, writing only decades after Jesus's death and resurrection about the revolt of the second-century BC Hasmonean zealots, characterized Rome by saying "where their friends and those who relied on them were concerned, they had always stood by their friendship" (1 Maccabees 8:12 JB); But on their enemies "they inflicted heavy casualties, carried off their women and children into captivity, pillaged their goods, subdued their country, . . . and reduced them to slavery" (1 Maccabees 8:10–11 JB).

Rome had defeated the regional powers around the Mediterranean, and "consequently, for Judea, Samaria, and Galilee of the first decades of the Common Era, this meant that Jewish leaders could expect Rome's protection from other equally brutal designing foes in the region provided they paid tributes and efficiently quelled local internal insurrections. Make no mistake, life in the ancient world was uniformly cruel and violent. But for Palestine of Jesus's lifetime, Rome had become more of an abhorrent meta-presence. It was both hated and tolerated by most of the

---

1. N. T. Wright, *The New Testament and the People of God,* 160.

ruling elites, who "played the political game" and who "rendered unto Caesar (more or less) what Caesar thought was due to him, and gave to their god what was left."[2]

So, if not the Romans, who can we call the real villains in this, the original Passion Play? The late Anthony Saldarini, one of the foremost scholars of late Second Temple and rabbinic Judaism, wrote that in addition to the Sadducees and the scribes, who were "part of the political alliance" against Jesus, the Pharisees were "the day to day opponents of Jesus par excellence." He wrote that they were an "ominous presence . . . allied with the chief priests in taking action against Jesus, especially in Jerusalem."[3] They constantly collided with "his teachings on sabbath, purity and other issues and they [tried] to destroy his reputation and influence with the people."[4] Saldarini cites New Testament scholar Rudolph Schnackenburg, who describes the Pharisees in particular as "ever watchful and suspicious adversaries of Jesus" that kept "the people under surveillance with their propaganda,"[5] continually threatening the delicate peace between the governed, the governing elite, and their overlords.[6]

For our purposes, Saldarini's identification of the Pharisees as the drama's "opponents par excellence" and an "ominous presence" will function only as a temporary label for the relationship between Jesus and the religious establishment of first-century Palestine.

The Gordian Knot

In Greek mythology, a peasant called Gordius secured his oxcart to a column in the public square of the city of Phrygia by means of an impossibly intricate knot. The oracles prophesied that the man who would someday undo the knot would go on to conquer all of Asia. The myth came to support the legend that the task of undoing the knot—an act fraught with political potential—fell to the young Alexander the Great of Macedonia.[7] Notwithstanding several versions of Alexander's solution, the Gordian knot has come to be a useful metaphor for intractable, obdurate, and maddeningly complex problems.

2. Ibid., 161.
3. Anthony J. Saldarini, *Pharisees, Scribes and Sadducees in Palestinian Society,* 188.
4. Ibid., 172.
5. Ibid., 188.
6. Ibid.
7. Britannica.com, s.v. "gordian-knot."

For us, the so-called Gordian knot is the religious and political context of Jewish Palestine in Jesus's lifetime prior to the war with Rome that produced the sacking of Jerusalem and the destruction of the Temple in AD 70. That knot includes innumerable large and small strands. We have selected several of the more important ones.

The Power of Class

The first tangle in the Gordian knot is the one we may label as the class structure of Jesus's Palestine. Jewish social classes were marked by kinship affiliations as well as by relationships of power and influence within a rigid, two-tiered, unbalanced structure. Both tiers contained many nuanced parts not stipulated to by the two general umbrella-like categories. The various classes within these two more general tiers tended to marry strictly within their own subgroups; connections to one tier or another were generally hereditary.[8] Separating the two tiers was a wide gulf that was essentially "unmediated by a middle class."[9]

In describing the class structure as two-tiered, we have purposefully excluded the Romans in Palestine as well as the monarchy and its attached retinues. We have done this because during Jesus's lifetime, the monarchy of Palestine was not only appointed and supported by Rome; they were educated in Rome and then reintroduced into Palestine as its client kings. Often colorfully referred to as "kings with strings," Herod and Herod's sons (and later the procurator of Judea) reigned as the on-site representatives of the empire. Their "class" was inextricably affiliated with Rome and in most respects was carefully self-segregated from the rest of Jewish society. Together with the monarchy's residential palaces, the city of Caesarea Maritima in Judea and the cities of Tiberius and Sepphoris in Galilee were Roman enclaves where pagan residents and a few Hellenized Jews lived far from other Jews.

On the other hand, a permanent and hereditary upper tier of Jews in Palestine controlled both the day-to-day political and the religious lives of its citizens. In this respect, Palestine was not unlike every other state in the ancient world where separation of religious and civil governments was nonexistent. Those Jews who belonged to the upper tier were partly the elites of Jesus's day who had descended from families of high priests. Others came from families of high officials and the old, wealthy kinship

8. Ibid., 24.
9. Ibid.

affiliations of Jerusalem. Finally and more important to our discussion here, another segment of this upper tier formed a small army of what sociologists refer to as "the retainers," who served the hereditary elites in a primarily urban environment.

The political, economic, and religious power of the sub-group we will hereafter refer to as retainers, who vastly outnumbered their patrons, was vested in the roles they played within their environment and in the influence they managed to amass and subsequently protect. Each subset of retainers was made up of professionals, trained in skills that made them of value to the governing Jewish elites. They existed simply to collectively and individually serve. Those classified as retainers included soldiers, educators, entertainers, artisans, and various religious functionaries such as lower-echelon priests.[10]

It is a critically important idea that Saldarini identifies the Pharisees, Sadducees, and even scribes as titles for groups among the heterogeneous urban retainers. He writes that the Pharisees and Sadducees were spawned more than a century and a half before the advent of Jesus, during the reign of Hyrcanus, and that they "competed for power with other political interest groups."[11] They were groups, not necessarily sects, whose members were retainers with various employment situations who always individually depended on the Jewish religious establishment as their employers. "Either alone or with other officials, [the Pharisees controlled] the synagogue and the judicial processes for removing those whom they oppos[ed],"[12] However, in much the same way that political parties today experience group homogeneity because of shared values and ideas, organized groups such as the Pharisees in Jesus's day were bound together by kinship, friendship, and the patronage of their elite employers. "*Reputed* to be more pious and accurate in interpreting the laws than others," they came together because they shared a passionate belief in how to maintain Jewish identity and purity in a world that constantly impinged upon that identity.[13] Saldarini also cites Josephus who defines the Pharisees as a *syntagma*, a Greek word aptly used today in linguistics to describe a phrase or component part of a larger work analyzed for its relationship to the whole of the text—a useful metaphor for both Pharisees and Sadducees because in the ancient world, the meaning of the word was similar to the appropriated linguistic one; a *syntagma*, often meant "a military group . . . or a civil group recognized by a constitution,"

10. Ibid.
11. Ibid., 46–48, 92–93, 157.
12. Ibid., 188.
13. Ibid., 93; emphasis added.

which bound its members to a structure of relationships that secured affiliation through sometimes secret rituals and ceremonies containing formal promises of commitment to other members of the group.[14]

As a proportion of the entire population of Jewish Palestine, this governing tier—descendants of the old elite families, together with their retainers—"seldom exceeded 5 to 7 percent of the entire population."[15] That left the remaining 93 to 95 percent of Palestinian Jews as the various substrata of the perpetually impoverished lower tier who also served the elites. This they did through agricultural production, supporting trades, and payment of taxes. This tier was populated by farmers, laborers, artisans, masons, carpenters, metalsmiths, and servants whose major goal was "wantlessness"—freedom from the constant concerns of penury.[16] These working classes knew all too well that drought, disease, corruption, dishonesty, and other natural or manmade disasters could spell immediate ruin, enslavement, or death. Saldarini's estimate of the size of the governing elite relative to the Jewish population goes directly to the motives of those who became Jesus's Jewish enemies. In first-century Palestine, the Pharisees' security within the elite upper tier—indeed, their status, power, and influence—was such a motivation.

As far as scholars are aware, neither the Pharisees nor the Sadducees left their own written records.[17] To better understand them we must depend on other contemporary sources, sparse though they may be—like Josephus, himself a one-time Pharisee, who described the Pharisees as a respected and influential "political interest group" on par with unions, alliances, political parties, or other fraternal organizations of our day. As such, the group "had its own goals for society, and [the membership] constantly engaged in political activity to achieve them."[18]

---

14. Ibid., 37.

15. Ibid., 38.

16. Ibid., 36–37.

17. An entry on Pharisees in a dictionary of Judaism acknowledges the difficulties and cites the four Christian Gospels (a polemic obviously favoring the Christian view of the Pharisees), Josephus's works (written with a bias for Roman consumption), and I and II Maccabees as the most contemporary sources. But like most academic investigations of Pharisee and Sadducee beliefs, the entry relies on the rabbinic schools and synagogues, developed in the second century, which the authors of the entry see as the successors to Pharisaic thinking. See Kaufmann Kohler, "Pharisees," 9:661, 666.

18. Saldarini, *Pharisees, Scribes and Sadducees*, 281.

Pharisees lived primarily in Jerusalem, where they "probably fulfilled administrative or bureaucratic functions."[19] There is no evidence to suggest that being a Pharisee constituted a job description. Rather, Saldarini's summary of their place in the context of Jewish society is helpful. They were "a literate, corporate, voluntary association" whose members belonged to the "army of retainers . . . dependent on the governing class and rulers for their place in society." Historically and socially, they were not a "sect-like table fellowship" that was withdrawn from everyday interactions. That is a critically important observation. It means that their "place" was by no means safe from those whom they deemed to be pretenders, like Jesus, who might challenge their legitimacy as monitors or interpreters of the people's strict observance of a Jewish way of life. Looking at them from that angle, these educated "servants of the governing class . . . had a program for Jewish society and influence with the people [as well as] their patrons."[20]

Jesus's renowned healing powers would have threatened their influence with people of both higher and lower stations. More important, however, his knowledge of both the Torah and the Oral Law (sometimes referred to as the Oral Traditions) loomed as a threat to those Pharisees who jealously protected their status as recognized interpreters of the laws in dealing with Sabbath-day observance and ritual purity. From the outset of Jesus's ministry until the destruction of the Temple in AD 70, the Pharisees "probably sought a new communal commitment to a strict Jewish way of life based on adherence to the covenant" of Moses.[21]

William Barclay insightfully described the situation between Jesus and some of the retainers as an "unsparing and sustained . . . indictment" of the various factions' abilities that from time to time "erupted into [Jesus's] blazing wrath" toward them.[22] Barclay explained that Jesus's public embarrassment of the Pharisees, centered as it was on his distaste for their rigid adherence to and enforcement of the Oral Traditions, dangerously destabilized their status among the population.

An early exchange in Mark illustrates the tensions between the Pharisees and Jesus. Jesus had accepted an invitation to eat at the home of a tax collector named Levi the Son of Alphaeus. Levi had included some whom Mark called "disreputable" in the dinner. He wrote, "When the teachers of religious law who were Pharisees saw [Jesus] eating with tax

19. Ibid.
20. Ibid., 284.
21. Ibid., 282.
22. William Barclay, *The New Daily Study Bible: The Gospel of Matthew*, 2:281.

collectors and other sinners," the Pharisees, who were apparently monitoring Jesus and his disciples, asked, "Why does he eat with such scum?" (Mark 2:14–18 NLT.)

For the Pharisees in Mark's text, Jesus flagrantly and seemingly with knowledge and forethought abused a number of oral statutes. He ate with those whose professions made them by definition sinners, and he did not follow the prescribed ablutions prior to eating with such individuals (Mark 7:1–4). Levi's dwelling was defiled by the presence of sinners. Therefore Jesus himself became unclean by crossing the home's threshold. Clearly, at this and every other encounter with the Pharisees, the son of a carpenter from the ranks of that lower tier who seemed to flout the authority of his betters, undermined social and religious norms by challenging the privileges and authority of these retainers of the upper tier.

The Sadducees, Scribes, and the Hellenization of Judaism

The years preceding the Maccabean Revolt of 167 BC brought some of the most impactful events to the long narrative of Jewish history. They must be factored into any understanding of the complex culture surrounding Jesus's ministry. Shortly after the death of Alexander the Great in 323 BC, his vast empire was shared among three of his generals into successor states. The thus-divided kings and kingdoms were hardly cordial to one another. Tiny Palestine lay between two of them: Ptolemaic Egypt in the south and the expanding Seleucid Empire to the north. For the next 150 years, what remained of the Promised Land was cruelly buffeted between them. Through it all, the looming presence of Alexander's Greek legacy slowly permeated the everyday lives of many Jews and most of the religious and civic culture. Josephus and the authors of the Maccabees tell us that especially during the reign of Antiochus IV Epiphanes (from 175 BC until his death in 164 BC), the Seleucid Empire was disintegrating under the weight of the madness of its Greek king.

Those eleven years of his reign were distinguished by overexpansion, terrible corruption, and the compulsory spread of Antiochus's brand of Hellenism. The city of Jerusalem suffered greatly. Observant Jews were forced to offer sacrifices to Greek gods, even at the Temple. The altar was utterly desecrated. Priests were forced to sacrifice and then offer swine or be slain themselves. Antiochus deposed the high priests who were descendants of Zadok, King David's high priest, as the leaders of the theocracy. Many of the ruling elite and their retainers of the upper tier absorbed

Greek language and cultural mores. They absorbed their philosophies into their theology. For example, as perhaps one of the more galling displays of Jewish capitulation to the ways of the Hellenic overlords, many Jewish young men who frequented the Greek gymnasium that was built in Jerusalem surgically disguised evidence of their circumcision for fear of embarrassment during the gymnasium's games contested in the nude.

Scholars of the period rely on Josephus and later rabbinic texts to tell us that the priestly brotherhood of elite Jews known as the Sadducees[23] was founded by men mostly from the ranks of the temple priesthood. These founders included men who could reliably trace their lineage to Levi, who referred to themselves as chief priests. The Sadducees included members of the various lower ranks of priests involved with the Temple, such as musicians, physical and religious custodians, temple guards—and groups such as the Levite priests who came to arrest Jesus at Gethsemane (Matt. 27:47). The duties of the lower-level temple priests also included making sacrifices and performing the rituals of the sanctuary. They burned incense and interceded in the Holy Place. They manned the tables set for money exchanges and purchases of birds and beasts for sacrifices. Lastly, these numerous ranks of professional priests were supposed to pass to succeeding generations the laws and rituals associated with acceptable temple worship (Deut. 33:9–10; Mal. 2:7).[24]

The Sadducees mainly recruited their members from temple retainers, who were controlled by the reigning high priest appointed by Rome and influenced by Greek culture. The four Gospels name the high priests who, although not royalty, wore the trappings and held the power of royalty during Jesus's ministry. Caiaphas, who ruled from AD 18 to 36, officiated over the groups that dispatched Jesus to Rome's procurator Pilate for crucifixion; and his father-in-law, Annas, who ruled from AD 6 to 15, was the first to scrutinize Jesus.

The office of high priest under Roman rule was not a lifetime appointment. As a result, there were other former high priests like Annas who also wielded power and influence in Jerusalem. They seem to have been "satisfied with the political life and committed to [maintaining] their own power as part of the ruling dynasty" of the high priests.[25]

---

23. The name Sadducees is believed to be derived from Zadok, the first High Priest of Solomon's Temple, whose name may be transliterated as "Sadduc."

24. Allen Ross, "The Religious World of Jesus: The Priests."

25. Ibid.

The brotherhood of the Sadducees was supported by the existing theocratic government, the high priest, and other elites who all gradually absorbed Greek ideas. As a brotherhood, Sadducees wanted only the Torah—the five books of Moses plus the Prophets—as their purity standard. They did not share "the most essential doctrines of the Messianic hope of the Pharisees."[26] Instead, their belief system included the Hellenic concept of the afterlife, which included the very Greek idea of a disembodied, ill-defined *psyche* that survived death and that wandered without consciousness in the underworld of the dead. The dead were therefore granted a sort of immortality only by means of the living who remembered their good deeds in life.

The Hellenized Sadducees' main concerns centered on obedience to the duties and commandments for observant Jews as set out in the Torah and centered in the Temple's sanctifying rituals rather than in the more numerous and extreme Oral Traditions the Pharisees strictly observed. Apparently, the Sadducees were satisfied with a more political life committed to their own power as part of a priestly dynasty.[27]

Only three encounters between Jesus and the Sadducees are recorded,[28] none of which come from John's Gospel.[29] Instead, we first see them in Matthew's Gospel as companions to the Pharisees at Jesus's baptism (Matt. 3:7). We next see them with a contingent of Pharisees in the region of the Galilee testing Jesus by "demanding that he show them a miraculous sign from heaven to prove his authority" (Matt. 16:1–4 NLT).[30] Matthew

---

26. Ibid.

27. Ibid.

28. Acts records the only other direct references to the Sadducees. In this passage, however, it is revealing that it refers to an altercation between Paul and Annas, the high priest, and his officials, some of whom are Sadducees and some Pharisees (Acts 23:1–10). This passage clarifies the character of the two groups. Only *some* of the Temple Mount officials belong to either of the two brotherhoods, whose members were affiliated by their beliefs and "debts of honor" described in this chapter.

29. John wrote that "priests and Levites," rather than Sadducees and Pharisees, came from Jerusalem (John 1:19 KJV).

30. In what may be a reference to the pollution brought about by the Hellenization of the Jewish elite, Jesus told the Sadducees that they were able to read the signs in the heavens, but only "*a wicked and adulterous generation* seeketh after a sign" (Matt. 16:4 KJV; emphasis added). The slight about the generation of Jews of Jesus's day was perhaps a reference to the pollution of purity laws and intermarriage with non-Jews. The problem for modern translators is that the passage does not appear in the earlier texts of the event those translators have

wrote that later Jesus and the disciples "crossed to the other side" of the lake. There, Jesus cautioned his disciples by way of a metaphor about the corrupting influence of the Sadducees and Pharisees. He reminded them of the recent miracle of feeding thousands of pilgrims with only five loaves and dried fishes. With reference to the bread of that miracle, he warned them that the Sadducees and Pharisees were like spoiled yeast that would ruin bread. At first the disciples did not think metaphorically. "Why can't you understand that I'm not talking about bread?" Jesus asked. So he told them again, "'Beware of the yeast of the Pharisees and Sadducees.' Then at last they understood that he wasn't speaking about the yeast in bread, but about the deceptive teachings of the Pharisees and Sadducees" (Matt. 16:5–12 NLT). The third and last reference to the Sadducees comes from an encounter on the Temple Mount during preparations for the Passover feast (Matt. 22; Mark 12; Luke 20), where they attempted to trip up Jesus on several highly technical parts of Torah law.

By comparison to the Pharisees, the Sadducees were considered worldly. They actively participated in the political and social affairs of the times. Many were the guardians of the Temple. Some who were well-educated became the equivalent of accountants in the temple treasury, where they shamelessly fleeced those who came to offer their oblations. Barclay said that practice of selling animals for sacrifice was "bare-faced extortion at the expense of the poor and humble pilgrims, who were practically blackmailed into buying their victims from temple booths." The high cost of exchanging money was such a "glaring social injustice" that it enflamed Jesus with rage.[31]

Finally, it was implicit that Sadducees would help the Roman leadership assigned to ancient Palestine's kingdoms or provinces. They were expected to keep at bay the more militant nationalist elements of Judaism that were intent on overthrowing their Roman overlords for the sake of the purity of covenant Israel.

The real power of the Sadducees was exercised through the Sanhedrin, or governing assemblies, that decided most of the secular and religious affairs of both the provincial and community levels. They did not have the universal support of the masses, and in the main recruited their members only from the priestly and wealthy elite of Jerusalem. Josephus claimed that the Hellenized Sadducees' association with the levers of Roman

---

relied upon. See for example the New Living Translation, The Revised Standard Version, and several others. The J. B. Phillips translation includes the reference.

31. William Barclay, *The New Daily Study Bible: The Gospel of John*, 1:110–11.

power made them more "boorish" and "heartless" than other Jews.[32] After Roman armies destroyed Jerusalem and the Temple in AD 70, the Sadducees, along with Jewish temple practices, came to an end.

The last group or association influenced by Greek thought and language we must highlight was formed by a loose coalition called scribes (with a lower-case designation). Called "teachers of religious law" in newer translations of the four Gospels, their familiarity with the Torah as copyists and educators qualified them as authoritative interpreters of the scriptures. In some cases their scholarship earned them a place alongside the priests (Jubilees 4:17–25). Scribes were often servants in elite households. Ezra the Scribe of the Old Testament brought the written form of Biblical text with him from captivity in Babylon. In their various capacities, the scribes, together with their fellow conservative Pharisees, were looked upon as guardians of the Traditions of the Patriarchs contained in both the canon texts as well as the Oral Traditions.[33]

The Bias of the Sources

The last thread in the knot relates to the problems that a Bible student or scholar who attempts a wider understanding of the text will invariably confront: The first problem is the amount of time and mental commitment required of anyone who makes a genuine effort, something most of us cannot muster. The second is what Saldarini calls the perils of "anachronistic retrojections"—a phrase used to discuss Bible criticism that projects contemporary interpretations onto ancient contexts. Applying modern cultural norms to ancient situations is what we twenty-first-century Bible students often do when we attempt to recreate the world of Jesus and his antagonists. We literally "throw backward" our own overlay onto the Gospel texts. Saldarini, in a direct caution about studying Jesus's time and place, says: "The Pharisees, scribes, and Sadducees must be understood as part of Palestinian Jewish society and ancient society, which differs significantly from modern society, in order to prevent an anachronistic

---

32. J. Dwight Pentecost, *The Words and Works of Jesus Christ*, 556.

33. "The Jews, especially the Pharisees, do not eat until they have poured water over their cupped hands, as required by their ancient *traditions*. Similarly, they don't eat anything from the market until they immerse their hands in water. This is but one of many *traditions* they have clung to—such as their ceremonial washing of cups, pitchers, and kettles" (Mark 7:3–4 NLT; emphasis added).

retrojection of modern categories and concepts."[34] Thus, finding a clear and accurate picture of the times means using as many extant contemporary sources, in addition to commentaries by reputable scholars, as time (especially time!) and expense can allow.

We must also remember that there are only a few informants who wrote reliably anywhere near the first-century AD on the political and religious environment of the Palestine of Jesus. The first are obviously the New Testament four Gospels, the Acts of the Apostles, and the Letters— all written by the end of the first century or early second century. (Some of the Pauline pseudepigraphical epistles were likely written up to six decades after Paul's death.)

Mark's is the earliest of the Gospels. It and Matthew's provide us with the most detailed and frequent contexts of Jesus's interactions with the Jewish elites. In Mark alone the Pharisees disputed with Jesus over fasting (Mark 2:18), Sabbath day observance (Mark 2:24; 3:2), and divorce (Mark 10:2). Together with the scribes they challenged Jesus over ritual purification of hands (Mark 7:1) and eating with sinners (Mark 2:16). They demanded that he provide a miraculous sign (Mark 8:11), and attempted to trap him in an argument over taxes (Mark 12:13). In the Gospels we note that exchanges between Jesus and the Pharisees outnumber interactions with the other groups by a factor of six.[35] Saldarini's claim that they are the "opponents par excellence" is well founded, at least by numeric calculations.

If we come to a study of the Pharisees, Sadducees, and scribes with the Gospels as our only source, we should acknowledge that the authors wrote with the bias of believers. As polemicists, they cast the Pharisees and others as Jesus's bitter and malignant antagonists and villains. They did not compile a history of the wider context. For that we can turn to only a few contemporary sources; the critical source mentioned over and over is Flavius Josephus.

Jews generally see Yosef ben Matityahu, remade as the Roman Josephus, as a turncoat. Christians cite him as an independent albeit brief contemporary corroborator of the historical Jesus. He wrote his *History of the Jewish Wars* (or simply *Wars*) for Roman consumption, so we must also concede his bias. However, sections of Josephus's writings are important as sources because he provides us with an insider's knowledge of Jewish soci-

---

34. Saldarini, *Pharisees, Scribes and Sadducees*, 34.

35. The Pharisees are mentioned eighty-nine times, with only six outside the Gospels. The Sadducees come in with fifteen entries, with only five in Acts. No mention of them appears in the epistles, and surprisingly, none appear in the Gospel of John.

ety of the day, including its so-called retainers: the Pharisees, Sadducees, Essenes, and scribes. His descriptions of the workings of the elite Jewish religious establishment and of those groups that were made from the elite's retainers are critical. From Josephus we understand that at the time of Jesus, Judaism was "in the grip of a chain of renewal movements which as a rule moved within the framework . . . of common convictions."[36]

The importance of the apocryphal 1 and 2 Maccabees should also not be underestimated when trying to understand these groups. These books provide historical context for the zealous devotion to Jewish identity and ritual purity. In them we read about the so-called Maccabean Revolt that began 160 years before the advent of Jesus. [37] It was led by Mattathias ben Johanan, a lower-echelon priest from the House of Hasmoni, together with his five sons and their descendants, against the pagan Greek Seleucid Empire. To this day the revolt stands as a glorious story of the renewal (if only for a brief time) of Jewish identity as God's covenant people.

We may assume that every first-century Jew knew the story. We may also assume that many Jews aligned themselves with one of the groups formed in response to the revolt, its prologue, and its aftermath. The Hasmonean state the Maccabees founded lost its independence when the Roman general Pompeii came from Egypt in 63 BC. He incorporated the little Jewish state into the Roman Empire's provincial state of Palestine. But the story injected into Jewish society from that time until arguably the present day what Jonathan Goldstein calls a militant nationalism.[38] And, Goldstein says, that militancy was on a slow boil beneath the surface of all Jewish society in the New Testament texts.[39]

Goldstein's translation of the Maccabees makes the claim that the most important legacy left to the Jews of Jesus's day from Mattathias ben Johanan and his sons was twofold: first, an absolute commitment to ridding the heresy of Hellenism from the Jewish way of life and attitudes of its citizens, and a recommitment to strict observance of Torah; and second, an absolute conviction that violence in the cause of restorative purity enjoyed God's approbation.[40] He writes that in Jesus's day, commitment to

---

36. Gurd Theissen, Annette Merz, *The Historical Jesus: A Comprehensive Guide*, 128.

37. The books get their title from a nickname given to Mattathias's son Judas. He was given the task of leading the warriors of the revolt. He did so with such courage that he came to be called Maccabaeus ("the Hammer").

38. Jonathan A. Goldstein, introduction *1 Maccabees*.

39. Ibid., 3–14.

40. Ibid.

the concept of a Jewish state had become the central issue of Judaism since the Maccabean Revolt, and probably played a major role in the formation of many Jewish groups, including the Pharisees. Because their autonomy and their religious practices were constantly threatened by encroachment of Hellenism and later the Romans, Jews defended their way of life in a number of ways—including violence—to recommit themselves and others to Jewish traditions and beliefs.

The Temple Mount as a Microcosm

Observant Jews in first-century Palestine were required to make pilgrimages to Jerusalem three times each year for the festivals of Shavuot (Pentecost), Sukkot (Tabernacles), and Pesach (Passover). Barclay writes that during those festival periods the crowds coming to Jerusalem, including Jesus and his disciples, swelled to enormous numbers, all seeking accommodations in Jerusalem or the surrounding towns and villages.

During the Passover, upward of a quarter of a million lambs were ritually slaughtered for the temple altar and taken to be eaten as part of the Seder supper commemorating the Israelites' release from bondage in Egypt. The various constituencies of the large crowds, not to mention the resident population of Jerusalem (the high priestly families, the chief priests, the wealthy old aristocratic families, thousands of retainers, and so forth) and the Roman guards garrisoned in Antonia fortress, must have made for a cacophony of smells, sights, and sounds. The Temple Mount itself was packed with throngs of men, women and children who became a microcosm of worldwide Judaism.

Matthew 21 through 23 record increasingly tense exchanges between Jesus and every class and group—as if we are to understand all the necessary context for Jesus's Passion in a more concentrated dose in a period of twenty-four to thirty-six hours before the Seder supper. If we read the intensely rich story of those hours all together rather than in its isolated parts, it is riveting.

The day before the events on the Temple Mount, Jesus entered the city on a white donkey. He and Lazarus of Bethany, recently brought back to life by Jesus's command, had been hailed with shouts of Hosanna. Matthew began with Jesus's entry through the southernmost gates of the Temple. It was there that the corrupt moneychangers, managed by the Sadducees and employed by Annas, the Rome-appointed high priest, set their tables. Other dishonest functionaries sold doves and other offerings at sometimes more than ten times their usual price outside the temple gates. The tables were referred to as the "Bazaars of Annas, and were the private property of [his] family."[41] Jesus swept all of them away with powerful disdain. "My house shall be called the house of prayer; but ye have made it a den of thieves" (Matt 21:13 KJV), referring to a place where robbers hid and hoarded their money. Jesus's language came from Jeremiah 7, which was explicitly directed against the priests of the Temple. The priests and money changers would have known exactly the point he was making. The disruption at the entrance to the Temple during the crush of Passover must have brought the Temple to a chaotic halt. But for the moment, his righteous anger and subsequent property destruction went unchallenged by temple authorities because multitudes of stunned men, women, and children continued to press through the same gates into the Court of the Gentiles.

Jesus then sat beneath Solomon's porch and taught them. Next he healed the blind and the lame, an act that made the watchful "leading priests and elders indignant." They demanded to know by what authority he had done those things (Matt. 21:15 NLT). And then, after more thrusts and parries throughout the waning day, Jesus finally left the Mount for the short three-mile walk to Bethany to stay the night with Mary, Martha, and Lazarus.

The following morning he returned to the Temple's courts. There the priests and elders were already assembled and challenged him again about the source of his authority. He skillfully outwitted them, humiliating them in front of the crowds. Then he sat to teach two parables: one about a land-owner and his son and corrupt tenants; another about a king and his guests at a wedding feast. Both were barely disguised analogies of his Messianic role, and both infuriated his antagonists. So, embarrassed, the priests and elders regrouped to prepare for the next encounter and to arrange for the temple guards to arrest Jesus. But they could not because the Passover pilgrims pressed around him for a glimpse or a blessing (Matt. 21:23–46; 22:1–14).

Next a group of Pharisees appeared from the crowds and attempted to provoke him into saying something incriminating to warrant his arrest. When they could not, they also temporarily withdrew—but this time to enlist the Herodians who had watched in the courtyard to help in yet another attack on Jesus. The famous exchange about Caesar's coin and taxes ensued (Matt. 22:16–17).

All the while, the animals bawled and squawked, the sacrifices continued, the blood drained from the sacrifices and ran like thick red rivers through special ditches to the Kidron River outside the city walls, and the

---

41. Barclay, *The Gospel of Matthew*, 2:286

crowds swelled as the wealthy and poor alike came to pay their temple taxes. Some of the most entitled deliberately parted the crowds as they preened in their costly attire (Mark 12:41–44; Luke 21:1–4). Matthew's Gospel adds that Jesus "knew their evil motives" and called them hypocrites. "Why are you trying to trap me?" he asked in a voice that must have carried over the noise of the court's crowds (Matt. 22:18–22 NLT).

The tension of those chapters builds inexorably as we become aware that every political, religious, and social faction of Jewish society from both upper and lower tiers was by then participating in the high stakes drama.

A phalanx of fresh troops began another wave of the assault. A group of Sadducees emerged. They had heard about the Pharisees' encounters hours before and had come to interrogate Jesus about marriage after the resurrection in a hypothetical case mandated by Torah law (Deut. 25:5–10). The question they asked involved a Levirate marriage in which a childless widow married a succession of her dead husband's brothers, all of whom also died. They were stymied by Jesus's reasoned teachings about the resurrection, as were the growing number of "astonished" pilgrims and Pharisees (Matt. 22:22–33 NLT).

As we proceed to Matthew 23, we can easily imagine the pent-up wrath, righteous indignation, and terrible sorrow that Jesus expressed as he excoriated his tormenters. He turned to "the crowds and to his disciples" to deliver his most extraordinary rebuke, sometimes referred to as the "Seven Woes" or the "Woes of the Pharisees." Each dreadful, itemized accusation became a scathing denunciation of the scribes and Pharisees, the genuine villains of the narrative. Each provoked the men of the brotherhood—humiliated before the pressing crowds and their peers as well as temple priests and perhaps Roman soldiers observing from the heights of the Antonia Fortress—to plot his death. His sermon was about pretense and duplicity—in short, *hypocrisy*.

The ancient meaning of that word brings us closer to the center of Jesus's censure. Originally the Greek word was *hupokrites*, meaning "one who answers." It then "came to be specially connected with the statement and answer of a dialogue" in Greek theater. Finally, it morphed into "the regular Greek word for *actor*."[42] Over time the term took on a pejorative meaning—a pretender, one who acts a part and covers up true feelings by putting on a show.

Jesus weaponized the word to especially describe the practices of the Pharisees. He perceived that they were pretenders or actors, religious leaders who did not practice what they taught. Their religion was for show, a

---

42. Ibid., 2:336.

checklist of sorts that purchased heaven. It was off-putting and ostentatious. By devising hundreds of hedges to prevent breaking Torah Law, they also had built barriers between God and the common man. They had substituted man-made teachings for God's teachings. They had relied on the technicalities of the traditions to avoid being honest and generous with those in and out of the faith. They focused on outward appearances and practices. In sum, Jesus accused the assembled scribes and Pharisees of turning Judaism into a religion that had lost sight of the "weightier matters of the law, judgment, mercy, and faith" (Matt. 23:23 KJV). Their Judaism had become a way of playacting in a drama of eternal consequence.

Jesus's opening remarks decried "the teachers of religious law and the Pharisees" because they "crush people with unbearable religious demands and never lift a finger to ease the burden" (Matt.23:2–4 NLT). He was not referring to the principles embodied in the Decalogue given to Moses on Sinai. Rather, he was referring to the thousands of rules and regulations— the protocols that discouraged whole classes of people from becoming truly religious. The common person found it difficult if not impossible to fully comply with this excessive list of rules.

Their purity system made even the everyday experience of eating into a religious ritual. The Oral Law prescribed what kind of food could be eaten, from whom food could be purchased (only those who tithed), what plates of food could be used, how a person should wash hands before eating, and what a person should wear while dining. Such requirements were entirely impractical and out of reach for people like shepherds who spent their days caring for their sheep in the countryside, where normal city conveniences were unavailable. As a result, shepherds were on the bottom rungs of the social ladder, on par with tax collectors and dung sweepers. It was in this context that Jesus lent support to these outcasts by referring to himself as the Good Shepherd.

He made it clear that the rules and regulations that the scribes and Pharisees cared for so much were more about how they could distinguish themselves from others and less about encouraging and making it possible for others to approach God. Their rules and regulations made religion an outward show. By becoming experts in the intricacies of the Oral Traditions, they could easily distinguish themselves as the most righteous in the community. They lived their religious practices not so much to please God but to be "seen by men." Jesus raged. Their supposedly superior behavior qualified them to "sit in the chief seats of the synagogue," to enjoy seats of honor at meals, and to be respectfully greeted in the marketplace as "rabbi" (Matt. 23:5 NLT). Jesus declared that to make that kind of religiosity even more apparent, the Pharisees wore special clothing that set them apart as holy. "They broaden phylacteries . . . [and] they wear outsized tassels"[43] (Matt. 23:5–12 Barclay) on the four corners of the outer garment. Originally meant as reminders of God's commandments, their ridiculously large tassels must have made them appear as silly pretenders, actors striking poses for ultimate effect.

For Jesus, "any religion which produced ostentation in action and pride in the heart was a false religion."[44] So it was for the Pharisees that Jesus reserved this "most terrible and . . . most sustained denunciation" on the Temple Mount in the midst of thousands of witnesses, what A. T. Robertson called "the rolling thunder of Christ's wrath."[45] He not only called them "hypocrites" but also "blind guides," "fools," "serpents," and a "generation of vipers" (Matt. 23:13, 16, 17, 33 KJV).

Jesus concluded his most public fiery reproach by saying, "You yourselves (Pharisees and the like) are not going into [the Kingdom of Heaven]; nor do you allow those who are trying to get into it to enter" (Matt. 23:13 Barclay). And why not? Because the scribes and Pharisees replaced true religion—love, faith, sacrifice, and mercy—with a set of rules that benefited themselves to the detriment of others.

Barclay has broadened the Temple Mount reprimand to include all who falsely profess to be his disciples: "The gravest danger which they encounter is that it should turn their own prejudices into universal principles and substitute their own ideas for the truth of God. When they do that, they are not guides but barriers to the kingdom of God—for, being misled themselves, they mislead others."[46] In one verse, Jesus stripped away the "mask of elaborate godliness"[47] worn by the Pharisees. "What sorrow awaits you teachers of religious law and you Pharisees. Hypocrites!

---

43. Phylacteries were little leather boxes that were strapped on their wrists or foreheads. Inside was a parchment roll with four passages of scripture carefully written on it—Exodus 13:1–10, 11–16; Deuteronomy 3:4–9, 11:13–21. The Pharisees required this practice by a literal interpretation of Exodus 13:9: "And it shall be for a sign unto thee upon thine hand, and for a memorial between thine eyes, that the Lord's law may be in thy mouth" (KJV; repeated in verse 16).

44. Barclay, *The Gospel of Matthew*, 2:287.

45. A. T. Robinson, *The Pharisees and Jesus*, 139.

46. Barclay, *The Gospel of Matthew*, 2:289.

47. Ibid.

For you cross land and sea to make one convert, and then you turn that person into twice the child of hell you yourselves are!" (Matt. 23:15 NLT).

As if to intensify the condemnation, Jesus went on to name a specific list of offenses. The Pharisees were hypocrites because they failed to live up to their agreements. They relied upon technicalities (what a person swore by when taking an oath) to invalidate contractual arrangements (Matt. 23:16–22). They pretended to be religious by making a show of tithing their small herb gardens (not strictly required by the law of tithing). Yet, they overlooked the weightier matters of the law: "justice, mercy, and faith" (Matt. 23:23–24 NLT).

The Pharisees and teachers of religious law, he said, taught that purity was a matter of ritualistic cleansing when in truth, purity was a matter of what is in and what comes out of a man's or woman's heart. Purity, he said, was not about eating utensils, dishes, clothing, and outward appearances, but rather the quality of a person's soul. He accused them of being like "whitewashed tombs—beautiful on the outside but filled on the inside with dead people's bones and all sorts of impurity" (Matt. 23:27 NLT).[48] The scorching comments could not have been more humiliating.

---

48. For Barclay's comments on the hypocrisy of the Pharisees, see ibid., 2:329–31. He writes that it was so well acknowledged that an entire nomenclature had grown up to describe their religious excess. There were the "Shoulder Pharisees," who meticulously observed the law and touted their good works to the world; the "Wait-a-Little Pharisees," who could always find a valid excuse for avoiding a good deed; the "Bruised" or "Bleeding Pharisees," who would not speak to or even glance at a women on the street and therefore would shut their eyes, stumble, fall, and bump into walls or buildings, cutting and bruising themselves; the "Pestle and Mortar Pharisees," the "Hump-backed Pharisees" or "Tumbling Pharisees," who walked humbly by bending over like a pestle in a mortar or hunchback; the "Ever-reckoning" or "Compounding Pharisees," who constantly kept a balance sheet between themselves and God, carefully noting every good deed so that they could obligate God; and, finally, the "Timid" or "Fearing Pharisees," who always feared divine judgment.

Despite Jesus's general criticism of the Pharisees, there was one category of Pharisee he did not lambast—the true God-fearing Pharisees, who loved God and delighted in living God's commandments. For Jesus, they were sincere, good people. Some of them became his followers. Nicodemus was a Pharisee and a member of the Jewish Sanhedrin. Just after Jesus's death, he assisted Joseph of Arimathea, another member of the Sanhedrin, in preparing Jesus's body for burial (John 19:39).

Conclusion

The Temple in Jerusalem sat atop Mount Zion. On that day during his last Passover pilgrimage, Jesus stood in the courtyard of the Temple in the midst of thousands of pilgrims and perhaps dozens of fuming, disgraced scribes and Pharisees whose minds must have been spinning with plots of revenge. We can picture him as he served up his final speech directed toward his assassins. His denunciation summoned an expression of unalloyed sorrow over the children of God who had once been given an extraordinary covenant:

> O Jerusalem, Jerusalem [he keened], the city that kills the prophets and stones God's messengers! How often I have wanted to gather your children together as a hen protects her chicks beneath her wings, but you wouldn't let me. Behold, your house is left unto you desolate." (Matt. 23:37–39 NLT)

And then he left.

In a chapter about Jesus and the religious establishment, it was important to us to lay out as accurately as possible the players in the drama. We mixed our metaphors to describe ancient Palestine as a knot of enormous complexity. We first spoke about what sociologists have written regarding the period and what those who lived inside the period said about each other. Then we wrote what Jesus said and did in the midst of it all.

It should be of no surprise that Jesus wept over what these Jewish elites had become. They were the product of legacies left by generations before his time—those who had been Hellenized by the Seleucid invasions, those whom the Maccabees had left with a taste for militant nationalism, those who had formed associations to purify and protect the covenant people through the Torah and the strictures of the Oral Law. It is not surprising that he was so forcefully vocal about what the religious elite did to take advantage of the rest of society. He said religion ought to be fixed on *love of neighbor,* not *love of self.* He understood that when religion becomes dependent upon the observance of external requirements instead of on an inner transformation, it leads to a life of profound self-preoccupation and selfishness rather than one of compassion and inclusion of others. Ultimately, when hypocritical piety and self-aggrandizement became the vehicle for obtaining riches and status, especially at the expense of the poor, it became intolerable. For Jesus, it brought out the wrath of God, a warning to all Christians who claim to take upon themselves his name and seek to become his disciples.

section Three
concluding Thoughts

chapter 17

Discipleship and the covenant of salt

This book—or even this book's title—is hardly an original idea. We consulted the internet to find a number of sermons and blogs incorporating Jesus's question: "Whom Say Ye that I am?" We also found more than a dozen books with the same question worked into their titles. For example, Father James Martin's introduction to his book on his pilgrimage to the Holy Land begins with the story of Jesus inquiring of his disciples about his identity as they walked north to Caesarea Philippi. Martin writes that "out of the blue," Jesus asked his disciples who he was because he had heard them "arguing" about his true identity.[1] The question frankly begs an answer from all Christians.

Our purpose in attempting to answer Jesus's inquiry was actually a good deal more of a personal effort than a public one. We wanted to more carefully consider the life and teachings of Jesus so as to leave a satisfactory testament for our children, their children, and, we hope, their children's children. Obviously we could not come away from such a project without realizing more than we ever had before at least two things: (1) how much we still have to learn about Jesus, and (2) how exemplary and compelling his life was. We hope we got most of it right. We are certain that in some respects we have not.

We make no claim that these essays are deep theological discussions; nor are they meant to be a Bible commentary. We certainly recognize that we are incapable of such volumes. We do not read Greek or Latin. We cannot claim the academic expertise of faculty members in a college of religious studies. We have certainly not read all there is written on the subject.[2] We can say that those whose books we have read have been quoted accurately and in context. We can also say that some time ago we became fascinated with the recent trend in scholarly literature on "the historical

---

1. James Martin, *Jesus: A Pilgrimage*, 1.
2. Judith openly acknowledges that James probably has gone a considerable distance beyond herself.

Jesus." We have become convinced of the value of contributions of men and women in that field.

The study itself was humbling. The entirety of Jesus's life is breathtaking. It deserves a lifetime of investigation and contemplation. Our study is more daunting still when we consider the changes we need to make in our own lives to become more like him.

One of the surprising aspects of asking serious questions about Jesus was finding unexpected answers. In many, if not most, cases, those answers have significantly changed our perspectives. We have been forced to reevaluate some of our cherished assumptions. The chapter on Jesus and the family, for example, was particularly challenging. His emphasis on the universal family of all humankind rather than on the small "nuclear" family caused us to wonder again and again about how we regard our brothers and sisters—those who are our kin and those in our *tribe,* or more important, those who lack the security of associations of religious affiliation or custom. This emphasis reminded us that from God's standpoint, inasmuch as we are quite literally all his children, we are all truly brothers and sisters, regardless of our ethnic origins or nationality.

In writing the chapter on Jesus and women, we realized once more that Jesus was living far beyond the tight manacles of first-century Jewish culture in Palestine. In very real respects, he purposefully did not differentiate between the sexes in ways that his own culture did. Rather, he included and encouraged women to be active and equal participants of the Kingdom of God.

In the chapters "Jesus and the Enemy" and "Jesus and the Romans," we came to understand his complete disavowal of the local and imperial assumptions held by the institutional culture of his day, a culture that saw violence as a means to get and keep power. And we were astonished not only at his emphasis of the importance of forgiveness, but also of his command for full-throated prayers for and love of one's enemies—our enemies, both personal and institutional! We have had more than a few sincere conversations on the implications and difficulties of Jesus's prescriptions for peace that all of us so often ignore in our contemporary violent and militaristic society.

In the chapter on Jesus and the poor, his concern for social and economic inclusion and opportunity stood out as vitally important. Every event in his life that we studied moved us because we witnessed over and over again his compassion for the most vulnerable in his society, those who were overlooked and exploited. We could picture him angrily toppling the tables of the moneychangers on the Temple Mount as he rebuked the temple priests lining their pockets with the humble contributions of others. How Jesus despised the systemic injustice that marginalized and disenfranchised God's less-fortunate children—slaves, widows, orphans, and the impoverished.

We likewise were reminded of how disquieted he became in confrontations with the corrupted and Hellenized elite classes of the religious establishment, who controlled the ritual orthodoxy of the masses making their pilgrimages to Jerusalem during festivals.

Finally, Jesus disdained the narcissistic religion of the self-important and self-absorbed retainers, who were members of several of the political and religious associations or groups the Gospels identified as the Pharisees, Sadducees, and teachers of religious law known as scribes. These men aggrandized themselves and their status as they paraded their own personal righteousness and monitored that of others. Rather than caring for and loving their neighbors, they built impossible walls of stones engraved with itemized uprightness. Their behavior literally leaped off every page of the Gospels, where we were confronted with a Jesus who time and again challenged our thinking as he pressed us to be more forgiving, nonjudgmental, charitable, inclusive, and concerned for others rather than for ourselves.

Nevertheless, it was one thing to search for and then to comprehend even a part of the person who we determined was the real Jesus of history and heaven, but it was another to then yearn to be more like him. But finding the resolve to act upon what we learned and yearned for—to become his *disciples*—continues to be the most difficult task of all. We were reminded of an imaginary conversation that John Dominic Crossan constructed in one of his many books on the historical Jesus. We preface the exchange by saying that Crossan, a former priest and now author of considerable influence in circles of academic Jesus scholarship, views the resurrection of Jesus as metaphorical:

> **Jesus:** "I've read your book, Dominic, and it's quite good. So now you're ready to live by my vision and join me in my program?"
>
> **Dominic:** "I don't think I have the courage, Jesus, but I did describe it quite well, didn't I, and the method was especially good, wasn't it?"
>
> **Jesus:** "Thank you, Dominic, for not falsifying the message to suit your own incapacity. That at least is something."
>
> **Dominic:** "Is it enough, Jesus?"
>
> **Jesus:** "No, Dominic, it is not."[3]

3. John Dominic Crossan, *Jesus: A Revolutionary Biography,* xiv.

Crossan's dialogue posed the question we had been asking ourselves: "Is it enough?" But it became all the more urgent because we made Jesus to be the one who answered us.

In our spiritual pilgrimage, we set out to find him in the four Gospels. We attempted to clothe the Gospels in the environment of first-century Palestine. We studied the most respected scholarship we could find on the historical Jesus, knowing that nearly two millennia of transmissions, interpolations, and translations would sometimes hinder our efforts as amateur historians. All along we made genuine, sincere efforts to guard against what Saldarini—the man who wrote about the Pharisees and Sadducees of Jesus's day—called "retrojection." Recall that this refers to the projection of our contemporary prejudices and judgments onto the texts at our disposal. We guarded against this so that we might deserve some small commendation for not, as Crossan put it, "falsifying the message to suit [our] own incapacity." But more important, Crossan reminded us of that most difficult inquiry: Do we have the courage to "live by [Jesus's] vision and join [him] in [his] program?" Put simply, are we willing to become true disciples of the Lord Jesus Christ?

We quickly found that the word "disciple" can mean widely different things to different people. Its Hebrew cognate once meant *punishment.* The Oxford English Dictionary says the noun "disciple" has several etymological origins. It is originally from the Greek word *mathetes,* meaning a teacher's pupil or artisan's apprentice. It moved into the Old English word *discipul* (the feminine form is *discipula*) from the Latin *discipulus,* meaning "pupil, student, follower," which in turn came from the verb *discere,* "to learn."[4]

In some instances, discipleship is simply a title used to mean someone who is temporarily called to perform a particular task, such as short-term missionary service. In other cases, a disciple can mean someone who voluntarily devotes himself or herself to the discipline (certainly not in the old Hebrew sense of punishment) of learning the teachings of a great mentor.

However, if the word *disciple* sometimes simply refers to the student of an exceptional teacher like Jesus, clearly when he spoke about becoming *his* disciple, he had something much more demanding in mind. In brief, he intended the term to mean someone who had taken steps to formally join him, by way of a covenant relationship, in establishing and then sustaining the Kingdom of God on earth. He meant that a disciple had promised,

---

4. Oxford English Dictionary, s.v. "disciple."

in the presence of God, witnesses, and attending angels, to live a life in conformity with his teachings. He meant that a disciple was more than a disciplined student who used "sound methods" of scholarship to learn "his record." Disciples, rather, were those who followed his example by behaving the way he behaved despite the burdens placed on their shoulders.

Jesus spoke on a number of occasions about the intensity of a disciple's commitment. On one such occasion, he taught with sincerity something that may feel particularly problematic: that his disciples must hate their families. Jesus prefaced this lengthy discourse, found in Luke 14, by a parable about guests invited to a feast who make inane excuses about their inability to attend. "None of those men which were bidden shall taste of my supper," said "a certain man [who] made a great supper" (Luke 14:16–23 KJV).

We might be forgiven if we scratch our heads and move past the next ten verses of chapter 14, which constitute Jesus's injunction on discipleship, because they are followed by the three great parables about a lost sheep, a lost coin, and a lost son we wrote about in chapter 8 (Luke 15).

However, we set out to find the meaning of that especially problematic passage on hating one's family in the context of the world of the New Testament. And we found that Luke's text was not unduly difficult, though it was certainly sobering. He clearly presented what Jesus expects, provided we seriously want to be his committed disciples.

We realized that Luke's text explains elements of a covenant relationship with the true messiah. It speaks with the urgency we would and should expect of a man who has bound to himself beloved men and women who would soon face the task of building the Kingdom of God without him.

At the end of chapter 14, Jesus set out three necessary elements of a disciple's covenant relationship. First, we must "hate" our father, mother, spouse, children, and siblings, and be willing to give up our very lives if necessary (Luke 14:26).

In the King James Version of this verse, Jesus said, "If any man come to me, and *hate* not his father, and mother, and wife, and children, and brethren, and sisters, yea, and his own life also, he cannot be my disciple (emphasis added). The New Living Translation reads nearly the same except that it adds a qualifier at the end of the directive: "If you want to be my disciple, you must hate everyone else *by comparison*" (emphasis added). By this Jesus did not suggest that a disciple should feel animosity toward those closest to him. Nor was he suggesting that a disciple should do something contrary to the Fifth Commandment to honor father and mother. An expository dictionary of the Old Testament helps clarify Luke's text. The word *hate*, used as a point of comparison of degrees, meant levels of preference rather than a binary choice. Hence, Jacob did not *hate* Leah in the sense of despising her, but rather he "preferred Rachel more."[5] Discipleship therefore must take preference over everything else!

It is helpful to read Luke 14:26 for a second time in the Amplified Bible, a translation that includes in brackets the range of meaning in the original Greek text. "If anyone," it reads,

> does not hate his [own] father and mother [in the sense of indifference to or relative disregard for them in comparison with his attitude toward God] and [likewise] his wife and children and brothers and sisters—[yes] and even his own life also—he cannot be my disciple.

In the Luke text, the second condition of true discipleship is that we must commit to bearing even heavy burdens and do our part in all things that might be asked of us (Luke 14:27). Therefore, because discipleship meant an undeviating commitment, it also meant sacrifice. A true disciple must "carry" his own "cross and follow me" (Luke 14:27 NLT).

Finally in Luke, Jesus cautioned the true disciples that they must consider and calculate the cost of such a lifelong commitment. He compared the decision to become a true disciple to constructing a building:

> For who would begin construction of a building without first calculating the cost to see if there is enough money to finish it? Otherwise, you might complete only the foundation before running out of money, and then everyone would laugh at you. They would say, "There's the person who started that building and couldn't afford to finish it." (Luke 14:28–30 NLT)

Jesus also compared discipleship to the life-and-death decision-making process undertaken before going into battle. We must count the cost of the conflict and make sure we can succeed before we begin (Luke 14:31–33). But the ultimate *cost* was elemental: "So no one can become my disciple without giving up everything for me" (Luke 14:33 NLT).

The Covenant of Salt

At the conclusion of the discourse on discipleship in Luke, Jesus made a seemingly abrupt transition to a comment on salt. He also made similar

---

5. Merrill F. Unger and William White Jr., eds., *Nelson's Expository Dictionary of the Old Testament*, 172.

references about salt in the two other synoptic Gospels. Each seems to come at different times in his ministry.

In Matthew, the reference to salt came early on as Jesus was teaching on the western shores of the Sea of Galilee. It followed the celebrated Beatitudes in the Sermon on the Mount. His fame was already widespread, so perhaps for more privacy upon "seeing the crowds, he went up on a hill" where "he sat down and was joined by his disciples," whom he taught. "You are the salt of the earth. But what good is salt if it has lost its flavor? Can you make it salty again?" he asked. "It will be thrown out and trampled underfoot as worthless" (Matt. 5:13 NLT).

In Mark, the salt reference was again directed to the disciples and followed shortly after the Transfiguration, in northern Galilee (Mark 9).

Luke placed the salt metaphor as part of what has been called his "travel log." Luke's reference to salt is often not included in charts that synchronize the sometimes-conflicting timelines of the Gospels, but it apparently came in the fall of the year as Jesus was making his way south through Perea, on his way to Jerusalem for the Feast of Tabernacles. He spoke to the disciples on that occasion about the three-part covenant of discipleship, including "counting the cost" of their lifetime commitments to the Kingdom of God (Luke 14:28–35).

The first sentences of the language on salt in both Mark and Luke are identical: "Salt is good for seasoning. But if it loses its flavor, how do you make it salty again?" Jesus asked the disciples. He finished the passage in Mark: "You must have the qualities of salt among yourselves [speaking only to the disciples] and live in peace with each other" (Mark 9:50 NLT). And Luke recorded: "Flavorless salt is good neither for the soil nor for the manure pile. It is thrown away. Anyone with ears to hear should listen and understand!" (Luke 14:35 NLT).

Jesus's three cautions on salt may have come at different times in his ministry, or might all be altered retellings of the same event. Whatever it may be is of little consequence to the several questions we have asked ourselves concerning these references to salt. First, was our understanding correct that Jesus was speaking to his disciples only, or was he teaching a broader audience referred to as the "multitudes," who shadowed him everywhere he went? We concluded that it is reasonable to presume that in each case the instruction about salt was for a more fully committed group of men and women. The larger crowds were, by contrast, mixed masses of people consisting of more mildly interested followers as well as the simply curious. They would also have been laced with Pharisees, Herodians, and others—even Romans who came to monitor the man who represented such an ominous challenge to the status quo.

Second, if we are correct that Jesus spoke about salt only to an intimate few, what was it about the metaphor—disciples as "the salt of the earth"—that was so impactful for those who had "ears to hear" (Luke 14:35)? And third (actually third through sixth), why then do we still use the salt-of-the-earth metaphor to describe someone who is somehow more trustworthy, steadfast, and straightforward than most, even in a post-enlightenment environment? Why do some jokingly say that "spilling salt" means bad luck? Or why do we laugh as if to say we know it is purely outdated superstition as we toss a pinch of salt over our shoulders to ward off more bad luck? Why, to this day, might we very occasionally hear about the custom of bringing "good luck" to a new home by scattering a pinch of salt on the floor of every room?

We found answers to questions two through six and more in a book by Mark Kurlansky. He is an American journalist who has written entire volumes on the history of single-item topics such as oysters, cod, and paper. In 2002, he published *Salt: A World History.* What we learned added immeasurably to our understanding of Jesus and the metaphor of salt.

The word *salt* is the root word of *salvation.* The Greeks called it "divine" (*theion*).[6] The Egyptians, Greeks, and Romans included salt in their sacrifices and offerings and invoked the blessing of the gods with libations of salt and water.[7] Because of its value—both symbolic and economic—in the ancient world, salt came to represent the serious nature of any legal agreement. Israel's immutable bargain with God was known as a "salt covenant."[8] The Book of Numbers recounts that the Lord gave Aaron, his sons, and his daughters, "a statute for ever: . . . a covenant of *salt* for ever before the Lord unto thee and to thy seed with thee" (Num. 18:19 KJV; emphasis added). Even today, at the beginning of the Jewish Sabbath, bread is dipped in salt to remind Jews of their covenant between God and his people.[9]

For any number of reasons, then, salt was a fitting metaphor for discipleship in the ancient world. It represented the most valuable promised blessings of a covenant God made with his chosen people. In context, salt served four principle purposes in the synoptic Gospels related to the role a discipleship.

---

6. William Barclay, *The New Daily Study Bible: The Gospel of Matthew,* 119.
7. Ibid.
8. Mark Kurlansky, *Salt: A World History,* 117.
9. Ibid.

First, salt was a symbol for purity. The Romans said salt was the purest substance on earth because it came from the "purest of all things, the sun and the sea."[10] Like salt, Jesus's disciples were to be examples of purity—virtuous, honest, and wholesome in speech and in deed. Or as the Apostle James put it, disciples were to keep themselves "unspotted from the world" or to "refuse to let the world corrupt" them (James 1:27 KJV, NLT). Through their example, disciples bound by the salt covenant became a "cleansing antiseptic in any society in which they happened to be: they must be the ones who by their presence defeated corruption and made it easier for others to be good."[11]

Second, salt was used as a preservative to keep meat and other perishable goods from putrefying. Kurlansky quotes the Roman historian Plutarch, who said that meat is a dead carcass and will decay. But salt preserves it and "keeps it fresh, and is therefore like a new soul inserted into a dead body."[12] In the same way that salt preserves meat, covenant disciples *preserved* the Christian community by embracing, to quote the Apostle Paul, all that is "true, honorable, right, pure, lovely, and admirable" (Philip. 4:8 NLT).

Third, in Jesus's day, people believed evil spirits caused disease. Salt was believed to be a protection from harm. Both Jews and Muslims believed that salt was an antidote to evil. It was a "well-known fact" that evil spirits "detest salt."[13] In Matthew's account of the calling of the Twelve Apostles, Jesus gave them authority over evil spirits, and they were expected to banish evil influences associated with the underworld. In this apostolic charge, Jesus "called unto him his twelve disciples, [and] he gave them power against unclean spirits, to cast them out" (Matt. 10:1 KJV).

Fourth, salt was used in the ancient world, as well as in today's kitchens, to accentuate flavor in food. Food without salt can be bland. True disciples were to a Christian community what salt was to taste. They were to bring out the best in each other and the church. They were to serve and protect and bring joy to one another.

"Emperor and Galilean," by nineteenth-century Norwegian playwright Henrik Ibsen, is in part a drama about the psychological conflict Ibsen imagined the fourth-century Roman emperor Julian suffered as a Christian who gradually reverts to the paganism of his ancestors. In Act

---

10. Barclay, *The Gospel of Matthew*, 119.
11. Ibid., 120.
12. Ibid.
13. Kurlansky, *Salt*, 117.

V, Julian delivers a meditation on his abandonment of the church and his Christian friends; it offers a valuable contradiction to the meaning of Jesus's metaphor on the value of salt and the salt covenant—especially when we understand Jesus's symbolism in the context of the ancient world. Julian rationalizes that Christians are ugly and boring. They live lives severed from a noble purpose or service to others, and they

> brood their lives away, unspurred by ambition; the sun shines for them, but they do not see it; the earth offers them its fullness, and they desire it not; all their desire is to renounce and to suffer that they may come to die."[14]

For Jesus, nothing could be further from the truth. Disciples were to be joyful, living proof that Christianity was not a dour religion that rejected the good things of mortality. Christians believed that the earth was created by God to bless mankind. At the conclusion of the days of creation, "God looked over all he had made, and he saw that it was very good!" (Gen. 1:31 NLT). The bounties of the earth were essential gifts from God, including salt. And like salt, disciples were to enhance the joy of life's abundance by nourishing and serving others.

Finally, in the context of the twenty-first century, the salt metaphor for discipleship may be even more potent than it was in Jesus's time. We now have scientific understanding of how salt sustains life itself. Salt is medically essential for digestion and respiration. Without it, the body cannot transport nutrients or oxygen, transmit nerve impulses, or move muscles.[15] Without it, a person experiences headaches, weakness, lightheadedness, and nausea, and if deprived of it long enough, succumbs to death. And so it is with our commitment to Jesus's "Good News." Like salt, Jesus's modern covenant disciples are to teach all God's children how to make choices that will sustain themselves and avoid spiritual death.

In the end, the distinctive characteristic of any true disciple is a willingness to subjugate individual will in order to be the servant of all. "He that hath my commandments, and keepeth them, he it is that loveth me" and the Father with "all [his] heart, and with all [his] soul, and with all [his] mind" (John 14:21 KJV; D&C 41:5; Matt. 22:37 KJV).

Jesus said this was the first and greatest commandment. But a second is *equally important*: "Love your neighbor as yourself" (Matt. 22:39 NLT). Jesus then pointed out that all other commandments were "based on these two" (Matt. 22:40 NLT). Therefore, the mark of a salt-covenant disciple

---

14. Henrik Ibsen, "Emperor and Galilean," loc. 2103–9, ebook.
15. Kurlansky, *Salt,* 104.

is love expressed by a willingness to minister to and bear the burdens of others. "By this shall all men know that ye are my disciples, if ye have love one to another" (John 13:35 KJV).

As we studied and thought about the ancient covenant of salt, we were reminded of contemporary covenants of commitment that call on us who enter into them to agree to "bear one another's burdens" (Mosiah 18:8), to obey the commandments, to live as Jesus asked us to live in the Gospels, to be chaste, to willingly sacrifice our lives for the sake of the Kingdom of God on earth, and to consecrate everything we might be blessed with in this life to that Kingdom.

Jesus returned to the theme of discipleship after the resurrection when he recommitted his disciples one morning on the shores of the Sea of Galilee. They had gone fishing overnight. At dawn, Peter, Thomas, Nathaniel, and two others saw someone on the beach but could not tell who it was. Jesus called out, "Friends, have you caught any fish?" "No," they replied (John 21:5 NLT). Then he told them to throw out their nets on the other side of the boat. They did and caught so many fish that they "couldn't draw in the net" (John 21:6 NLT). Suddenly, Peter recognized Jesus, "jumped into the water, and swam ashore" (John 21:7 NLT). The other disciples soon followed in the boat.

As Jesus and his band of disciples ate breakfast on the beach by dawn's light, he challenged Peter with the same challenge he poses to all who profess to follow him. Jesus asked, "'Simon, . . . do you love me?' 'Yes, Lord . . . you know I love you,'" was the first reply. "Then feed my lambs," Jesus told him. Jesus repeated the question: "'Simon . . . do you love me?' 'Yes, Lord, . . . you know I love you.'" So that there would be no mistaking what Jesus meant, he responded again. "*Then take care of my sheep*," And a third time he asked him, "'Simon, . . . do you love me?' Peter was grieved that Jesus asked the question a third time. He said, 'Lord, you know everything. You know I love you.' Jesus said, 'Then feed my sheep'" (John 21:15–17 NLT; emphasis added).

In a very real way, Jesus's admonition to love and serve others controverts the "performance principle" at work in our modern Western culture. All of our lives we busily work to show why and how we are better than our competition. In fact, we are predisposed to live our religion in the same way we work to become successful in our culture: What can I do to better myself? What do I have to do to be the best by comparison to others? How many hours must I work to show that I am committed? How can I make the most money? How should I dress to fit in and impress other people? What kind of car do I need to drive to look successful?

Marcus Borg describes the stress and anxiety many of us feel as a result of such endless striving to be successful. He says our culture is centered on what he calls the three A's: *appearance, affluence,* and *achievement.* He writes, "All of us, at least in the first half of our lives, are to a large extent driven by these values" and we "become blind to much else as well as burdened and preoccupied as to how we measure up to those values."[16] When we live this way, "we are profoundly preoccupied with ourselves—how well we are doing."[17]

Conventional wisdom and social media constantly tell us what we need to do to be successful. These ideas are so deeply engrained in many of us that it can be difficult to break free enough to see life from Jesus's vantage point. That is because the so-called truths of our day constitute some of our "culture's most taken-for-granted notions about two things—what is real and how to live."[18] Born of a "covenant of [being] cool," selfish habits become part of us as we grow up, rarely if ever to be challenged.

But the road to discipleship or the covenant of salt is an invitation out of a life centered exclusively on the values of the world to one centered on others so that we see "things as they really are, and . . . really will be" (Jacob 4:13). It is understanding and living by Jesus's exquisite couplet: "He that findeth his life shall lose it: and he that loseth his life for my sake shall find it" (Matt. 10:39 KJV). Salt-like discipleship means acting on the recognition that we will find our greatest fulfillment when we are occupied with the needs of others.

We came to understand a little better what N. T. Wright observes—that what mattered to Jesus in the end was that his true disciples were "the kind of people through whom the kingdom will be launched on earth."[19] Being like Jesus meant that *each of us* qualified for heaven through serving his "lambs." Being like Jesus was about loving *others* and thereby transforming the earth, making it a Godlike place. It was what Jesus earnestly prayed for and by example asked us to pray for: "Thy kingdom come. Thy will be done *in earth,* as it is in heaven" (Matt. 6:10 KJV; emphasis added).

---

16. Marcus Borg, "Jesus and the Christian Life."

17. Ibid.

18. Ibid.

19. N. T. Wright, *The Day the Revolution Began: Reconsidering the Meaning of Jesus's Crucifixion,* 3559–67, Kindle.

The true disciple was to "demonstrate the way in which God's kingdom will actually be put into operation."[20]

> They are the people of the Beatitudes who will learn the way of forgiveness and reconciliation (Matt. 5:13–16), the way of purity (Matt. 5:27–32), the way of truthfulness (Matt. 5:33–37). And, in particular, as Chapter 5 [of Matthew] comes to its climax, they will learn the way of nonviolence, the way of love for enemies, and the way of prayer for persecutors (Matt. 5:38–48). They will turn the other cheek; they will go the second mile; they will allow someone to strip them of both shirt and cloak. And they will thereby demonstrate that they truly are [disciples] and children of their Father in heaven.[21]

God's ultimate rule on earth will come about because we, as true disciples of Jesus Christ, are the light of the world and the salt of the earth (Matt. 5:13, 14 KJV). We have covenanted. We have come away from this pilgrimage with a resolve to "have salt in yourselves, and have peace one with another" (Mark 9:50 KJV).

---

20. Ibid.
21. Ibid.

in search of the personality of jesus

By Dean Collinwood

In 2015, James and Judi McConkie, along with James's sister, Kathleen, and her husband, Dean Collinwood, served together as tour guides in Israel. Dean holds a PhD from the University of Chicago and has been a university professor, teaching sociology and cultural anthropology. Our tour group consisted of about forty-five people. Each morning before we went to see the sights, we spent an hour or two in class preparing our students for what we were about to see. Each of us had prepared in advance so that we could make a meaningful contribution when it was our turn. In one of those advance-planning meetings before we left for Israel, Dean shared with us an essay he had written on Jesus's personality. It provoked an energetic discussion among the four of us. Having posed the question "What is Jesus really like?" in these pages, we could not help but ask Dean if we could share his essay in this book. With his permission, we do.

Hollywood does not know what to do with Jesus. Because the Christian world reverences him as God or the Son of God or some other divine being, and because no one knows what divinity is like, the moviemakers are at a loss. As a result, they often default to portrayals of Jesus that are akin to a person in a trance. He is made to walk slowly, raise his hands and arms reverentially, and speak somberly as if he were experiencing a heavenly vision at all times.[1] He hardly seems human—and that, most likely, is the point.

But Jesus *was* human. He was born like every other human is born; he grew up with several brothers and sisters (and probably lots of other relatives); he worked for a living; and like everyone else, he grew hungry, felt pain, and became tired. For ordinary mortals, the daily interplay between our sociological and physiological realities produces our personalities. The

---

1. Some recent movies have taken the opposite approach, depicting Jesus as very much a human being with all the typical strengths and weaknesses of regular people.

question is, therefore, did that interplay apply to Jesus? Did Jesus have a personality?

Think of relatives, friends, and workmates; they have personalities. The combination of qualities and characteristics that form their distinctive *selves* is often casually mentioned: one person is said to be "optimistic," another is "introverted," and yet another is "lazy." But with Jesus, people usually recount what happened to him or what he did but not what he was *like*. Think of describing him after spending an afternoon with him. Would he have seemed pleasant or irritable, distant or engaged? Would he have been off-putting or easy to talk to? Would he have come across as a "red" or a "yellow"? Would he have seemed like a Type A or a laid-back person? Would he have appeared jovial or severe, superior or supportive?

Surely, Jesus had a personality, but few people think about it.[2] It is not that people or Hollywood are entirely to blame; the historical record is sparse, to say the least. And no one at the time could have asked Jesus to take something like a Meyers-Briggs Type Indicator psychometric assessment or an online Keirsey Temperament Sorter.[3] However, if one studies the Gospels carefully, it is possible to deduce at least a few qualities that might help illuminate part of Jesus's personality. The historical evidence does not allow anything close to a complete description, but it does support at least a few tentative guesses. First, however, some comments on the meaning of the term "personality."

Personality as Traits on a Continuum

Most people define personality by listing traits: so-and-so is honest, shy, hardworking, and so on. The implication is that there are equal but opposite traits: dishonest, gregarious, and lazy. This approach to personality comes from the work of Harvard psychologist Gordon Allport (1897–1961). His trait theory identified cardinal or dominant traits versus stylistic or weaker traits. He avoided the psychoanalyzing of Sigmund

---

2. One who has thought about it is seminarian John W. Miller, who argues that Jesus was not generic and formless but unique and "traited." See John W. Miller, *Jesus at Thirty: A Psychological and Historical Portrait.*

3. For insight into contemporary empirical assessment tools, see the work of Cambridge psychologist Peter J. Rentfrow et al, "Divided We Stand: Three Psychological Regions of the United States and their Political, Economic, Social, and Health Correlates,"996–1012.

Freud in favor of identifying the current context or immediate experiences of a person in order to determine personality.[4]

Over the decades since Allport's work, psychologists have settled on a handful of dichotomous traits that they believe successfully describe most people. Most people, they say, are either open or closed to new experiences, conscientious or irresponsible, extraverted or introverted, agreeable or disagreeable, and neurotic or stable.[5] Of course, there are many other dual traits.

That is how this essay is structured—around binary or ideal-type categories; Jesus is assumed to be this or that, one or the other way. In reality, of course, people's personalities do not congregate at polar opposite points; rather, they fall somewhere along a continuum from honest to dishonest, from shy to gregarious, from hardworking to lazy. Given the inadequacies of the historical record, however, it is impossible to say that Jesus was an eight or nine on an introversion scale or a six or seven on a confidence scale. The best we can suggest is that Jesus may have had a greater tendency toward one type of attitudinal position than another; we cannot say how intense that propensity was.

Certain traits often capture people's attention, and those are what end up in the historical record. Or, just as often, a trait is unintentionally implied by the recorder of a narrative. When studying a person who lived two thousand years ago, we have no alternative but to rely on the written record, however sparse and haphazard it may be. We must rely on the preferences, implications, and biases of the writers who watched Jesus live his life.[6]

Personality as a Tendency

In normal circumstances, it is assumed that people act in ways consistent with others' image of them. That is, there is an expected permanency or stability to personality. Certain life-changing events, such as a mental breakdown or post-traumatic stress, may alter the anticipated behavior, but in the absence of such trauma, people's behavior is expected to be fairly

---

4. See Gordon W. Allport, *Personality: A Psychological Interpretation.*

5. As applied to Jesus, see James R. Beck, *Jesus and Personality Theory: Exploring the Five-Factor Model.*

6. Bias clearly affects those who attempt to describe Jesus's personality today. As one of many examples, J. C. O'Neill openly admits that his purpose in describing Jesus was "to defend the truth of the doctrines of the Trinity and the Incarnation." J. C. O'Neill, *Who Did Jesus Think He Was?* 3.

predictable, assuming their personalities have been "pegged" correctly in the first place. But, in reality, people do not always behave as expected; personality means a *tendency* to act in certain ways. A few instances of inconsistent behavior can be expected and should not undermine our image of a person's personality as long as the behavior matches what we expect most of the time.

Also, some traits are considered to be dominant, or "cardinal," as Allport labeled them, while others are simply "stylistic," appearing less frequently or only in certain, unusual, or unique circumstances. Where Jesus is concerned, we must understand at the outset that the historical record is so incomplete that deciphering which are dominant and which are nondominant traits is simply impossible. Multiple occurrences in the record of a behavior-trait episode do not imply that the trait in question is dominant. What we have to work with is what the Gospel writers reported, not necessarily what was most important.

Keeping all these limitations and disclaimers in mind, we now cautiously proceed to sketch out seven possible personality traits of Jesus as found in the Gospels. Accompanying and serving as "proof text" for each likely personality trait are stories, contextual summaries, or quotations from various Bible translations. These proof texts are labeled "evidence." In brackets are alternative translations, sometimes inconsistent or even contradictory, of the key words or phrases. The initial quotations as well as the bracketed translations come from the King James Bible, the New International Version, the New Revised Standard Version, the Young's Literal Translation, and some twenty other translations of the Bible. Analysis follows at the end of each trait section.

Compassionate or Cold?

The Gospels clearly document Jesus's acceptance and defense of the poor, of women, and of other marginalized people. But was that part of his personality? Did he *feel* for the poor? Were his statements on behalf of the poor just political, or were they emotional, from the heart? If Jesus grew up poor, on the edge of destitution, he may have gained his compassion from his own difficult life experiences.[7] If he was somewhat more fortunate than others in his village, he might have sensed the opportunity

---

7. John Dominic Crossan, *Jesus: A Revolutionary Biography*, New York: HarperCollins Publishers, 1994, 25.

to use his slightly advanced status to help others. Evidence that Jesus was compassionate and empathetic comes from Mark, Luke, and John.

Evidence: "A leper came to him, imploring him, and kneeling said to him, 'If you will, you can make me clean.' Moved with pity [or compassion, or feeling indignant, or sorry for him], he stretched out his hand and touched him and said to him, 'I will [or I want to, or I am willing]; be clean'" (Mark 1:40–41).

Evidence: "In those days the multitude being very great, and not having what they may eat, Jesus having called near his disciples, saith to them, 'I have compassion upon [I share the suffering of] the multitude, because now three days they do continue with me, and they have not what they may eat; and if I shall let them away fasting [or send them home hungry] to their home, they will faint [or they will collapse] in the way, for certain of them are come from far'" (Mark 8:1–3).

Evidence: "Having come forth, Jesus saw a great multitude, and was moved with compassion on them [or was very sorry for them] that they were as sheep not having a shepherd [or beaten down and helpless], and he began to teach many things" (Mark 6:34).

Evidence: In Nain, Jesus saw a dead man being carried out of town. He had been his mother's only son, and she also was a widow. "And the Lord having seen her, was moved with compassion [or had compassion, or his heart overflowed with compassion, or his heart went out to her] towards her, and said to her, 'Be not weeping [or Don't cry].'" He then brought the man back to life and "gave him [or gave him back, or delivered him] to his mother" (Luke 7:13–15).

Evidence: Jesus went to Bethany because Mary's brother, Lazarus, had died, and he was a friend of the family. A bereaved Mary went out to meet him as he approached the village. "When Jesus saw her weeping, and the Jews who came with her also weeping, he was greatly disturbed in spirit and deeply moved [or groaned in the spirit and was troubled, or a deep anger welled up within him and he was deeply troubled]. . . . Jesus began to weep" (John 11:33–35).

Analysis: From these and other passages not referenced, one can say with reasonable confidence that Jesus possessed the capacity to feel the pain and suffering of others. He was not like narcissists, whose viewpoints are limited to their own needs and whose thoughts center only on their own creature comforts. Rather, Jesus felt the emotions of others, and he reacted to them, crying when they cried, feeling sorrow when they felt sorrow. The evidence also suggests that he was not only empathic in his heart, but that he also acted on his empathy, willingly alleviating the sorrow, pain, and hunger of others. His was active empathy. So, was Jesus compassionate or cold?

Driven or Laid Back?

Was Jesus hardworking or relaxed about life? Did he have a serious, driven, goal-directed, Type A personality, or the opposite? Jesus's work as an adult was that of a teacher—an itinerant teacher. Did he take that work seriously? Some people who are innately laid back sometimes show temporary excitement about specific projects and work enthusiastically at them, but only for a while. Was Jesus that way, or was he naturally and persistently a hardworking person who enjoyed work over play? Luke, Mark, and Matthew provide an answer to the question.

Evidence: When Jesus was in Jerusalem, probably for his bar mitzvah at around age twelve, he wanted to stay in the temple listening to the elders and asking them questions. This seemed more interesting to him than the excitement of a trip home with his parents. Many boys would have preferred to be out and about, playing games, riding donkeys, or doing other *action* things, but not Jesus. "After three days they found him in the temple courts, sitting among [or sitting amidst] the teachers, listening to them and asking them questions [or both hearing them and questioning them]" (Luke 2:45–47).

Evidence: As an adult, Jesus liked to start his workdays early in the morning; he also sometimes continued working late into the night. He started his day with prayer. "The next morning Jesus got up long before daylight [or while it was still dark, or rising up a great while before day]. He went out to a place by himself [or a deserted place, or a solitary place]. There he talked with God [or prayed]" (Mark 1:35).

He went to the temple early to teach. "Early in the morning all the people came to hear him in the temple" (Luke 21:38). "Early the next morning [or at dawn] he came again to the temple. All the people came to him [or rose early in the morning to hear him]. He sat down and taught them [or gave them a lesson on a Torah topic]" (John 8:2). "Jesus taught in the temple every day. But at night he went out and stayed on the hill called the Mount of Olives. And all the people would get up early in the morning to listen to him in the temple" (Luke 21:37–38). "About that time Jesus went out of the city on the hill to talk with God. He talked with God all night" (Luke 6:12).

Sometimes, he apparently was on the road even before having breakfast. "In the morning when they were on the way out of Bethany, Jesus was hungry" (Mark 11:12). He did some very important work in the morning. "In the morning [or at daybreak] he called his disciples to him. He chose twelve of them and called them apostles [or special messengers]" (Luke 6:13). "When it was almost morning [or early in the morning or shortly before dawn or the fourth watch of the night—3:00 a.m. to 6:00 a.m.], Jesus came to the disciples. He was walking on the water. He was going to pass by them" (Mark 6:48).

Evidence: "Jesus went around to all the cities and towns [or going up and down all the cities and villages]. He taught people in their meetinghouses [or synagogues] and told them the good news of the kingdom of heaven [or proclaimed the good news of the reign]. He healed all the sick and weak people" (Matt. 9:35). "Jesus went out again by the seaside. Many people came to him. So he taught them" (Mark 2:13). "Jesus then left that place and went into the region of Judea and across the Jordan. Again, crowds of people came to him, and as was his custom [or as he always did], he taught them" (Mark 10:1).

There is no indication that Jesus ever spent afternoons at the theater or arena (popular things to do under both Greek and Roman rule), relaxed on weekends, or took a vacation. "They went to the town of Capernaum. As soon as it was the Sabbath day [or immediately or straightway], Jesus went into their meeting house [or synagogue] and taught the people" (Mark 1:21). Note that this would have been about 6:00 p.m. on a Friday night. Note also that he apparently did this each week, for some of the translations say "Sabbath days," not just "day." Moreover, rather than delivering a one-hour lecture the way college professors or public guest speakers do, he sometimes taught the people continuously for several days at a time. "Jesus called his disciples to him. He said, 'I share the suffering of the people [or I have compassion on the multitude]. They have been with me for three days [or they continue with me] and they have nothing to eat'" (Matt. 15:32).

Did Jesus ever have fun? He went to dinners as an invited guest, and we know he attended a wedding feast once. But at these events, he seemed to maintain a serious, sometimes combative tone, as we will see below. Apparently, he enjoyed the company of children. But note, the record does not say that he *played* with them; rather, it says that he "blessed" them. So, even with children, he seemed to be about his business. "And he took the children in his arms, placed [or laid or put] his hands on them and blessed them" (Mark 10:16). Pronouncing a Jewish blessing, or *bracha*, was different than just patting a child on the head and saying, "You're a good child." Rather, it was a formal way of giving thanks to God, similar to saying the blessing or saying grace before a meal, and it usually began with the words, "Blessed are you, Lord our God." At the end, those hearing the blessing were expected to say "amen." In other words, it was serious, ritualized business.

Jesus apparently did not like to stop working and had to be begged to stop, even when the day was almost done. "They came near the village to which they were going. It looked as if he was going on further [or acted as though he wanted to go farther]. But they begged him not to go further. They said, 'Stay with us. It will soon be night [or it is toward evening]. The day is almost finished.' So he went in to stay with them" (Luke 24:28–29).[8] After Jesus fed the five thousand men who came to hear him, he continued to talk with them even after he sent his disciples on ahead. After he bid his farewell, he did not stop working but continued his mission by climbing up a hill to pray. "Then Jesus said to the disciples, 'You get into the boat right away and go over to Bethsaida. I will send the people away.' When he had sent the people away [or led the multitude away, or after saying farewell], he went up on the hill [or he went away to the mountain, or he went up a mountainside] to talk with God" (Mark 6:45–46).

Evidence: Jesus described his own goal-driven, dutiful orientation toward work. "There is one who has sent me. I must do his work while it is still daylight [or it behoveth me; in other words, I have a duty or responsibility to be working the works of him who sent me]. Night is coming. Then it will be too dark to work" (John 9:4). He also bemoaned the fact that there were too few laborers compared to the amount of the harvest to be taken in. "The harvest is much, but there are not many people to gather it [or the laborers are few]. So talk to the Lord of this harvest and ask him to send out people to his harvest" (Luke 10:2).

Analysis: The record is strong that Jesus liked to work. He was a man with a mission. He liked to get up early, work all day, and then either continue working into the night or go away to pray, sometimes all night. He often slept outside on the ground (think Garden of Gethsemane) rather than in a comfortable bed, yet he was up early to resume his business. As we have seen, this serious approach to life was apparently with him since his youth. It is possible that it was a part of his core personality, not just a stylistic or temporary enthusiasm. So, was Jesus hardworking or laid back? Was he driven by internal goals, or did he prefer to relax and smell the roses?

---

8. This and a few other episodes referenced in this chapter are post-resurrection events.

Temperate or Quick to Anger?

Was Jesus always measured in his comments to others or did he display behavior that observers would have defined as "anger"?

Evidence: Jesus went to the synagogue in Capernaum and started to heal a man who had a withered hand. But those Jews who were of the Pharisaic school of Judaism "watched him to see whether he would cure him on the Sabbath, so that they might accuse him." Although the Pharisees just watched and said nothing, Jesus "looked around at them with anger [or with wrath, or Jesus was angry as he looked at them]; he was grieved [or deeply distressed or sad, feeling both anger and sympathy for them at the stoniness of their hearts; or very upset, deeply disturbed, furious, deeply hurt, or indignant] at their hardness of heart" (Mark 3:1–5).

Evidence: "People were bringing little children to him in order that he might touch them; and the disciples spoke sternly to them. But when Jesus saw this, he was indignant [or greatly displeased or angry; or grew angry or much displeased; or became irritated, upset, or irate; or was moved with indignation]" (Mark 10:13–14).

Evidence: "Then they came to Jerusalem. And he entered the temple and began to drive out [or cast out, throw out, cast forth, or send out] those who were selling and those who were buying in the temple, and he overturned [or overthrew, turned upside down, upset, kicked over, knocked over, or pushed over] the tables of the money changers and the seats of those who sold doves; and he would not allow [or stopped everyone, would not let, refused to let, suffered not, would not permit, or did not let] anyone to carry anything through the temple" (Mark 11:15–16).

John describes the temple scene this way: "Having made a whip [or a scourge, or a whip out of ropes] of small cords, he put all forth out of the temple [or drove all from the temple courts], also the sheep, and the oxen; and of the money-changers he poured out [or scattered, spilled left and right, scattered over the floor, or sent in all directions] the coins, and the tables he overthrew" (John 2:15).

Analysis: It appears that Jesus could show quick anger at a range of people. In the Capernaum synagogue episode, he displayed anger at his *challengers* even though they had remained silent. In the children episode, he expressed indignation or anger at his *closest supporters,* the disciples, when they did something he did not like. And in the temple at Jerusalem, he displayed anger against *strangers,* violently disrupting commerce, overturning tables and chairs, and driving out not just the animals but also the people with a whip he himself had made. How long did it take him to find the materials and make the whip? While making it, did he become angrier—angry enough to inflict violence on objects, animals, and people? Was this hot blood, or did he have malice aforethought? These questions are important because, Mark says, he had gone into the temple the night before this violent act and "had looked around at everything [or had looked round about upon all things], but it being late, he left, returning the next day" (Mark 11:11). So were his actions premeditated? Did he make the whip in advance or on the spot? Had he brooded all night about the temple situation?

These events are attested to in all four Gospels, and they do not paint Jesus in the best light, despite having been written by those who believed in him and were converts to his message. That such unfavorable episodes were recorded by his supporters makes the stories more reliable. In fact, in one instance early Christian scribes apparently altered a passage to remove evidence of this part of his personality. The earliest manuscripts of Mark 1:41 state that Jesus was "moved with anger" before healing the leper; however, later scribes likely felt uncomfortable with this description and altered it to read: "Moved with *compassion*, Jesus reached out and touched [the leper]." The narrative makes it clear why Jesus was angry. After instructing the healed man, "Don't tell anyone about this. . . [T]he man went and spread the word, proclaiming to everyone what had happened. As a result, large crowds soon surrounded Jesus, and he couldn't publicly enter a town anywhere" (Mark 1:44–45). This, however, does not mean that Jesus lacked compassion. Despite anticipating that healing the leper would make his mission to preach the Kingdom more difficult, he healed him nevertheless. For our purposes, we need to ask what these events tell us about Jesus's personality. Was he temperate and emotionally self-disciplined, or was he quick to anger?

Patient or Intolerant?

The length of Jesus's ministry is disputed. Some say it was less than a year. Most believe it was just under three years. During that time, it is clear that Jesus visited some villages several times, while calling upon other villages only once. Yet he expected people to believe him immediately. He also expected his apostles to understand him without his having to explain himself to them. When people did not believe him immediately, he cursed their towns, and when his apostles did not understand, he expressed exasperation at them.

Evidence: "Jesus began to speak against [or denounce, rebuke, upbraid, or scold] the cities where he had done most of his miracles. The people there had not turned away from their sins. So he said, 'How terrible it will be for you, Korazin! How terrible for you, Bethsaida! . . . And what about you, Capernaum? Will you be lifted up to heaven? No! You will go down to the place of the dead [or be brought down to Hades or to hell]'" (Matt. 11:20–23).

He urged his apostles to take the same approach to conversion. If the inhabitants of a town did not immediately welcome them or believe their message, Jesus instructed them to reproach or curse the town. "Whenever you enter a town and they do not welcome you, go out into its streets [or broad places] and say, 'We wipe the dust [or even the very dust] of your town from our feet as a public announcement of your doom'" (Luke 10:10–11).

Evidence: Jesus's disciples failed in their attempt to drive an evil spirit out of a boy. Jesus, sounding frustrated at either the disciples or the community, complained out loud, "How long must I put up with you [or be with you and put up with you, or have patience with you]?" (Mark 9:19). Matthew tells the story this way: "You unbelieving [or perverted, faithless, or perverse] and evil people! How long do I have to stay with you [or must I be with you]? How long do I have to put up with you [or endure you]?" (Matt. 17:17). Then the boy's father implored Jesus to do something, if he could. "But if you can do anything, please take pity on us and help us" (Mark 9:22). Was Jesus annoyed at the tentative request, *"If you can do anything?"* ["What do you mean, 'If I can?'" Jesus asked. "Anything is possible if a person believes."] "Everything is possible to the man who believes [or if thou art able to believe]" (Mark 9:23). Is there a hint of impatience in Jesus's answer?

Evidence: The apostles frequently did not understand Jesus's parables and other teachings. As Luke said, "They did not grasp what was said" (Luke 18:34). However, when they asked him to explain the meaning to them, notwithstanding he was the teacher and they were the students or trainees, Jesus at times responded caustically. "Do you not understand this parable? Then how will you understand all the parables?" (Mark 4:13). In response to the apostles' inability to understand the meaning of the five loaves of bread, an exasperated Jesus said, "You of little faith, why are you talking about having no bread? Do you still not perceive? How could you fail to perceive that I was not speaking about bread?" (Matt. 16:8–11). Of the related incident of feeding four thousand, Jesus once again chastised his apostles: "Do you still not perceive or understand? Are your hearts hardened? Do you have eyes, and fail to see? Do you have ears, and fail to hear?" (Matt. 16:5–11).

Evidence: After Jesus had told a parable about clean and unclean food, Peter asked him to explain it. Jesus's reply was cutting: "Are you still so dull [or without understanding or intelligence, or don't you understand yet]? Don't you see [or do you not yet understand, perceive ye not, or understand ye not]?" (Matt. 15:16–17).

Analysis: People today who work as missionaries to non-believers know that it often takes years or decades to convert enough people to one's message to establish even a small congregation of believers. It takes years to build faith and faith communities. Yet Jesus seemed to expect people to see a few of his miracles, listen to him for a few hours or days, and then fully understand him or at least quickly change their worldviews or religious practices. His expectations seem unrealistic in light of ordinary human behavior.

Clearly, Jesus pushed his disciples to become more discerning, to think symbolically rather than concretely, to not be so "dull." Perhaps his answers were not offensive to the apostles in the culture in which they lived. Maybe that kind of tough love is what students of a rabbi were expected to endure in that day, especially from a teacher whom they believed had their best interests at heart. Jesus giving pet names to Simon as "the rock" and to James and John as "sons of thunder" sheds light on his ability to see the irony in things, and it shows a good-natured, even familial intimacy with those around him. Yet his impatience with his apostles cannot be gainsaid.

What about other followers or general audiences? Is it possible that those who did not immediately grasp the meaning of his teachings received his reaction as impatient rather than uplifting? Was it his personality to be short-tempered with slow learners? Did he come across as superior and holier than thou? Certainly, the Jewish leaders thought so; what about others? Was Jesus patient or intolerant?

Diplomatic or Acerbic?

Was Jesus pragmatic and reserved to avoid controversy or did he freely express his thoughts—even if they may have been construed as caustic or offensive? The analysis of this next possible trait is implied in the foregoing, but it deserves its own category because of Jesus's role as a public figure.

Evidence: Jesus was once invited to be the dinner guest of a Pharisee. After taking his place at the table but not ritually washing his hands before eating (which surprised and probably annoyed the host), he began to attack Pharisees in general. "Now you Pharisees clean the outside of the cup and of the dish, but inside you are full of greed [or extortion, rapine, violence, or robbery; or you are maggoty] and wickedness [or evil, or iniquity]. You fools [or foolish, or unthinking people]!" Then Jesus, becoming more energized in his condemnation of Pharisees in general (remember that he is a dinner guest at a Pharisee's house), said, "Woe to you [or how horrible, or how terrible] Pharisees! For you love to have the seat of honor in the synagogues. . . . Woe to you" (Luke 11:37–44).

When oral comments are written down, much of the richness of live speech is lost—the raising of an eyebrow, the inflection of the voice, the twinkle in the eye. Therefore, it is often difficult for readers to know if a speaker was talking seriously or in jest, with irony or with condescension. Without these unrecorded clues, it is often difficult to know the impact of speech on one's listeners. But, fortunately, in this case, we know: The other guests at dinner were insulted by what Jesus said, because the record shows that one of the lawyers, that is, an expert in the Torah, said to him, "Teacher, when you say these things, you insult us [or reproach us] too" (Luke 11:45). Jesus was not deterred; he did not apologize or temper his words. Instead, he attacked the lawyers too: "Woe also to you lawyers! For you load people with burdens hard to bear, [or burdens grievous to be borne] and you yourselves do not lift a finger to ease them. Woe to you! For you build the tombs of the prophets whom your ancestors killed. . . . Woe to you lawyers! For you have taken away the key of knowledge; you did not enter yourselves, and you hindered those who were entering" (Luke 11:46–47, 52).

His remarks provoked acrimonious and antagonistic responses from his fellow guests, for when they went outside (where they were no longer constrained by the rules of guest etiquette) at the end of dinner, "the scribes and the Pharisees began to be very hostile toward him [or strongly opposed or assailed him, or they were angered, or they opposed him bitterly or violently] and to provoke him [or to disparage his words]" (Luke 11:53). In other words, the argumentative and accusatory demeanor he had displayed during the dinner continued in the form of bellicose hostility toward him afterward.

Evidence: Jesus, speaking to a general audience as well as to his disciples, made a long series of attacks on the scribes and Pharisees. He called them "fools," "hypocrites," "sons of hell," and "blind guides." Here are two excerpts from his speech: "Woe to you [or a curse on you, you are hopeless, you are horrible or terrible], scribes and Pharisees, hypocrites [or frauds]! For you are like whitewashed tombs which indeed appear beautiful outwardly, but inside are full of dead men's bones and all uncleanness [or filth or rottenness]" (Matt. 23:27). "Woe to you, scribes and Pharisees, hypocrites! For you travel land and sea to win one proselyte, and when he is won, you make him twice as much a son of hell [or child of hell] as yourselves" (Matt. 23:15).

This kind of blunt talk may have been characteristic of rural Galileans (the birthplace of many violent rebels against Roman rule), just as some New Yorkers today are perceived as being in-your-face when they talk. Perhaps such language was considered *de rigueur* for prophets and iconoclasts, because Jesus's ascetic cousin, John the Baptizer, used equally acerbic language when addressing the multitudes who came to him to be baptized. "You brood of [or children of] vipers [or poisonous snakes], how can you who are evil [or being evil] say anything good? For out of the overflow [or abundance] of the heart, the mouth speaks" (Matt. 12:34).

Evidence: A man wanted to follow Jesus, but his father had just died, and he needed to take care of the burial. Instead of soothingly commiserating with the man, Jesus bluntly said to him, "Follow me, and let the dead [or spiritually dead ones] bury their own dead" (Matt. 8:22).

Evidence: In a dispute with his opponents, Jesus was asked, "Who are you?" Jesus said to them, "Why do I speak to you at all? [or Why should I even speak to you at all?]. I have much to say about you and much to condemn [or There is a lot more I could say to condemn you]" (John 8:25–26).

Analysis: Jesus is recorded as having a very sharp tongue. Indeed, he appears to have enjoyed baiting certain people and intentionally provoking anger and rejection. His comments were iconoclastic and provocative. He was in-your-face if you were a Pharisee or a Sadducee. Just *being* a Pharisee or Sadducee—even without saying anything, as in the instance of Jesus in the synagogue in Capernaum—was enough to ignite Jesus's fiery tongue. However, it is also clear from the record that Jesus had the loyalty of thousands of ordinary followers, people who were willing to spend several days at a time listening to him. It is unlikely they would have remained in his camp had he always been acerbic and aggressive. He must have often spoken salutary words of peace and comfort, as in the Sermon on the Mount. So, was Jesus diplomatic or acerbic? Was he situationally diplomatic and situationally acerbic? Could people count on the manner with which Jesus would talk to them?

Extrovert or Introvert?

During his ministry, Jesus was a public person. Crowds numbering in the hundreds or thousands followed him wherever he went. People stood outside the door when he tried to eat dinner, and they followed after him in boats when he tried to leave town. Did he enjoy the attention, or was it hard for him to cope with it? Was he energized or drained by his audiences? We do not know. But the record does show Jesus often retiring by himself to pray, sometimes for hours at a time.

Evidence: "The next morning Jesus went away to a place by himself" (Luke 4:42). "After he had dismissed them, he went up on a mountainside by himself to pray. When evening came, he was there alone" (Matt. 14:23). "But Jesus often withdrew to lonely places and prayed" [or He kept himself apart in the wilderness and prayed; or He repeatedly left the crowds, stealing away into the wilderness to pray; or He would often slip away to the wilderness and pray in seclusion]" (Luke 5:16).

As Jesus apparently saw it, private prayer was part of his mission, part of his work. Therefore, it is not certain that his retreat to private places to pray can be used as evidence of an introverted personality. Yet, during his youth and young adulthood, Jesus may have spent hours each day working with objects, maybe wood or stone. Perhaps he had become used to hours of solitary privacy or alone time while working as a craftsman. On the other hand, he was perhaps the oldest of a large family and must have been accustomed to regularly interacting with siblings and other family members.

We know that Jesus was extremely gifted in sharing stories, one-liners, and aphorisms. He must have accumulated an arsenal of such material in order to keep his audience's attention for hours or days at a time. Therefore, is it safe to assume that he had spent much time alone prior to his ministry in contemplation and mental planning?

Analysis: It is possible that Jesus belonged to a category of people that some psychologists call "pseudo-extroverts"—people who are skilled at public discourse and public presentation but at their core prefer solitude. Some actors who shine on stage retreat quickly to the privacy of their dressing rooms as soon as the performance ends and the curtain falls (and for such people, it would be a *performance*, not necessarily an expression of their cores selves) rather than linger to enjoy the adoration of their fans. When he performed a miraculous cure, Jesus often told people not to talk about it. Was this to avoid engendering more public scrutiny and attention? Is it possible that Jesus's mission drove him to become a public person but that his core self was more introverted? Was Jesus an extrovert or an introvert?

Confident or Insecure?

Jesus often found himself or placed himself in debates with the Pharisees or others, and the Gospels show him as so clever that his challengers almost always lose the arguments and end up being silenced or looking stupid. But the reality is that he did not always win debates. His debate challengers sometimes used his rhetorical tools against him and got the upper hand. When that happened, how did he respond, and will those responses give us insight into whether he was a confident or an insecure person?

Evidence: A Gentile woman asked Jesus to heal her daughter. But Jesus wanted to give his message only to the Jews, and so he declined to help her, explaining, "Let the children [or Jews] be fed first, for it not fair [or not good, or not meet, or not right] to take the children's food and throw it to the dogs [or little dogs]." Perhaps he thought he had silenced the woman, but she, cleverly using his metaphor, shot back, "Sir, even the dogs [or little dogs] under the table eat the children's crumbs." He had to agree; she had bested him at his own folksy metaphor, and so he relented, complimented her on her faith, and healed her daughter (Mark 7:26–29).

Is it possible that Jesus said what he said as a joke or with a twinkle in his eye? Maybe the dog metaphor was intended to be humorous. But the Matthew version of the story makes it clear that Jesus intentionally ignored the woman at first, even though she was crying out after him. He declared to her that he was sent only to the lost sheep of the house of Israel. Moreover, the term "little dogs" suggests condescension. There is no evidence of humor (some irony but not humor) in any story of Jesus in any of the Gospels. Even at social events, such as the wedding at Cana, where people might be expected to be in a festive mood, Jesus is portrayed as severe—seeming to rebuke his mother for asking him to perform a miracle before his time. Thus, based on contextual evidence, it is likely that Jesus used the dog metaphor seriously rather than humorously—but was bested by his female interlocutor.

Evidence: Two of Jesus's apostles, James and John, wanted (or at least their mother wanted) Jesus to promise that they could sit on his right hand and on his left hand when he attained his glory. Jesus tried to dissuade them by putting up what he apparently thought was an airtight case for "no." "Are you able to drink the cup that I drink, or be baptized with the baptism that I am baptized with?" he challenged. He must have assumed they would realize that they could not do those things and that that would end the matter. Instead, they retorted, "We are able." Jesus must have been surprised because he had to concede that they would, in fact, drink the same cup he would—be baptized just as he was and then be killed for the cause. So, having lost his rhetorical point, Jesus retreated to a different argument so that he would not have to grant them their wish. Your request "is not mine to grant," he argued. (Matt. 20:21–23). The episode seems similar to that of a parent trying to reason with a stubborn child; upon failing to convince the child, the parent resorts to "because I said so." Jesus did not grant their wish, so, in that sense, they lost, but he lost the debate point because they used his own argument against him and won, forcing him to resort to a second, rather weaker, argument to bring closure.

Analysis: It is not clear how Jesus felt about losing these mini-debates. Was he upset? Humiliated? Was his self-esteem wounded? The written evidence does not allow us to draw a firm conclusion, but the evidence from silence suggests that he took the losses in stride, that he did not get angry, withdraw, or go on the attack against those who bested him in verbal sparring. At least there is no record of his having reacted in these ways. In the case of the Gentile woman, he even complimented her for her faith. If he had felt the need to win at all costs, we might discover evidence of insecurity, but that does not seem to be the case based on the sparse record. So was Jesus gracious in defeat or defiant to the end? What does that tell us about his self-confidence? Was he confident or insecure?

This last question carries much baggage. As it turns out, Jesus may have been considered by Jewish detractors in his day to be the child of Mary's immorality or rape—in other words, an illegitimate child, a bastard. This claim was thrown at Jesus during his ministry and may have plagued him during his youth as well. When Jesus was in a dispute with the Pharisees, they asked him, "Who are you?" Whereupon Jesus went into a sharp discourse about God, Abraham, and so on, causing the men to become more and more agitated with him. Finally, they mocked him, saying, "We are not children of people who weren't married to each other" [or born of fornication or illegitimate children, or our ancestry isn't in question, or we were not born of sexual immorality, or we were not born out of wedlock, or we of whoredom have not been born]" (John 8:31–42).[9]

---

9. James F. McGrath argues that the Gospels do not support a claim that people in Jesus's day thought he was illegitimate. James F. McGrath, "Was Jesus Illegitimate? The Evidence of His Social Interactions."

One cannot imagine a more personal attack on one's sense of self. Yet, given this type of possible lifelong humiliation, it is a telling commentary about Jesus's inner strength that he was able to demonstrate great self-confidence at all times. He was frustrated that people did not accept his message, yet he always seemed confident about his own identity, never publicly questioning it. Was Jesus confident or insecure?

Comment on Somatotype

We have addressed a handful of possible personality traits of Jesus. We now turn to a slightly different component of, or contributor to, personality. Personality is often confounded, rightly or wrongly, with physical appearance. In different cultures at different times, certain facial or body types are associated with positive or negative personality traits. Studies show, for example, that people today are considered to be more likeable if their facial features are completely symmetrical; if they have fat, baby-like cheeks; or if their mouths turn up naturally in a smile while at rest.[10]

Such features, in turn, influence personality, as does one's overall appearance of health. If someone goes through life receiving positive responses from everyone because of a pleasant-looking face or because of robust health, those experiences will shape that person's personality and worldview. Therefore, knowing what Jesus looked like and how society would have evaluated his appearance would have provided helpful insights into his personality. Unfortunately, descriptions of Jesus's physical appearance are not found anywhere in the Gospels or in any other reliable source.[11]

However, there are a few logical assumptions we may safely make, one of which is that Jesus was probably a healthy and energetic person.

At the time Jesus was preaching, he apparently was in his early 30s and had likely spent his youth and early adulthood as a physical laborer or craftsman (a *tekton* in Greek), perhaps wielding heavy iron tools and carrying and positioning lumber or other materials. Like most people, he must have walked wherever he went. In Galilee, the pathways snake up and down many steep hills. He might have walked from his home in tiny

---

10. See, for example, Gillian Rhodes et al., "Facial Symmetry and the Perception of Beauty," 659–69, where facial symmetry was correlated with attractiveness.

11. Some Christians interpret Isaiah 53:2 to be a prophetic description of how Jesus would look during his mortal ministry. "My servant grew up in the Lord's presence like a tender green shoot, like a root in dry ground. There was nothing beautiful or majestic about his appearance, nothing to attract us to him" (NLT).

Nazareth to the boom town of Sepphoris, where construction workers were in demand—a distance of eight miles round-trip, with the return trip mostly uphill. Moreover, his town was located in the highlands, away from the malaria-infested locales of the coastal villages. Thus, unlike Paul the Apostle, who often alluded to some kind of personal handicap, there is no evidence of Jesus ever having been sickly or disabled in any way.

Consequently, it is logical to assume that Jesus was probably in good physical shape and could easily have presented an image of energy and vigor. For example, he might have bounded up the stairs to the temple at Jerusalem or the synagogue at Capernaum rather than becoming winded as he ascended—or slowly floating up the steps in a stupor or trance, as is sometimes depicted in movies. That he was not able to carry the crossbeam on the way to his crucifixion was probably not due to natural weakness but to his having been severely flogged, perhaps kept all night in a pit, and denied food.

We do not know how tall Jesus was or if he was taller or shorter than average. (The average male of his day was between five-foot-two and five-foot-six). Many Jewish men wore short beards, so perhaps he did as well, although the earliest depiction of him, a painting on a church in Syria, seems to show him beardless. The fashion for men in Roman Palestine (and in Galilee a region heavily influenced by Greek and Roman culture) was short hair, so perhaps he had short hair. The standard long-hair image of him came from a now strongly disputed claim that Jesus was a Nazarite ascetic like John the Baptist. The only human male hair ever found in an archeological investigation (a tomb near Jerusalem) from first century Israel was that of a man whose hair had been trimmed or cut evenly, was short to medium—three to four inches long—and reddish in color.[12]

Comment on Speech

Speaking style also figures prominently in people's personality profiles. With no audio recordings, we will never know how Jesus spoke. Did he speak quickly, tripping over words to get to his point, or did he speak slowly, enunciating every syllable? Was his voice volume low and soothing or loud and animated? Was his grammar prim and proper or sloppy?

It is frequently recorded that in the temple, Jesus "cried" out [or shouted, or spoke with a loud voice] (John 12:44). "It was the last and

---

12. James Tabor, "The Only Ancient Jewish Male Hair Ever Found."

most important day of the Feast. Jesus stood up and spoke in a loud voice" (John 7:37). When raising Lazarus, "Jesus called in a loud voice. He said, 'Lazarus, come out!'" (John 11:43). We know he spoke for days at a time, speaking while walking, speaking while sitting on a mountainside, speaking while standing or sitting in the temple, and speaking at dinners. It is likely that he adjusted his volume to the setting, but it is clear that he had the capacity to speak loudly and to cry out, and that he used that capacity frequently. We also know that the Galilean accent in which Jesus, Peter, and others of his inner circle spoke was mocked by the Jerusalem elites as hick talk or country slang. In some circles, Jesus's accent would have produced a negative reaction, regardless of what he said.

Conclusion

The record shows that Jesus's personality may have been characterized by at least the seven personality traits outlined above, although it is entirely possible that some of these traits represent exceptions to Jesus's core self, that they were stylistic or situational rather than core traits. Perhaps his cardinal traits were not even recorded for history. Some people think, for example, that his violent and aggressive behavior in the temple, or his condescending allusion to the Gentile woman as a little dog, are instances of atypical or marginal acts. Perhaps they were added to the original texts by those with axes to grind or a specific viewpoint to promote. No one has enough information to make a final decision about these matters. But the record, as presented, suggests that the temple behavior and the dog story were actual events, not later emendations or fabrications. They are both found in Mark, our earliest and most unlayered Gospel account, and they are consistent with other aspects of Jesus's personality, such as his undiplomatic comments toward his Pharisee dinner host and guests.

Recoiling at unflattering descriptions of Jesus likely springs from theological or personal preference. That is, for two thousand years, people have conjured up whatever kind of Jesus they needed at the moment to satisfy their emotional, political, ecclesiastical, or other agendas. His interpreted behavior has been used to justify militarism and genocide on the one hand, and love and compassion on the other. Thus, those who prefer to think of Jesus as an exclusively kind, loving, and supportive friend will likely find the in-your-face traits sketched out by the Gospel writers to be jarring. Others may even deploy the descriptions recorded in the Gospels to reject Jesus as a role model or Savior. While no one is ever completely free of bias, this present effort to identify Jesus's personality has been conducted without any theological or personal agenda.

In sum, from this reading of the Gospels, Jesus can be cautiously identified as possessing the following personality traits:

1. Jesus was compassionate and sensitive, able to feel the pain and sorrow of others, particularly the poor and marginalized, and he often acted quickly to alleviate their suffering.

2. Jesus was hardworking and mission driven. He worked long hours, and never deviated from the task at hand. He probably appeared to others to embrace his calling with energy, strength, and determination.

3. Jesus was quick to anger, particularly, but not exclusively, toward those who had transformed the Jewish religion from a community of refuge and love into an institution of rituals and regulations.

4. Jesus was impatient with people, including his closest allies, when they did not quickly believe him or understand him.

5. Jesus was intentionally but situationally acerbic and undiplomatic in many of his debates and conversations with those who opposed him. While he gathered many loyal followers from the masses with his engaging stories and parables, he alienated the community's leaders and others by unleashing upon them harsh, provocative, and demeaning denunciations.

6. Jesus may have been mildly introverted or pseudo-extroverted; that is, he may have preferred solitude but understood that his mission required him to engage in intensely public activity, which he did successfully for long periods before retreating for alone time.

7. Jesus was self-confident; he did not always win verbal debates, but when he lost, he seemed to do so graciously rather than defiantly, suggesting a strong sense of self-esteem. He could lose without taking it personally. He never publicly questioned his own identity or self worth.

Epilogue

As Providence would arrange it, just as we were preparing our thoughts to write the last few paragraphs of this book, we were asked to lead a tour of pilgrims to the Holy Land. The tour gave us one final opportunity to think about how we should bring this book to a close. It also provided a chance to review, during a compressed eleven-day period, the life of the Savior from his birth to his death and resurrection. The tour gave us a chance to consider Jesus in geographical and religious context. How was it that he, an obscure boy who grew up in the rather small and inconsequential town of Nazareth, with none of the accouterments of power, so profoundly influenced billions of followers down through the centuries?

On our trip together, away for the daily interruptions of life—family, work, students, clients, church, and even our weekly date to the movies—we realized, more than we ever had before, that for us and many others, nothing could diminish the importance of Jesus's life and teachings.

What our eleven-day experience meant to us on an individual level came on the last day of our trip in an unexpected way. We were scheduled to meet a guide at the entrance to a tranquil garden owned and administered by a Christian nondenominational charitable trust based in the United Kingdom. Known locally as simply "the Garden Tomb," the garden is a walled enclave outside the old city walls that surrounds a rock-cut tomb unearthed in 1867. Many Protestants consider it to be the site of the burial and resurrection of Jesus.

The guide assigned to be our escort at the Garden Tomb was Gord Reeve, a retired Baptist minister from British Columbia. When our group arrived, Gord explained to us that this lovely garden could very well be the location of the borrowed tomb belonging to Joseph of Arimathea. And if it was not the precise place, it is still a peaceful oasis in the midst of a noisy, dirty, and chaotic modern city that represents what that place must have been like.

It just so happened that this day was Gord's first opportunity to explain what possibly happened at this place. Something that changed the trajectory of the Christian movement and the course of history. Something, Gord said, that rejuvenated the movement that seemed to have died with Jesus on the cross. Something that invigorated the leaders to oppose violence, vengeance, and the spiritual narcissism of the world. Something that confirmed that love of neighbor would ultimately overcome selfishness, greed, and cruelty.

Gord closed his remarks only steps away from an empty tomb by referring to a conversation he previously had with a Jewish friend who told him about a traditional thanksgiving hymn in praise and adoration of what God has done. The hymn, called *Dayenu,* is part of the Jewish Passover celebration. Roughly translated, it means "It would have been enough" or "It would have sufficed." The word *day* in Hebrew means "enough," and *enu* is the first-person plural suffix meaning "to us." The song is over a thousand years old. It is about being grateful to God for all his gifts and blessings to Israel. Each verse gives thanks to God for a particular blessing and then ends with a refrain that means if this were all that the Lord God had ever done for us, it would have been enough; four lines give a sense of the whole:

> If He had brought us out of Egypt and had not carried out judgments
> against them—Dayenu, it would have been enough.
> If He had supplied our needs in the desert for forty years, and had not
> feed us the manna—Dayenu, it would have been enough.

Gord made the point, however, that in Christianity, the individual deeds of Jesus, taken alone, would not have been *Dayenu.* If Jesus had only given us his teachings, though superlative, they would not have been enough. If Jesus had only performed mighty miracles, although astounding, they would not have been enough. If Jesus had died on the cross in torment for us, it would not have been enough. If Jesus had been placed in a tomb and venerated over the years by thousands of pilgrims, it would not have been enough.

But what *is* enough is Jesus's transcendent revivification—when as the Son of God he defied death after three days and walked out of the tomb clothed with a perfected corporeal body of flesh and bone.

That *is* enough because it is certain proof that he is the promised Messiah, the Anointed One, the Son of God. He is what he said he was. Everything hinges on this. "If Christ be not raised, your faith is vain; ye are yet in your sins" (1 Cor. 15:17 KJV). "But now is Christ risen from the dead" (1 Cor. 15:20 KJV).

His resurrection is also enough because inherent in the acknowledgment that Jesus is risen from the dead is the promise that we (and our loved ones) will also be raised. It is a guarantee that every human being can look forward to a life full of tangible social relationships—the kind of loving and tender associations that give meaning to life (D&C 130:2). It means that Jesus's death is inseparably connected to the ultimate destiny of humankind in the Kingdom of God because what is enough is that the "purpose" of the resurrection, as twentieth-century Jesuit theologian Ignacio Ellacuria wrote, "means not only a verification or consolation, but the assurance that His work must continue and that He remains alive to continue it."[1] Those who killed Jesus did so in an effort to end his movement to confront injustice and establish the Kingdom. Just as the physical body of Christ could not be destroyed, neither could the metaphorical and communal Body of Christ (his followers) be destroyed. The work of God's kingdom became and continues to be the work to root out the systemic injustice of poverty, oppression, suffering, and hate.

It is what keeps us marching forward one step at a time in a life that is at times joyous but far too often is a veil of tears. His resurrection assures us that the travails we experience are worthwhile because our future perfected body will share in the glory of God and his Son. It offers us hope that we can build the Kingdom by following the example of the Jesus of Nazareth.

Paul understood all of this. It was the reason the first generation of Christians—although misunderstood, persecuted, beaten, and martyred—were joyous:

> For we know that God, who raised the Lord Jesus, will also raise us with Jesus. . . . *That is why we never give up.* Though our bodies are dying, our spirits are being renewed every day. For our present troubles are small and won't last very long. Yet they produce for us *a glory that vastly outweighs them and will last forever!* So we don't look at the troubles we can see now; rather, we fix our gaze on things that cannot be seen. For the things we see now will soon be gone, but the things we cannot see will last forever. . . . For we know that when this earthly tent we live in is taken down (that is when we die and leave this earthly body), we will have a house in heaven, an *eternal body made for us by God himself.* . . We grow weary in our present bodies, and we long to put on our heavenly bodies like new clothing. For we will . . . *not be spirits without bodies.* . . . While we live in these earthly bodies we groan and sigh, but it's not that we want to die and get rid of these bodies that clothe us. Rather, we want to put on our new bodies so that these dying bodies will be *swallowed up by life*" (2 Cor. 4:14–18; 5:1–4 NLT; emphasis added).

This is what Jesus meant when he said, "I am come that they might have life, and that they might have it more abundantly" (John 10:10 KJV).

---

1. Ignacio Ellacuria, "The Crucified People," 584.

It was this effulgent and whole life that Jesus was speaking about at the time he electrified the crowds by raising Lazarus from the dead and said of himself, "I am the resurrection, and the life" (John 11:25).

James's father died of polio in 1953 when James was just seven years old. The disease struck without warning and required periods of quarantine, during which families were separated from each other. The disease brought to mind disquieting images of crutches, leg braces, wheelchairs, and breathing devices. In his father's case, his lungs were paralyzed and he was left unable to take a breath. He was placed in an iron lung, an apparatus powered by an electric motor that enabled him to breathe. It was a long, horizontal iron and glass tube that exposed only his head. When the pressure on the inside was lowered, his chest cavity would expand. When it was increased, his chest cavity would contract, thus allowing him to breathe. After only two weeks, he died at age thirty-two, leaving James's mother with three young children to raise.

All of us to one extent or another have been affected by the death of a friend or a loved one. Death is a nemesis that destroys and afflicts us all. Nephi speaks of "that awful monster, death" (2 Ne. 9:26). Paul describes it as "the last enemy that shall be destroyed" (1 Cor. 15:26). It is the one universal experience we all face sometimes with faith and often with existential dread. But thanks to Christ Jesus, "We shall not all sleep, but we shall all be changed, in a moment, in the twinkling of an eye, at the last trump: for the . . . dead shall be raised incorruptible, and we shall be changed" (1 Cor. 15:51–52 KJV).

James Sr. was a remarkably good man and an exceptional musician. He taught music at the University of Minnesota until the time of his death. For what appears to be no good reason, he was a casualty of the 1950s polio epidemic that particularly afflicted Minneapolis and took more than 25,000 lives each year before the Salk polio vaccine came to the rescue. He wrote a Christmas hymn that expresses our feelings of anticipation that James will once again, in the flesh, clasp his father's hand and feel the warmth of his embrace—as well as that of so many other loved ones whose bodies sleep for a moment in the grave:

> Sing we now this day. Alleluia!
> Songs of praise and cheer! Alleluia!
> The risen Lord our King will be.
> From chains of death we are set free.
> Alleluia! Alleluia!

We say *Dayenu*—it is enough!

Bibliography

Albright, W. F. and C. S. Mann. *Matthew.* The Anchor Yale Bible Commentaries 26. New York: Doubleday and Co., 1971.

Allport, Gordon W. *Personality: A Psychological Interpretation.* New York: Henry Hold and Co., 1938.

Barclay, William. *And He Had Compassion: Signs and Wonders.* King of Prussia, PA: Judson Press, 1994.

———. *And Jesus Said: A Handbook on the Parables of Jesus.* Philadelphia: Westminster Press, 1970.

———. *The New Daily Study Bible.* 17 vols. Louisville: Westminster John Knox Press, 2003.

Baron, Joseph L., ed. *A Treasury of Jewish Quotations.* New York: Rowman and Littlefield Publishers, Inc., 1985.

Bartchy, S. Scott. "Slaves and Slavery in the Roman World." In *The World of the New Testament: Cultural, Social, and Historical Contexts,* edited by Joel B. Green and Lee Martin McDonald, 169-78. Grand Rapids: Baker Publishing Group, 2013.

Beck, James R. *Jesus and Personality Theory: Exploring the Five-Factor Model.* Weston, IL: IVP Academic, 1999.

Bird, Michael F. "Gentiles." In *The Routledge Encyclopedia of the Historical Jesus,* edited by Craig A. Evans. New York: Taylor and Francis Group, 2010.

Borg, Marcus J. *The God We Never Knew: Beyond Dogmatic Religion to a More Authentic Contemporary Faith.* San Francisco: Harper San Francisco, 1977.

———. *Meeting Jesus Again for the First Time: The Historical Jesus and the Heart of Contemporary Faith.* New York: HarperCollins Publishers, 1995.

———. *Reading the Bible Again for the First Time: Taking the Bible Seriously but Not Literally.* New York: HarperCollins Publishers, 2001.

———. *Speaking Christian: Why Christian Words Have Lost Their Meaning and Power—And How They Can Be Restored.* New York. NY: HarperOne, 1989.

Borg, Marcus J., and Dominic Crossan. *The First Paul: Reclaiming the Radical Visionary Behind the Church's Conservative Icon.* New York: HarperCollins Publishers, 2009.

———. *The Last Week: What the Gospels Really Teach about Jesus's Final Days in Jerusalem.* San Francisco: HarperSanFrancisco, 2006.

Borg, Marcus J., and N. T. Wright. *The Meaning of Jesus: Two Visions.* San Francisco: HarperOne, 1998.

Bouquet, A. C. *Everyday Life in New Testament Times.* New York: Charles Scribner's Sons, 1954.

Brooks, David. "The Art of Presence." *The New York Times,* January 20, 2014. https://www.nytimes.com/2014/01/21/opinion/brooks-the-art-of-presence.html.

Brueggemann, Walter. *Finally Comes the Poet: Daring Speech for Proclamation.* Minneapolis: Fortress Press, 1989.

Burge, Gary M., Lynn H. Cohick, and Gene L. Green. *The New Testament in Antiquity.* Grand Rapids: Zondervan, 2010.

Clark, J. Reuben. *Behold the Lamb of God.* Salt Lake City: Deseret Book, 1991.

Cohick, Lynn H. "Women, Children, and Families in the Greco Roman World." In *The World of the New Testament: Cultural, Social, and Historical Contexts,* edited by Joel B. Green and Lee Martin McDonald, 179-87. Grand Rapids: Baker Publishing Group, 2013.

Conway, Moncure Daniel, ed. *The Writings of Thomas Paine.* New York: Putnam & Sons, 1896.

Crossan, John Dominic. *The Greatest Prayer: Rediscovering the Revolutionary Message of the Lord's Prayer.* New York: HarperOne, 2011.

———. *In Search of Paul: How Jesus's Apostle Opposed Rome's Empire with God's Kingdom.* New York: HarperSan Francisco, 2004.

———. *Jesus: A Revolutionary Biography.* New York: HarperCollins Publishers, 1995.

Edwards, Douglas R. "Court of the Gentiles." In *The Anchor Bible Dictionary,* edited by David Noel Freedman. 6 vols. New York: Doubleday, 1992.

Ehrman, Bart D. *Lost Christianities: The Battles for Scripture and the Faiths We Never Knew.* New York: Oxford University Press, 2003.

Ellacuria, Ignacio. "The Crucified People," translated by Phillip Berryman and Robert R. Barr. In *Mysterium Liberationis: Fundamental Concepts of Liberation Theology,* edited by Ignacio Ellacuria and Jon Sobrino. Maryknoll, 580-603. New York: Orbis Books, 1993.

Ferguson, Everett, ed. *Encyclopedia of Early Christianity.* London: Routledge, 1990

Freedman, David Noel, ed. *The Anchor Bible Dictionary.* 6 vols. New York: Doubleday, 1992.

Ganjavi, Nizami. "The Eye of Charity." In *Nizami: Selected Poems,* introduction and translations by Paul Smith, loc. 296-97, Kindle. N.p.: Createspace, 2012.

Goldstein, Jonathan A. *I Maccabees: a New Translation, with Introduction and Commentary.* Yale University Press, 2008.

Goleman, Daniel. "Rich People Just Care Less." *The New York Times,* October 5, 2013. https://opinionator.blogs.nytimes.com/2013/10/05/rich-people-just-care-less/.

Good, Deirdre. *Jesus' Family Values.* New York: Church Publishing, 2006.

Haidt, Jonathan. *The Righteous Mind: Why Good People Are Divided by Politics and Religion.* New York: Vintage Press, 2013.

Haidt, Jonathan, and Jesse Graham. "When Morality Opposes Justice: Conservatives Have Moral Intuitions that Liberals May Not Recognize." *Social Justice Research* 20, no. 1 (2007): 98-116.

Hanson, K. C., and Douglas E. Oakman. *Palestine in the Time of Jesus.* Minneapolis: Fortress Press, 1998.

Hendricks, Obery M., Jr. *The Politics of Jesus: Rediscovering the True Revolutionary Nature of Jesus' Teachings and How They Have Been Corrupted.* New York: Doubleday, 2006.

Hengel, Martin. *Crucifixion*. Minneapolis: Fortress Press: 1977.

Hinckley, Gordon B. "Funeral of Elisa Young Wirthlin." August 2006. Transcript in possession of authors.

Holland, Jeffrey R. "Whom Say Ye That I Am?" *Ensign*, September 1974, 6–11.

Horsley, Richard A. "Messianic Movements in Judaism." *The Anchor Bible Dictionary*, edited by David Noel Freedman. 6 vols. New York: Doubleday, 1992.

Hughes, Robert. *Rome: A Cultural, Visual, and Personal History*. New York: Random House Inc., 2011.

Hutchinson, Anthony A. "Women and Ordination: Introduction to the Biblical Context." *Dialogue: A Journal of Mormon Thought* 14, no. 4 (Winter 1981): 58–74.

Ibsen, Henrik. "Emperor and Galilean." In *The Complete Works of Henrik Ibsen* 12, translated by William Archer, 2103-9, ebook. Hastings, East Sussex, UK: Delphi Classics, Ltd, 2017.

Josephus, Flavius. *The Antiquities of the Jews*, translated by William Whiston. Radford, VA: Wilder Publications, 2009.

Kakutani, Michiko. "An Idea as Much as a City." *The New York Times*, November 21, 2011. http://www.nytimes.com/2011/11/22/books/rome-a-personal-history-by-robert-hughes-review.html.

Khatry, Ramesh. *The Authenticity of the Parable of the Wheat and the Tares and Its Interpretation*. Boca Raton, FL: Universal Publishers, 2000.

Keener, Craig S. *The Gospel of Matthew: A Socio-Rhetorical Commentary*. Grand Rapids: William B. Eerdmans Publishing, 2009.

Klawans, Jonathan. *Josephus and the Theologies of Ancient Judaism*. New York: Oxford University Press, 2016.

Kohler, Kaufmann. "Resurrection." In *The Jewish Encyclopedia*. 12 vols, 9:661–66. New York: Funk and Wagnalls, 1901–1906.

Köstenberger, Margaret Elizabeth. *Jesus and the Feminists: Who Do They Say That He Is?* Wheaton, IL: Crossway Books, 1900.

Kurlansky, Mark. *Salt: A World History*. New York: Walker and Company, 2003.

Kushner, Harold S. *When Bad Things Happen to Good People*. New York: Schocken Books Inc., 2004.

Lee, Martin McDonald. "Tax, Tax Collectors." In *Encyclopedia of the Historical Jesus*, edited by C. A. Evans, 620-22. New York: Routledge, 2008.

Leeming, H., and K. Leeming, eds. *Josephus' Jewish War and Its Slavonic Version: A Synoptic Comparison*. Boston: Brill Leiden, 2003.

Lewis, C. S. *Mere Christianity*. New York: Macmillan Publishing Co., Inc., 1979.

Lind, Michael. "The Five Worldviews That Define American Politics." *Salon*, September 25, 2011. http://www.salon.com/2011/01/12/lind_five_worldviews/.

Macarthur, John. *New Testament Commentary*. Chicago: Moody Bible Institute of Chicago, 1987.

Martin, James. *Jesus: A Pilgrimage*. San Francisco: HarperOne, 2014.

McDonald, Lee Martin. "Tax, Tax Collectors." In *The Routledge Encyclopedia of the Historical Jesus*, edited by Craig A. Evans. New York: Taylor and Francis Group, 2010.

McGrath, James F. "Was Jesus Illegitimate? The Evidence of His Social Interactions," *Journal for the Study of the Historical Jesus* 5, no. 1 (2007): 81–100.

Meier, John P. *A Marginal Jew: Probing the Authenticity of the Parables*. New Haven, CT: Yale University Press, 2016.

Miller, John W. *Jesus at Thirty: A Psychological and Historical Portrait*. Minneapolis: Fortress Press, 1997.

Miller, Robert J., ed. *The Complete Gospels*. Sonoma, CA: Polebridge Press, 1994.

Morris, Leon. *The Gospel According to Matthew*. Grand Rapids: William B. Eerdmans Publishing, 1992.

National Geographic Channel. "The First Jesus?" *National Geographic*, accessed December 13, 2017. http://www.nationalgeographic.com.au/tv/the-first-jesus/.

Neil, William. *The Rediscovery of the Bible*. London: Hodder & Stoughton, 1954.

Neusner, Jacob. *Invitation to the Talmud: A Teaching Book*. Atlanta: Scholars Press, 1998.

Nibley, Hugh. *The Message of the Joseph Smith Papyri: An Egyptian Endowment*. Salt Lake City: Deseret Book, 1975.

O'Neill, J. C. *Who Did Jesus Think He Was?* Boston: Brill, 1995.

Oppenheimer, Mark. "C. S. Lewis's Legacy Lives On, and Not Just through the Wardrobe." *The New York Times*, March 4, 2011. http://www.nytimes.com/2011/03/05/us/05beliefs.html.

Patterson, Stephen J. *The God of Jesus: The Historical Jesus and the Search for Meaning*. Salem, OR: Trinity Press, 1998.

Pentecost, J. Dwight. *The Words and Works of Jesus Christ: A Study of the Life of Christ*. Grand Rapids: Zondervan, 1984.

Perrin, Nicholas. "The Imperial Cult." In *The World of the New Testament: Cultural, Social, and Historical Contexts*, edited by Joel B. Green and Lee Martin McDonald, 124-35. Grand Rapids: Baker Publishing Group, 2013.

Phillips, J. B. *Ring of Truth*. London: Hodder & Stoughton, 1967.

Pokorny, Peter. "Jesus' Death on the Cross." In *Jesus Research: New Methodologies and Perceptions*, edited by James H. Charlesworth, 897-909. Grand Rapids: William B. Eerdmans Publishing, 2007.

Polkinghorne, John. *Faith, Science, and Understanding*. New Haven, CT: Yale University Press, 2000.

Pruitt, Dean G., and Sung Hee Kim. *Social Conflict: Escalation, Stalemate, and Settlement*. New York: McGraw Hill, 2004.

Rentfrow, Peter J., Samuel D. Gosling, Markus Jokela, David Stillwell, Michal Kosinski, and Jeff Potter. "Divided We Stand: Three Psychological Regions of the United States and their Political, Economic, Social, and Health Correlates." *Journal of Personality and Social Psychology* 105, no. 6 (December 2013): 996-1012.

Rhodes, Gillian, Fiona Proffitt, Jonathon M. Grady, and Alex Sumich. "Facial Symmetry and the Perception of Beauty." *Psychonomic Bulletin & Review* 5, no. 4 (1998): 659-69.

Robinson, A. T. *The Pharisees and Jesus: The Stone Lectures for 1915–16: Delivered at the Princeton Theological Seminary*. New York: Charles Scribner's Sons, 1920.

Saldarini, Anthony J., *Pharisees, Scribes and Sadducees in Palestinian Society*. Grand Rapids: William B. Eerdman's Publishing Co., 2001.

Saunders, William. "Who Added the Doxology?" *Arlington Catholic Herald*, March 17, 1994. http://www.ewtn.com/library/ANSWERS/DOXOLOG.HTM.

Scanzoni, Letha and Nancy Hardesty. *All We're Meant to Be: A Biblical Approach to Women's Liberation*. Waco, TX: Word, 1974.

Scullard, H. H. *From the Gracchi to Nero: A History of Rome from 133 BC to AD 211*. 5th ed. London: Routledge, 1982.

Sergio, Lisa. *Jesus and Women: An Exciting Discovery of What He Offered Her*. McLean, VA: EPM Publications, 1975.

Simundson, Daniel J. "Suffering." In *The Anchor Bible Dictionary*, edited by David Noel Freedman. 6 vols. New York: Doubleday, 1992.

Smith, Joseph. *History of the Church of Jesus Christ of Latter-day Saints*. 7 vols. Salt Lake City: Deseret Book, 1951.

Sprinkle, Preston. *Fight: A Christian Case for Nonviolence*. Colorado Springs: David C. Cook, 2013.

Stein, Robert H. "N. T. Wright's *Jesus and the Victory of God*: A Review Article." *The Journal of the Evangelical Theological Society* 44, no. 2 (June 2001): 207-18.

Stern, Ken. "Why the Rich Don't Give to Charity." *The Atlantic*, April 2013. https://www.theatlantic.com/magazine/archive/2013/04/why-the-rich-dont-give/309254/.

Tabor, James. "The Only Ancient Jewish Male Hair Ever Found." *Bible History Daily*, September 27, 2012. https://www.biblicalarchaeology.org/daily/ancient-cultures/ancient-israel/the-only-ancient-jewish-hair-ever-found/.

Talmage, James E. *The Articles of Faith*. Salt Lake City: The Church of Jesus Christ of Latter-day Saints, 1924.

Thayne, Emma L. "Where Can I Turn for Peace?" *Hymns*, 129. Salt Lake City: The Church of Jesus Christ of Latter-day Saints, 1985.

Theissen, Gerd, and Annette Merz. *The Historical Jesus: A Comprehensive Guide*. Minneapolis: Fortress Press, 1998.

Tolstoy, Leo. *The Complete Works of Leo Tolstoy*. O'Connor Books, 2009. Ebook.

———. *The Gospel in Brief: The Life of Jesus*. New York: Harper Perennial, 2011.

———. *The Law of Love and the Law of Violence*. Mineola, NY: Dover Publications, 2010.

———. *Lift Up Your Eyes: The Religious Writings of Leo Tolstoy*. New York: The Julian Press, 1960.

———. *My Religion: What I Believe*. Guilford Surrey, UK: White Crow, 2009.

Torjesen, Karen Jo. *When Women Were Priests: Women's Leadership in the Early Church and the Scandal of their Subordination in the Rise of Christianity*. New York: HarperSanFrancisco, 1993.

Unger, Merrill F., and William White. *Nelson's Expository Dictionary of the Old Testament*. Nashville: T. Nelson, 1980.

Wheeler, Mortimer. *Roman Art and Architecture*. London: Thames and Hudson, Ltd., 1990.

Whiston, William, trans. *The Genuine Works of Flavius Josephus, the Jewish Historian*. New York: William Borradaile, 1825.

Widtsoe, John A. *Rational Theology as Taught by the Church of Jesus Christ of Latter-day Saints*. Salt Lake City: General Priesthood Committee, 1915.

Wilson, Lynne Hilton. *Christ's Emancipation of Women in the New Testament*. Palo Alto, CA: Good Sound Publishing, 2015.

Wilson, R. McL., trans. *The Gospel of Philip*. London: A. R. Mowbray & Co. Limited, 1962.

Wright, N. T. *The Challenge of Jesus: Rediscovering Who Jesus Was and Is,* Downers Grove: IVP Academic, 1999.

———. *The Day the Revolution Began: Reconsidering the Meaning of Jesus's Crucifixion*. New York: HarperOne Publishing, 2016.

———. *Following Jesus: Biblical Reflections on Discipleship*. Grand Rapids: William B. Eerdmans Publishing, 1995.

———. *Jesus and the Victory of God*. Minneapolis: Fortress Press, 1996.

———. *The Kingdom New Testament: A Contemporary Translation*. New York: HarperOne, 2011.

———. *Matthew for Everyone, Part I*. Louisville: John Knox Press, 2004.

———. *The New Testament and the People of God*. Minneapolis: Fortress Press, 1992.

———. *Simply Jesus: A New Vision of Who He Was, What He Did, and Why He Matters*. New York: HarperCollins Publishers, 2011.

———. *Surprised by Hope: Rethinking Heaven, the Resurrection, and the Mission of the Church*. New York: HarperOne, 2008.

———. *Surprised by Scripture: Engaging in Contemporary Issues*. New York: HarperCollins Publishers, 2014.

Wright, N. T., Sinclair B. Ferguson, and J. I. Packer, eds. *New Dictionary of Theology*. Westmont, IL: IVP Academic, 1988.

Wylen, Stephen M. *The Jews in the Time of Jesus*. Mahwah, NJ: Paulist Press, 1952.

Young, Brad H. *Jesus the Jewish Theologian*. Ada, MI: Baker Academic, 1993.

Zwemer, Samuel M., ed. *The Moslem World*. New York: Missionary Review Publishing Co., 1917.

scripture index

Matt. 20:16 — 24
Matt. 20:21–23 — 257
Matt. 21:13 — 219
Matt. 21:15 — 219
Matt. 21:23–46 — 219
Matt. 21:31 — 124
Matt. 22 — 214
Matt. 22:1–14 — 219
Matt. 22:15–17 — 197
Matt. 22:16–17 — 219
Matt. 22:18–22 — 220
Matt. 22:21 — 197
Matt. 22:22–33 — 220
Matt. 22:29–30 — 24
Matt. 22:30 — 36
Matt. 22:37 — 79, 236
Matt. 22:37–40 — 78
Matt. 22:39 — 236
Matt. 22:40 — 147, 236
Matt. 23:2–4 — 221
Matt. 23:4 — 188
Matt. 23:5–12 — 222
Matt. 23:12 — 24
Matt. 23:13 — 222
Matt. 23:15 — 223, 254
Matt. 23:15–16 — 152
Matt. 23:15–17 — 188
Matt. 23:16 — 222
Matt. 23:16–22 — 223
Matt. 23:17 — 222
Matt. 23:23 — 221
Matt. 23:23–24 — 223
Matt. 23:27 — 223, 254
Matt. 23:33 — 188, 222
Matt. 23:37–39 — 224
Matt. 24:14 — 118
Matt. 24:45–51 — 184n12
Matt. 25:14–30 — 184n12
Matt. 25:31–46 — 55
Matt. 26:11 — 45
Matt. 26:39 — 132, 163
Matt. 26:52 — 146
Matt. 26:64 — 198
Matt. 27:11 — 198–199
Matt. 27:12 — 199

Matt. 27:16 — 133
Matt. 27:22–31 — 133
Matt. 27:46 — 132
Matt. 27:47 — 212
Matt. 27:57 — 65
Matt. 28:1–10 — 18

Mark
Mark 1:7 — 179
Mark 1:12–13 — 172
Mark 1:21 — 247
Mark 1:35 — 246
Mark 1:40–41 — 245
Mark 1:40–42 — 123
Mark 1:41 — 250
Mark 1:43–45 — 173
Mark 1:44–45 — 250
Mark 2:13 — 247
Mark 2:14 — 119
Mark 2:14–18 — 211
Mark 2:15–17 — 84
Mark 2:16 — 216
Mark 2:18 — 216
Mark 2:24 — 216
Mark 3:1–5 — 249
Mark 3:2 — 216
Mark 3:9 — 93
Mark 3:10 — 93
Mark 3:21–22 — 30
Mark 4:1–20 — 105
Mark 4:13 — 251
Mark 4:23–25 — 93
Mark 5:15–20 — 118
Mark 6:31–44 — 47
Mark 6:34 — 245
Mark 6:45–46 — 248
Mark 6:48 — 247
Mark 6:55 — 93
Mark 6:56 — 93
Mark 7:1 — 216
Mark 7:1–4 — 211
Mark 7:3–4 — 215n33
Mark 7:6 — 81
Mark 7:7 — 35, 41
Mark 7:9 — 81
Mark 7:11 — 81

Mark 7:17–19 — 31
Mark 7:18–19 — 81
Mark 7:20–22 — 79
Mark 7:20–23 — 81
Mark 7:26–29 — 256
Mark 7:36 — 97
Mark 8:1–3 — 245
Mark 8:1–9 — 47
Mark 8:11 — 216
Mark 8:30 — 97
Mark 9 — 233
Mark 9:19 — 251
Mark 9:22–23 — 251
Mark 9:50 — 104, 233, 239
Mark 10:1 — 247
Mark 10:2 — 216
Mark 10:13–14 — 249
Mark 10:14–15 — 34
Mark 10:16 — 248
Mark 10:21 — 67
Mark 10:45 — 85
Mark 11:11 — 250
Mark 11:12 — 247
Mark 11:15–16 — 249
Mark 12 — 214
Mark 12:13 — 216
Mark 12:30 — 79
Mark 12:37 — 52
Mark 12:40–41 — 52
Mark 12:41–44 — 63, 220
Mark 12:43–44 — 52
Mark 13:24 — 41
Mark 14:7 — 45
Mark 14:34 — 132
Mark 15:40–41 — 17
Mark 15:43 — 182
Mark 15:46 — 65
Mark 16:1 — 17
Mark 16:2–8 — 18
Mark 16:9–11 — 164
Mark 16:10–11 — 166
Mark 16:14 — 164

Luke
Luke 1:5 — 178n3
Luke 1:15 — 178n3

subject index

and systemic poverty, 54
on taxes, 196
Temple confrontation, 218–19
temptations of, 171–73
titles of, 195
on turning other cheek, 144, 199
two great commandments, 78
use of parables, 105–6. *See also* parables.
value of a soul, 68–69
violates tradition, 77–78, 80
on violence, 146
visits Americas, 34
voice, 259–60
on walking extra mile, 144, 198
on wealth disparity, 59
and widows, 52
and women, 13–18
Job, 89, 92, 127–28
John the Baptist
   appearance of, 178
   condemns Pharisees, 177–78
   on Jesus, 179, 182
   preaches of messiah, 177
Johnson, Gary R., 74
Joseph ben Matiyaha, 216
Joseph of Arimathea, 65–66
Joseph, 183
Josephus
   on destruction of Temple, 47
   on Jesus, 159
   on Jewish festivals, 218
   on messiahs, 157
   on non-violent resistance, 143–44
   on Pharisees, 208–10
   on temple taxes, 46
   on women, 11
justice, 201–2

K

Keller, Phillip W., 107
King James Bible, x
Kingdom of God, 151–52
   all things in common, 175
   economic equality of, 188
   ideal family, 38

new family, 29–30
no poor in, 44
non-compulsory, 175
not of this world, 199
Knohl, Israel, 157
Kushner, Harold S., 127–28

L

Lazarus, 97
LDS Humanitarian Services, 54–55
leprosy
   healing of, 94, 122–23, 245
   outcasts, 121
   symptoms of, 121–22
   unclean, 122
Levites, 150
Lewis, C. S., 23, 39
Lind, Michael, 176
Lord's Prayer, 71–73
lost, 103–4
love, 31
   opposite of sin, 78
   perfect, 145–47

M

marriage, 36–39, 110. *See also* family.
   households, 25–29
   Levirate, 220
   women's roles in, 11–13
Martin, James, 227
   on parables, 105
   on rich young man, 67
Mary (mother of Jesus), 35–36, 42n2
Mary Magdalene, 17–18
   and reported marriage to Jesus, 38
   sees resurrected Jesus, 164
Masterman, W. G., 121–22
materfamilias, 28
McConkie, James Sr., 266
Meier, John P., xvoo
Menahem ben Judah, 158
mental illness, 89
messiahs 97–98, 196
   expectations of, 156–57
   in Isaiah, 41

Stern, Ken 63
suffering
  and Jesus, 125–35
  nature of, 127–29
  responsibility to, 127–29
  theological limitations of, 133–34
systemic injustice, 182–88, 185
systemic poverty. *See* poor.

T

table commensality, 50–51. *See also*
  eating customs.
Talmage, James E., 99
tares, 152. *See also* parables.
tax collectors, 66s, 119
taxes, 119–20
  taxes Palestine, 46
  taxes Roman, 180, 195–96
  taxes Temple, 46, 195–96
tekton, 183. *See also* artisan.
Temple
  corruption of, 214
  destroyed, 139
  taxes, 46, 195–96
Temple Mount, xiv–xv
Ten Commandments, 75, 145
teteletai, 133
Thayne, Emma Lou, 126, 135
The Lamentation, 125–26
Third Servile War, 140
Thomas, 165
Tolstoy, Leo, 137–38, 204
Twain, Mark, 4
two great commandments, 31, 201

W

wealth
  and camel through a needle, 64–68
  disparity of, 57–69, 183
  hoarding of, 62–64
  insecurity of, 68–69
  in Palestine, 57–59
  rich young man, 62–63
Welch, James, 23

Weltanschauung, 173–74
"Where Can I Turn for Peace," 126, 135
widow's mite, 52, 63
widows, 28. *See also* women.
Widtsoe, John A., 99
women
  apostles, 18
  deacons, 18
  disciples, 17–20
  and divorce, 10–12
  in early Christianity, 18–21
  and marriage, 11–13
  not allowed in Temple, 16
  preach gospel, 16
  in Palestine, 10–13
  and priesthood, 19–20
  priests, 21
  roles of, 10–13
  sinful, 12
  sold into slavery, 10
  widows, 28
Women's Court, 16
Wright, N. T., 4
  on bearers of God, 202
  on Christian family, 31–32
  on discipleship, 238–39
  on enemies, 151
  on good vs. evil, 152–53
  on healings, 100
  on historical context, 3
  on Jesus as messiah, 167
  on Kingdom of God, 203
  on non-violence, 85–86
  on non-violent resistance, 143–44
  on Roman violence, 205
  on Rome, 193
  on self-validating Jesus, 2
  on us vs. them, 153
  on violence, 138, 142
Wylen, Stephen M., 76

Z

Zacchaeus, 66, 120
Zealots, 158

Also available from
GREG KOFFORD BOOKS

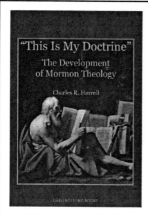

"This is My Doctrine":
The Development of Mormon Theology

Charles R. Harrell

Hardcover, ISBN: 978-1-58958-103-6

The principal doctrines defining Mormonism today often bear little resemblance to those it started out with in the early 1830s. This book shows that these doctrines did not originate in a vacuum but were rather prompted and informed by the religious culture from which Mormonism arose. Early Mormons, like their early Christian and even earlier Israelite predecessors, brought with them their own varied culturally conditioned theological presuppositions (a process of convergence) and only later acquired a more distinctive theological outlook (a process of differentiation).

In this first-of-its-kind comprehensive treatment of the development of Mormon theology, Charles Harrell traces the history of Latter-day Saint doctrines from the times of the Old Testament to the present. He describes how Mormonism has carried on the tradition of the biblical authors, early Christians, and later Protestants in reinterpreting scripture to accommodate new theological ideas while attempting to uphold the integrity and authority of the scriptures. In the process, he probes three questions: How did Mormon doctrines develop? What are the scriptural underpinnings of these doctrines? And what do critical scholars make of these same scriptures? In this enlightening study, Harrell systematically peels back the doctrinal accretions of time to provide a fresh new look at Mormon theology.

"This Is My Doctrine" will provide those already versed in Mormonism's theological tradition with a new and richer perspective of Mormon theology. Those unacquainted with Mormonism will gain an appreciation for how Mormon theology fits into the larger Jewish and Christian theological traditions.

Re-reading Job: Understanding the Ancient World's Greatest Poem

Michael Austin

Paperback, ISBN: 978-1-58958-667-3
Hardcover, ISBN: 978-1-58958-668-0

Job is perhaps the most difficult to understand of all books in the Bible. While a cursory reading of the text seems to relay a simple story of a righteous man whose love for God was tested through life's most difficult of challenges and rewarded for his faith through those trials, a closer reading of Job presents something far more complex and challenging. The majority of the text is a work of poetry that authors and artists through the centuries have recognized as being one of--if not the--greatest poem of the ancient world.

In *Re-reading Job: Understanding the Ancient World's Greatest Poem*, author Michael Austin shows how most readers have largely misunderstood this important work of scripture and provides insights that enable us to re-read Job in a drastically new way. In doing so, he shows that the story of Job is far more than that simple story of faith, trials, and blessings that we have all come to know, but is instead a subversive and complex work of scripture meant to inspire readers to rethink all that they thought they knew about God.

Praise for *Re-reading Job*:

"In this remarkable book, Michael Austin employs his considerable skills as a commentator to shed light on the most challenging text in the entire Hebrew Bible. Without question, readers will gain a deeper appreciation for this extraordinary ancient work through Austin's learned analysis. Rereading Job signifies that Latter-day Saints are entering a new age of mature biblical scholarship. It is an exciting time, and a thrilling work." — David Bokovoy, author, *Authoring the Old Testament*

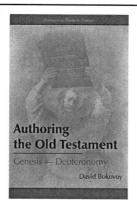

Authoring the Old Testament: Genesis–Deuteronomy

David Bokovoy

Paperback, ISBN: 978-1-58958-588-1
Hardcover, ISBN: 978-1-58958-675-8

For the last two centuries, biblical scholars have made discoveries and insights about the Old Testament that have greatly changed the way in which the authorship of these ancient scriptures has been understood. In the first of three volumes spanning the entire Hebrew Bible, David Bokovoy dives into the Pentateuch, showing how and why textual criticism has led biblical scholars today to understand the first five books of the Bible as an amalgamation of multiple texts into a single, though often complicated narrative; and he discusses what implications those have for Latter-day Saint understandings of the Bible and modern scripture.

Praise for *Authoring the Old Testament*:

"Authoring the Old Testament is a welcome introduction, from a faithful Latter-day Saint perspective, to the academic world of Higher Criticism of the Hebrew Bible. . . . [R]eaders will be positively served and firmly impressed by the many strengths of this book, coupled with Bokovoy's genuine dedication to learning by study and also by faith." — John W. Welch, editor, *BYU Studies Quarterly*

"Bokovoy provides a lucid, insightful lens through which disciple-students can study intelligently LDS scripture. This is first rate scholarship made accessible to a broad audience—nourishing to the heart and mind alike." — Fiona Givens, co-author, *The God Who Weeps: How Mormonism Makes Sense of Life*

"I repeat: this is one of the most important books on Mormon scripture to be published recently. . . . [*Authoring the Old Testament*] has the potential to radically expand understanding and appreciation for not only the Old Testament, but scripture in general. It's really that good. Read it. Share it with your friends. Discuss it." — David Tayman, The Improvement Era: A Mormon Blog

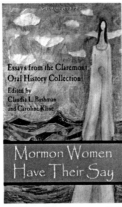

Mormon Women Have Their Say: Essays from the Claremont Oral History Collection

Edited by Claudia L. Bushman and Caroline Kline

Paperback, ISBN: 978-1-58958-494-5

The Claremont Women's Oral History Project has collected hundreds of interviews with Mormon women of various ages, experiences, and levels of activity. These interviews record the experiences of these women in their homes and family life, their church life, and their work life, in their roles as homemakers, students, missionaries, career women, single women, converts, and disaffected members. Their stories feed into and illuminate the broader narrative of LDS history and belief, filling in a large gap in Mormon history that has often neglected the lived experiences of women. This project preserves and perpetuates their voices and memories, allowing them to say share what has too often been left unspoken. The silent majority speaks in these records.

This volume is the first to explore the riches of the collection in print. A group of young scholars and others have used the interviews to better understand what Mormonism means to these women and what women mean for Mormonism. They explore those interviews through the lenses of history, doctrine, mythology, feminist theory, personal experience, and current events to help us understand what these women have to say about their own faith and lives.

Praise for *Mormon Women Have Their Say*:

"Using a variety of analytical techniques and their own savvy, the authors connect ordinary lives with enduring themes in Latter-day Saint faith and history." --Laurel Thatcher Ulrich, author of *Well-Behaved Women Seldom Make History*

"Essential. . . . In these pages, Mormon women will find *ourselves*." --Joanna Brooks, author of *The Book of Mormon Girl: A Memoir of an American Faith*

"The varieties of women's responses to the major issues in their lives will provide many surprises for the reader, who will be struck by how many different ways there are to be a thoughtful and faithful Latter-day Saint woman." --Armand Mauss, author of *All Abraham's Children: Changing Mormon Conceptions of Race and Lineage*

Common Ground—Different Opinions:
Latter-day Saints and Contemporary Issues

Edited by Justin F. White
and James E. Faulconer

Paperback, ISBN: 978-1-58958-573-7

There are many hotly debated issues about which many people disagree, and where common ground is hard to find. From evolution to environmentalism, war and peace to political partisanship, stem cell research to same-sex marriage, how we think about controversial issues affects how we interact as Latter-day Saints.

In this volume various Latter-day Saint authors address these and other issues from differing points of view. Though they differ on these tough questions, they have all found common ground in the gospel of Jesus Christ and the latter-day restoration. Their insights offer diverse points of view while demonstrating we can still love those with whom we disagree.

Praise for *Common Ground—Different Opinions*:

"[This book] provide models of faithful and diverse Latter-day Saints who remain united in the body of Christ. This collection clearly demonstrates that a variety of perspectives on a number of sensitive issues do in fact exist in the Church. . . . [T]he collection is successful in any case where it manages to give readers pause with regard to an issue they've been fond of debating, or convinces them to approach such conversations with greater charity and much more patience. It served as just such a reminder and encouragement to me, and for that reason above all, I recommend this book." — Blair Hodges, Maxwell Institute

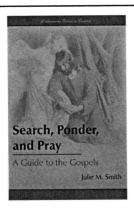

Search, Ponder, and Pray:
A Guide to the Gospels

Julie M. Smith

Paperback, ISBN: 978-1-58958-671-0
Hardcover, ISBN: 978-1-58958-672-7

From the author's preface:

During my graduate studies in theology, I came to realize that there is quite a bit of work done in the field of biblical studies that can be useful to members of the Church as they read the scriptures. Unfortunately, academic jargon usually makes these works impenetrable, and I was unable to find many publications that made this research accessible to the non-specialist. In this book, I have endeavored to present some of the most interesting insights of biblical scholars—in plain language.

It was also important to me that I not present the work of these scholars in a way that would make you feel obligated to accept their conclusions. Since scholars rarely agree with each other, I can see no reason why you should feel compelled to agree with them. My hope is that the format of this book will encourage you to view the insights of scholars as the beginning of a discussion instead of the end of an argument. In some cases, I have presented the positions of scholars (and even some critics of the Church) specifically to encourage you to develop your own responses to these arguments based on your personal scripture study. I certainly don't agree with every idea in this book.

I encourage you to read the Introduction. Although I have endeavored to keep it as short as possible, there are several issues related to the interpretation of the scriptures that should be addressed before you begin interpreting.

It is my experience that thoughtful scripture study leads to personal revelation. I hope that through the process of searching the scriptures, pondering these questions, and praying about the answers, you will be edified.

Life is full of unanswered questions. Here are over 4,500 more of them.

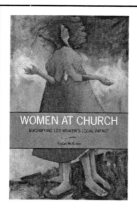

Women at Church: Magnifying LDS Women's Local Impact

Neylan McBaine

Paperback, ISBN: 978-1-58958-688-8

Women at Church is a practical and faithful guide to improving the way men and women work together at church. Looking at current administrative and cultural practices, the author explains why some women struggle with the gendered divisions of labor. She then examines ample real-life examples that are currently happening in local settings around the country that expand and reimagine gendered practices. Readers will understand how to evaluate possible pain points in current practices and propose solutions that continue to uphold all mandated church policies. Readers will be equipped with the tools they need to have respectful, empathetic and productive conversations about gendered practices in Church administration and culture.

Praise for *Women at Church*:

"Such a timely, faithful, and practical book! I suggest ordering this book in bulk to give to your bishopric, stake presidency, and all your local leadership to start a conversation on changing Church culture for women by letting our doctrine suggest creative local adaptations—Neylan McBaine shows the way!" — Valerie Hudson Cassler, author of *Women in Eternity, Women of Zion*

"A pivotal work replete with wisdom and insight. Neylan McBaine deftly outlines a workable programme for facilitating movement in the direction of the 'privileges and powers' promised the nascent Female Relief Society of Nauvoo." — Fiona Givens, co-author of *The God Who Weeps: How Mormonism Makes Sense of Life*

"In her timely and brilliant findings, Neylan McBaine issues a gracious invitation to rethink our assumptions about women's public Church service. Well researched, authentic, and respectful of the current Church administrative structure, McBaine shares exciting and practical ideas that address diverse needs and involve all members in the meaningful work of the Church." — Camille Fronk Olson, author of *Women of the Old Testament* and *Women of the New Testament*

Future Mormon:
Essays in Mormon Theology

Adam S. Miller

Paperback, ISBN: 978-1-58958-509-6

From the Introduction:

I have three children, a girl and two boys. Our worlds overlap but, already, these worlds are not the same. Their worlds, the worlds that they will grow to fill, are already taking leave of mine. Their futures are already wedged into our present. This is both heartening and frightening. So much of our world deserves to be left. So much of it deserves to be scrapped and recycled. But, too, this scares me. I worry that a lot of what has mattered most to me in this world—Mormonism in particular—may be largely unintelligible to them in theirs. This problem isn't new, but it is perpetually urgent. Every generation must start again. Every generation must work out their own salvation. Every generation must live its own lives and think its own thoughts and receive its own revelations. And, if Mormonism continues to matter, it will be because they, rather than leaving, were willing to be Mormon all over again. Like our grandparents, like our parents, and like us, they will have to rethink the whole tradition, from top to bottom, right from the beginning, and make it their own in order to embody Christ anew in this passing world. To the degree that we can help, our job is to model that work in love and then offer them the tools, the raw materials, and the room to do it themselves.

These essays are a modest contribution in this vein, a future tense apologetics meant for future Mormons. They model, I hope, a thoughtful and creative engagement with Mormon ideas while sketching, without obligation, possible directions for future thinking.

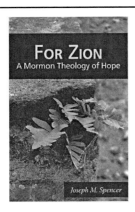

For Zion:
A Mormon Theology of Hope

Joseph M. Spencer

Paperback, ISBN: 978-1-58958-568-3

What is hope? What is Zion? And what does it mean to hope for Zion? In this insightful book, Joseph Spencer explores these questions through the scriptures of two continents separated by nearly two millennia. In the first half, Spencer engages in a rich study of Paul's letter to the Roman to better understand how the apostle understood hope and what it means to have it. In the second half of the book, Spencer jumps to the early years of the Restoration and the various revelations on consecration to understand how Latter-day Saints are expected to strive for Zion. Between these halves is an interlude examining the hoped-for Zion that both thrived in the Book of Mormon and was hoped to be established again.

Praise for *For Zion*:

"Joseph Spencer is one of the most astute readers of sacred texts working in Mormon Studies. Blending theological savvy, historical grounding, and sensitive readings of scripture, he has produced an original and compelling case for consecration and the life of discipleship." — Terryl Givens, author, *Wrestling the Angel: The Foundations of Mormon Thought*

"*For Zion: A Mormon Theology of Hope* is more than a theological reflection. It also consists of able textual exegesis, historical contextualization, and philosophic exploration. Spencer's careful readings of Paul's focus on hope in Romans and on Joseph Smith's development of consecration in his early revelations, linking them as he does with the Book of Mormon, have provided an intriguing, intertextual avenue for understanding what true stewardship should be for us—now and in the future. As such he has set a new benchmark for solid, innovative Latter-day Saint scholarship that is at once provocative and challenging." — Eric D. Huntsman, author, *The Miracles of Jesus*

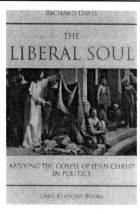

The Liberal Soul: Applying the Gospel of Jesus Christ in Politics

Richard Davis

Paperback, ISBN: 978-1-58958-583-6

The Liberal Soul offers something lacking in LDS culture. That is the presentation of a different way for Latter-day Saints to examine the question of how to be faithful disciples of Christ and good citizens. It shows public policy decision-making regarding government role as the manifestation of the "liberal soul" rather than as the libertarianism advocated by past Mormon speakers and writers such as Ezra Taft Benson, Cleon Skousen, or Vern Andersen. It also takes a different approach from the less radical but still traditional economic conservative attitudes of well-known politicians such as Orrin Hatch or Mitt Romney.

Davis suggests that a Latter-day Saint can approach economic policy, war, the environment, and social issues with the perspective that society is basically good and not evil, tolerance and forbearance are desirable qualities instead of bad ones, and that government can and does play a positive role as a vehicle of society in improving the lives of citizens. He describes how Latter-day Saints can apply the Gospel of Jesus Christ to our roles at each of these three levels—individual, group, and society—rather than assuming the societal level violates the principles of the Gospel. The result is that Latter-day Saints can help bring about a Zion society—one where all benefit, the most vulnerable are aided and not ignored, inclusion is the rule and not the exception, and suspicion and fear are replaced by love and acceptance.

Praise for *The Liberal Soul*:

"Davis provides a thoughtful exploration into the principles of generosity, equality, and Christian discipleship and their important relationship to democratic government. This book clearly explains the strong connection between liberalism and Mormonism. I would recommend it to anyone who has ever asked me, 'How can you be a Democrat and a Mormon?'"

— U.S. Senate Majority Leader Harry Reid

CPSIA information can be obtained
at www.ICGtesting.com
Printed in the USA
FSOW01n0447080118
42896FS